"The same surgeon general who required cigarette packages to say 'Warning, this product may be dangerous to your health' ought to require that 99 out of 100 books written on personal finance carry that same label. The exceptions are rare. Benjamin Graham's *The Intelligent Investor* is one. Now, it is high praise when I endorse *Bogle on Mutual Funds* as another."—From the foreword by Nobel Laureate Paul A. Samuelson

---

HIGH PRAISE FOR
BOGLE ON MUTUAL FUNDS

"Move over, Peter Lynch!"—*Kiplinger's Personal Finance*

"GOOD CRITICAL ADVICE FROM THE 'BAD BOY' OF VANGUARD. It takes only a few minutes to discover that Bogle, a man with an attitude, has written a book with an attitude."
—*The Washington Post*

"ADVICE AND PHILOSOPHY WITH A PROVOCATIVE EDGE."—*The New York Times*

"[This] book includes a wealth of information to help make intelligent choices in mutual funds. It is a refreshing change from the stream of books claiming to offer easy paths to wealth."
—*The Miami Herald*

"PERCEPTIVE . . . STRAIGHTFORWARD . . . PROVOCATIVE . . . LEVELHEADED."—*Individual Investor*

Please turn the page for more extraordinary acclaim . . .

BOGLE ON MUTUAL FUNDS
New Perspectives for the Intelligent Investor

John C. Bogle

A Dell Trade Paperback

A DELL TRADE PAPERBACK

Published by
Dell Publishing
a division of
Bantam Doubleday Dell Publishing Group, Inc.
1540 Broadway
New York, New York 10036

This publication is designed to provide accurate and authoritative information in regard to the subject matter covered. It is sold with the understanding that neither the author nor the publisher is engaged in rendering legal, accounting, or other professional service. If legal advice or other expert assistance is required, the services of a competent professional person should be sought.

From a Declaration of Principles jointly adopted by a Committee of the American Bar Association and a Committee of Publishers.

Reprinted by arrangement with Irwin Professional Publishing

Printed in the United States of America

Published simultaneously in Canada
October 1994
10 9 8 7 6 5 4 3 2 1
BVG

Dedication

To my parents, for setting my values.
To my brothers, for their sacrifices.
To Eve, my beloved wife, for her devotion, patience, and support.
To my children, for their understanding and pride.

Foreword

The same surgeon general who required cigarette packages to say: "Warning, this product may be dangerous to your health" ought to require that 99 out of 100 books written on personal finance carry that same label. The exceptions are rare. Benjamin Graham's *The Intelligent Investor* is one. Now it is high praise when I endorse *Bogle on Mutual Funds* as another.

I do not speak for myself. What is one person's opinion worth? It is the statistical evidences of economic history that I speak for. Over half a century, professors of finance have studied various strategies for prudent investing. A jury of economists is never unanimous—how could it be in such an inexact science?—but on these lessons of experience there is a remarkable degree of agreement.

1. *Diversification* does reduce, but not eliminate, risk. Buying many stocks, critics say, is "settling for mediocrity." When I was a trustee on the finance committee of the largest private pension equity fund in the world—which handled the old-age savings of the whole university community—we had 30 billion reasons to look into this critique alleging mediocrity. We discovered that the hundreds of money managers who believe in putting only a few eggs in one basket and then "watching fiercely those eggs," alas, produce long-term investment returns that are significantly below those of diversified portfolios. No exceptions? Yes, a few; but a changing group, hard to identify in advance, and prone to regress toward the mean even before you can spot them.

2. For those not in the millionaire class, the need to diversify implies that the sensible and cost-efficient strategy is *not to handle personally* investments needed for those future days of retirement, of home purchases, and of sending offspring to college. "Leave the driving to Greyhound" is not counsel of cowardice and modesty. It's just plain good sense when you reckon the facts about brokerage commissions and the need to keep tax records. All this applies even if you will not go all the way toward "index investing," my next topic.

3. The most efficient way to diversify a stock portfolio is with a low-fee

index fund. Statistically, a broadly based stock index fund will outperform most actively managed equity portfolios. A thousand money managers all look about equally good or bad. Each expects to do 3% better than the mob. Each puts together a convincing story after the fact. Hardly ten of one thousand perform in a way that convinces a jury of experts that a long-term edge over indexing is likely. (For bond and money market portfolios, the canny investor will select among funds with high quality and lean costs.)

4. Enough said about the testimony of economic science. Where John Bogle has added a new note is in connection with his emphasis upon low-cost, no-load investing. I have no association with The Vanguard Group of funds other than as a charter member investor, along with numerous children and innumerable grandchildren. So, as a disinterested witness in the court of opinion, perhaps my seconding his suggestions will carry some weight. John Bogle has changed a basic industry in the optimal direction. Of very few can this be said.

May I add a personal finding? Investing sensibly, besides being remunerative, can still be fun.

Paul A. Samuelson
Institute Professor Emeritus
Cambridge, Massachusetts

June 1993

Acknowledgments

Two centuries ago, it was said that if we stand on the shoulders of giants, we may see further than the giants themselves. The principal giant upon whose shoulders I have stood in writing this book is Benjamin Graham; the further distance brings the mutual fund industry into perspective.

My objective is to provide the same sort of framework for investing in mutual funds as Benjamin Graham provided for investing in individual stocks and bonds. His book *The Intelligent Investor* was first published in 1949. Revised and updated frequently thereafter, it set the standard against which other "how to invest" books are measured. It is no coincidence that the subtitle of this book, "New Perspectives for the Intelligent Investor," echoes his title. Whether I have succeeded in accomplishing the demanding objective that I set for myself, I leave to your judgment.

If this is a good book, it is importantly because of the comments, criticisms, and even editing that I have received from numerous readers of the early drafts. Hesitant as I am to single out any of the commentators, I simply cannot ignore the priceless assistance of Peter L. Bernstein, founding editor of *The Journal of Portfolio Management* and writer of what is without doubt the most thoughtful and respected newsletter in the field; Warren E. Buffett, chairman of Berkshire-Hathaway and probably the nation's most successful investor; and R. H. (Tad) Jeffrey, president of The Jeffrey Company and a remarkable combination of the academic and the practitioner. The time and effort each of them invested in this book place me in their eternal debt.

Many of my associates at Vanguard were also staunch readers and critics, and their comments too were invaluable. But I must single out James M. Norris, my principal staff assistant, for his countless hours of reading, suggesting, calculating, editing, and even typing, all of which have helped to make this the best book that I could write. I also want to thank my other staff assistants, Emily A. Snyder and Mortimer J. (Tim) Buckley III, for their remarkable dedication and support, manifested not

v

only in the substance of their work but also in their extraordinary commitments of time and energy.

I especially appreciate the willingness of Paul A. Samuelson, Professor of Economics Emeritus at Massachusetts Institute of Technology and Nobel Laureate in Economics, to write the foreword. In a sense, I have been his student since 1947, when, as a freshman at Princeton University, I studied his classic textbook, *Economics*. Through the numerous and impressive journal articles on investing he has written over the years, I remain his student and admirer today. His foreword brings this 46-year relationship to full circle.

Finally, in this day and age when it is said that every project needs a champion, I want to thank Amy Hollands Gaber of Irwin Professional Publishing. She spent four long years persuading me to write this book, and her enthusiasm, then as now, helped to give me strength to carry on. Because of her determination, an idea has become a reality.

J.C.B.

Preface

The purpose of this book is to guide investors in developing and implementing an intelligent investment program through mutual funds. It does not attempt to tell you how to attain wealth without risk, nor does it attempt to tell you how to select the next "number one" equity fund. Both of these tasks are, in a word, impossible, and I fear this book would lack all credibility if I did not acknowledge that fact at the outset.

Rather, what I hope to provide is a sensible framework for establishing a long-term investment program that will meet your financial needs. Such a program must take into account: (1) your investment attitudes, whether conservative or venturesome; (2) your position in the life cycle of investing, as you move from the accumulation of assets during your earning years to the enjoyment of income during your retirement years; and (3) the behavior of the securities markets over the long run, from which much (but not too much) should be learned.

This book deals solely with mutual funds. It does not deal with the analysis and evaluation of individual stocks and bonds. In my view, attempting to build a lifetime investment program around the selection of a handful of individual securities is, for all but the most exceptional investors, a fool's errand. To be sure, by owning individual equities, some active investors will inevitably enjoy spectacular results. But others perforce will lose much of their capital. Earning extraordinary returns from the ownership of individual stocks is a high-risk, long-shot bet for most investors. Specific stock bets should be made, if at all, in small portions, and more for the excitement of the game than for the profit. Serious money belongs elsewhere; it belongs in a widely diversified investment program. For nearly all investors, mutual funds are the most efficient method of achieving this diversification.

This book covers not only equity funds but bond funds and money market funds as well. Together, these two new (post-1970) segments of the mutual fund industry are larger than the equity fund base that had dominated the industry since the inception of the first U.S. mutual fund back in 1924. Of the industry's current total assets of $1.6 trillion, equity-oriented (common stock and balanced) funds comprise $517 billion, bond funds $510 billion, and money market funds $555 billion. Diversification in bonds and in short-term instruments is every bit as important as in equities: a portfolio comprising, say, 100 fixed-income obligations vastly reduces the risk of any single default, without any reduction whatsoever in return.

While mutual funds are an ideal vehicle to mitigate substantially the risk of holding specific stocks and bonds, market risk still remains. The central task of a lifetime investment strategy is to allocate financial resources so as to balance the different market risks among the three basic classes of liquid assets: (1) common stocks, which carry the greatest short-term price volatility and uncertainty, but—based on the underlying fundamentals of corporate earnings, dividends, and dividend growth—promise the highest expected returns over the long term; (2) bonds, which normally provide lower returns than stocks and, depending on the length of maturity, carry significant risk of principal fluctuation but remarkable stability of income; and (3) money market reserves, which usually engender minimal risk to capital and thus the lowest rewards but, given their short-term nature, create an inevitable risk of income volatility. An intelligent approach to allocating your assets among these three investment classes is a key theme of this book.

Risk and return are normally considered the central elements of asset allocation, and this book will not abandon the careful evaluation of these two fundamentals. However, I will add a third critical element, cost. The cost of an investment program is the third leg of what I would define as the eternal triangle of investing. In the mutual fund field, taking into account the impact of sales charges (if any), operating expenses, and advisory fees, annual costs may run from less than 0.3% to more than 3.0% of the value of your investment. If pre-tax, pre-inflation annual returns on a balanced portfolio of financial assets (i.e. stocks, bonds, and reserves) are assumed to run in the range of +10%, after-tax, inflation-adjusted annual returns will cluster around +4%. In such an environment, the difference between expenses of 0.3% and 3.0% commands, on the face of it, a powerful influence on returns. Other factors held equal, if the real after-tax return is +4% annually, the low-expense fund will earn a net return of +3.7%, nearly four times the net return of +1.0% for the high-expense fund. Maintaining minimal investment costs, then, is also an important theme of the book.

CAVEAT EMPTOR

The Latin phrase *caveat emptor,* literally translated, means "let the buyer beware." In ancient Rome, this warning was often posted in the marketplace to remind prospective buyers to carefully examine what they were purchasing before the sale was completed, so that in case of later disappointment they could not blame the seller. The same type of warning should alert today's mutual fund investors to possible disappointment in their investment selections. So I use *caveat emptor* boxes like this one throughout the book to highlight subjects that demand special caution on the part of the intelligent investor. In a few cases, I also use this format to direct your attention to what I hope will be interesting anecdotes and historical perspectives.

There is, of course, a point at which you must act on general principles and implement your asset allocation decision. You will usually want to choose among fund families that offer scores of mutual funds with different investment objectives and performance characteristics. Then you will have to select and monitor those equity, bond, and money market funds that best meet your specific requirements. Your choices among bond and money market funds will involve a limited number of critical judgments. Your choices among stock funds will usually require many more considerations, although, if you should elect to participate in the entire U.S. stock market through an index fund, the critical issues will be few. Helping you to make wise choices among individual mutual funds is yet another key theme.

While I assiduously avoid any specific reference to the mutual funds in The Vanguard Group, it will be obvious that much of the philosophy that I express in this book is a reflection of the Vanguard philosophy. For this parallelism, I make no apology. It is not because Vanguard has particular goals that I emphasize their importance in this book; rather, it is because I regard these goals as critically important that Vanguard adopted them in the first place. Only because I believed, for example, that low cost made a difference did we set out in 1974 to become the world's lowest-cost provider of financial services. Only because I believed that passive investing—holding all stocks in the market as distinct from actively managing a portfolio of selected stocks—should become an investment option did we form in 1976 the mutual fund industry's first market index fund. Only because I believed that millions of investors could make their own decisions without the advice—and cost—of an intermediary securities broker did we convert to a no-load (no sales commission) distribution system in 1977. I hope that you will consider the reaffirmation of these (and other) Vanguard principles throughout this book, not as a conflict of interest on my part, but as an exercise in integrity.

I have come to be known as the iconoclast of the mutual fund industry. Among industry participants, I am surely its sharpest critic. It is not that I consider this to be a bad industry; rather, it is an industry that can be so much better than it is. Somewhere along the road, the industry has lost its way. In my view, too many fund complexes have put the business need for asset gathering, the better to enhance the profits earned by fund managers, ahead of the fiduciary duty to provide efficient asset management at the lowest reasonable price, the better to enhance the returns earned by fund shareholders.

That said, let me affirm my positive belief in this industry: mutual funds, in general, have done a good job for their shareholders. Specifically, the industry is to be commended for four particular accomplishments.

1. Mutual funds have provided an essential diversification that has greatly reduced the risk of owning individual stocks and bonds.
2. Mutual funds have provided investment services—account information, transaction ease, efficient recordkeeping, and so on— that make them an extraordinarily convenient means of investing.
3. Mutual funds have been created in a remarkable variety of types and objectives, and they are in a position to meet even the most particular needs of investors.
4. Mutual funds have provided professional investment management that has, broadly speaking, delivered returns reflecting those earned in the market segments in which they participate.

These are not trivial accomplishments. Indeed, they provide the basic rationale for the growth of mutual fund industry assets from $94 billion at the beginning of 1980 to $1.6 trillion as 1993 began.

The central aim of this book is to make you a more knowledgeable and successful mutual fund investor. There are no easy answers in the fallible field of investing, where there are risks of one sort or another no matter *what* you do, and costs of one magnitude or another no matter *how* you do it. But there are intelligent investment programs that rely largely on simplicity and common sense. You can create for yourself a program that will meet your own objectives. If the new perspectives presented in this book help you to do so, you should be well served and financially rewarded.

John C. Bogle

Note: John C. Bogle is the founder of The Vanguard Group of Investment Companies, a mutual fund complex formed in 1974, and has been its Chairman and Chief Executive Officer since then. Assets of the Vanguard Funds totaled $112 billion on May 31, 1993. Under the Vanguard corporate structure, the Funds own all of the stock in The Vanguard Group, Incorporated, which provides essential services—management, investment, and distribution—on an at-cost basis. This structure is unique in the mutual fund industry.

Contents

Caveat Emptor Index

I

BUILDING BLOCKS

P art I provides basic background information on the rewards of investing, the risks of investing, and the principles and practicalities of investing through mutual funds.

If you are an experienced investor, well-acquainted with the financial markets and the mutual fund industry, you may wish merely to browse through the material in this section. However, I believe that, even for knowledgeable investors, each chapter will provide at least several new perspectives on familiar financial issues.

Chapter One

The Rewards of Investing
The Magic of Compounding

"The greatest mathematical discovery of all time." That is how Albert Einstein is said to have described compound interest. This first chapter emphasizes the magic of compounding—the interaction of rate of return and time—in the search for optimum long-term rates of return on your financial assets. I believe virtually every financial goal you may have—building capital, obtaining income to meet your day-to-day financial needs, saving for your child's college education, putting away money for your retirement, or any other wealth-building purpose—can be met through a disciplined approach to the ownership of financial instruments.

This is, first and foremost, a book about mutual funds and the mutual fund industry. To set the stage, I will discuss the fundamentals of the different classes of financial assets and their unique investment characteristics. While this is not a textbook on the financial markets, I believe the intelligent, and ultimately successful, investor must consider and understand the three major categories of liquid financial securities: stocks, bonds, and cash reserves.

I hope this first part helps eliminate some of the mystery of the financial markets. This is no mean task. I have realized over the years that many individual investors regard the financial markets as enigmatic, occult, and driven by forces unseen. Mysterious though the markets may seem in the short run, in the long run it is the basic fundamentals of investing that determine the returns on financial assets. For stocks, returns are driven by earnings and dividends; for bonds and money market instruments, by interest coupons over specified periods. It is the reality of underlying financial forces, not the illusion of superficial emotions—optimism and pessimism, hope and fear, greed and satisfaction—that is at the heart of intelligent investing.

CAVEAT EMPTOR: *The Real World*

The rates of return actually experienced by investors in the aggregate will fall short of the returns of the three unmanaged measurement standards: the S&P 500, the 20-year government bond, and the 90-day U.S. Treasury bill (or T-bill). If you own an actively managed equity portfolio, you may easily incur annual investment expenses ranging from 0.50% or less to 3.00% or more, including advisory fees and portfolio transaction costs. (Even if you invest in an index portfolio, you may incur annual charges of 0.20%.) Expenses of this magnitude are not incurred in the ownership of a U.S. Treasury bond or a U.S. T-bill, but in a high-grade bond portfolio or a money market portfolio you may incur investment expenses of 0.30% to 1.50%. For a large institutional investor, these costs would be lower; for a small individual investor, the costs would be much higher. Whatever the case, the returns actually realized by investors as a group would have fallen short of those in our historical, but theoretical, study.

A LONG-TERM PERSPECTIVE

The magic of compound interest is simply a combination of time and rate of return. Let us begin by taking a truly long-term look at the financial markets. Complete data tracing the returns on financial assets are available beginning in 1872. I use primarily the Standard & Poor's 500 Composite Stock Price Index (and a predecessor index prior to 1926) as the measure of common stock returns, the long-term (20-year) U.S. government bond as the measure of bond returns, and the 90-day U.S. Treasury bill as the measure of the returns on cash reserves.

During the 1872–1992 period, the annual return on U.S. common stocks averaged +8.8%, the annual return on long-term bonds averaged +4.6%, and the annual return on cash reserves averaged +4.2%. The differences in returns—which may appear small—result in a staggering dispersion in the final value of $1 invested in each asset class on December 31, 1871. The summary figures are in Table 1–1. A mere 0.4 percentage point increase in return, from +4.2% in bills to +4.6% in bonds, increases the final value of the $1 initial investment by more than 70%. A further 4.2 percentage point increase, to 8.8% in stocks, causes the final value to

TABLE 1-1
The Financial Markets (December 31, 1871, to December 31, 1992)

	Annual rate of return	Final value of $1 initial investment
Common stocks	+8.8%	$27,710
Long-term bonds	+4.6	240
Cash reserves	+4.2	140

increase an additional 115 times. This is the magic of compounding writ large. Figure 1–1 presents the cumulative returns since December 31, 1871, for each of the three basic asset classes.

I have used this dramatic example to get your attention and to show you that time and rate of return, inextricably linked, are a powerful combination. However, we all have time horizons that are somewhat shorter than 120 years. But even if the sizes of the ultimate capital wealth created are quite different, the principles remain intact whatever the holding period. For example, the value of $1 invested in each of the three asset classes

---

CAVEAT EMPTOR: *How Now the Dow?*

When they ask, "How's the market?" many investors are thinking about the Dow Jones Industrial Average of 30 stocks, weighted by their current share prices. The Dow Jones Average, because of its high numeric value (3300 at the end of 1992), is fun. It magnifies market moves to heroic dimensions, with but a 3% market increase or decrease reflecting a 100-point leap (or plunge). The fact is a 3% move in a typical stock selling at $30 per share is only 90 cents. Despite the Dow's popularity, I chose the Standard & Poor's 500 Index as my market standard. Since it is weighted by each corporation's total market capitalization, it is a much more reliable indicator of the actual experience of aggregate investors as a group at any given point in time. That said, over long time periods the records of the two indicators have been quite similar. From December 31, 1970, to December 31, 1992, for example, the annual rates of returns were Dow Jones Average, +12.6%; Standard & Poor's 500 Index, +12.2%.

FIGURE 1-1

Cumulative Returns on U.S. Financial Assets (December 31, 1871, to December 31, 1992)

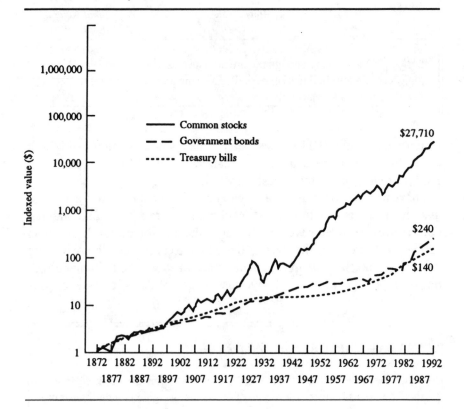

after 25 years would be $2.80 for bills, $3.10 for bonds, and $8.30 for stocks. Hence, the final value of the stock investment would be two and one-half times that of bonds, and nearly three times that of reserves. A detailed tabulation showing the crucial relationship between rate of return and length of holding period is presented later in this chapter (see Table 1-7).

While compound rates of return determine the ultimate success of any investment program, they are a simplistic way of measuring performance. For it is not enough to know what aggregate rates of return have been; we must also know how consistent these returns have been over time and what contributing forces have driven them. Reliable data needed to examine the

---

CAVEAT EMPTOR: *A Lantern on the Stern*

Financial history is important, and studying historical rates of return provides useful perspectives. But beware of concluding too much from past
returns in the financial markets. Especially beware of past returns for
periods that seem long enough but are not (such as post-World War II, an
almost continuous bull market period). Even the period beginning in 1926
has its limitations, especially considering the low level of interest rates
that prevailed from 1933 to 1958, suppressed first by the Depression and
then by national fiscal and monetary policies. Financial returns do not lend
themselves to actuarial tables. Samuel Taylor Coleridge tells us "the light
which experience gives is a lantern on the stern." Treat history with the
respect it deserves—neither too much nor too little.

---

elements of return are available from 1926 to the present, constituting
essentially the modern financial history of the United States.

TOTAL RETURNS ON COMMON STOCKS

In discussing the total returns on common stocks, I refer not to individual
equities but to widely diversified equity portfolios. For this purpose I will
use the Standard & Poor's 500 Composite Stock Price Index, probably the
most accurately constructed of all of the myriad indexes of market returns.
The returns generated by this diversified index correlate closely with the
returns of diversified equity mutual funds.

Before I begin discussing the history of returns on common stocks, I
want to emphasize that stock returns are driven by two critical factors:
dividends and earnings. Without dividends, which are made possible by
earnings, an investment in any stock would be purely speculative in nature.
Why are dividends and earnings so vital to stock returns? The most basic
way to answer that question is to recall that a share of company stock
represents a share in a business firm. If you are considering purchasing
shares in a firm, you have two broad expectations for that firm: (1) it will
pay annual dividends and the amount of these dividends will grow over
time; or (2) rather than paying dividends, it will retain its earnings so as
to build the business.

FIGURE 1–2
Common Stock Returns (Decades Ended 1935–92)

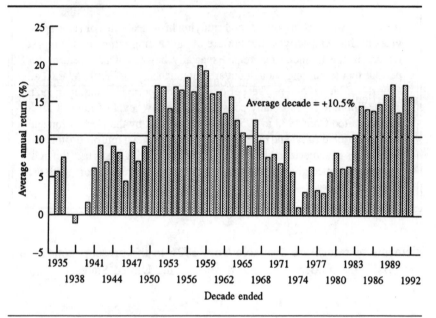

While the second expectation suggests that dividends need not always be a critical determinant of the returns on stocks, even when a company does not pay a dividend investors implicitly value the firm's stock based on the presumption of future dividends. When the earnings of a business are retained each year, investors expect that the earnings will increase over time, resulting in future dividends that will be higher than if they had been distributed currently. In sum, while the consideration of stock returns may encompass any number of qualitative and quantitative factors, any valuation judgment must ultimately rely on dividends and earnings.

Since 1926, the average *annual* total return (taking into account both capital appreciation and dividends) on common stocks has been +10.3%. While it is important to know what to expect from the stock market in the long run, you should also consider how stock returns have varied over different periods. Since this book is addressed to the long-term investor, I use a decade as my standard for analysis. Figure 1–2 shows the annualized total return on common stocks for the average decade during the 67-year period ended December 31, 1992, and for each of the 58 "moving decades" within it (1925–35, 1926–36, continuing through 1982–92).

As you can see, the variations in total return from one decade to the next were substantial. During the worst decade (1928–38), one of only two with a negative return, stocks provided an average annual return of −0.9%. During the best decade (1948–58), the average annual return was +20.1%. Nine decades witnessed returns of less than +5% and 16 of more than +15%. The majority, 33 decades, were in a middle range of +5% to +15%. If you had put your money to work at the beginning of any particular decade, there would have been roughly a 50-50 chance that your return would have been better than the +10.5% decade norm and a 50-50 chance that it would have been worse.

Figure 1–2 suggests that the decade returns offer little in the way of definitive judgments about stock returns except that they vary widely and randomly. But determining the composition of those returns adds substantial value to the analysis. In substance, three principal elements comprise the return on stocks:

1. Initial dividend yield.
2. Growth in dividends.
3. Change in price-dividend multiple.

The first two factors are financially driven and fundamental: (1) the actual dividend yield at the start of each decade and (2) the dividend growth generated by stocks over each of the past rolling decades. Ultimately, these two factors are the essential, dominant determinants of stock returns. The third factor is market-driven and technical. It is based on the opinion of investors at any point in time as to what is a fair price to pay for each $1 of corporate dividends—not just current dividends, but expected future dividends as well. I have used the price-dividend multiple rather than the more conventional price-earnings multiple, due mainly to the inexactness of earnings calculations compared to the precision of dividends actually paid. The price-dividend ratio is the reciprocal of the dividend yield (a price of $25 for $1 of dividends equates to a yield of 4%).

There are wide variations from year to year in the price-dividend multiple, just as in the price-earnings multiple. Many of these variations are based on the emotions of investors. In times of optimism, as was the case prior to the great crashes of October 28, 1929, and October 19, 1987, the price of $1 of dividends had been as high as $40. In times of gloom, so often the case during the post-Depression era through the mid-1950s, it had been as low as $10. The long-run average going back to 1926 is $24.

CAVEAT EMPTOR: *The Price-Dividend Multiple*

My shift from the customary concept of price-earnings multiple to the less familiar price-dividend multiple is based largely on the fact that, especially in recent years, wide gaps have opened up between *reported* corporate earnings and *operating* corporate earnings. The difference between the two is accounted for by write-offs of discontinued operations, write-downs of assets such as real estate, and changes in generally accepted accounting principles. As a result, reported price-earnings multiples have soared and, I would argue, have lost touch with reality. This chart reflects the sharp divergence of price-earnings and price-dividend multiples over the past 15 years. If reported earnings are less than operating earnings in any given year, there are two consequences: (1) the current price-earnings ratio rises and (2) the rate of past earnings growth declines. In 1991, for example, reported earnings on the S&P 500 totaled $15.97 per share, compared with operating earnings of $21.61 per share. Thus, the price-earnings ratio was 26.1 times, the highest in the entire period illustrated. If operating earnings were used, a more realistic ratio of 19.3 times would result. Using the reported earnings number results in an annual earnings growth rate of only +0.4% during the decade ended December 31, 1991, while operating earnings grew at a rate of +3.5% annually and dividends grew at +6.3% annually. If 1991 were unique, the problem might be ignored, but there were substantial write-offs again in 1992. In the long run, earnings must be generated for dividends to be paid, but the durability of dividends makes them a more solid baseline for analysis.

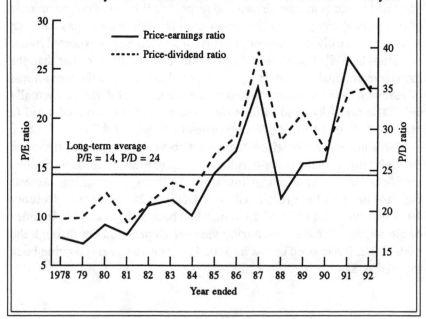

FIGURE 1-3
Price of $1 of Dividends (1926-92)

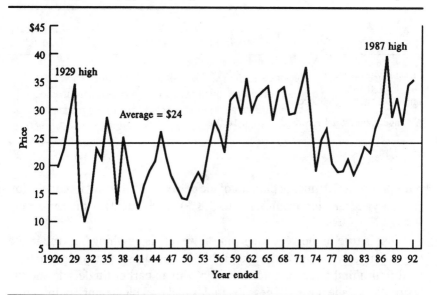

It is very important to understand that changes in the price-dividend multiple have a huge impact on stock returns. A decline in the price of $1 of dividends from $30 to $20 would result in a decline of −33% in stock prices. If this decline took place over a decade, the reduction in return would be −4.0% a year.

To some degree, the level of the price-dividend ratio is affected by the general level of interest rates, because stocks must compete with fixed-income securities for investor favor. Thus, when bond yields are relatively low, the price of $1 of dividends tends to be high (that is, the dividend yield tends to be low). When bond yields are high, the price of $1 of dividends tends to be low. Figure 1-3 traces the level of the price-dividend ratio during the 1926-92 period.

By way of contrast, the fundamental factors for the long-term investor are dividends and dividend growth. Taken together, these two basic elements account for about 90% of the average ten-year return on stocks during the 1926-92 era. Specifically, the average decade return of +10.5% annually included an average initial yield of 4.7% and an average ten-year dividend growth rate of +4.8%. A rise in the price-dividend

TABLE 1-2
Components of Stock Returns

	Golden decade 1981-91	Tin decade 1968-78	Average decade 1926-92
Initial dividend yield	+5.4%	+3.0%	+4.7%
Dividend growth rate	+6.3	+5.1	+4.8
Impact of multiple change	+6.3	-5.6	+1.0
Average annual total return	+18.0%	+2.5%	+10.5%

multiple, from 20 times at the start of the period to 35 times at its conclusion (i.e., a yield decline from 5.1% to 3.8%), accounted for the remaining +1.0%.

What is true in the very long run, however, is anything but true in the shorter run, even over a decade. Table 1-2 contrasts the components of total return in the recent golden decade with an earlier tin decade and the historical decade norms. These examples make an elementary point: large swings in the price-dividend ratio often make the difference between a golden decade and a tin decade. During the former decade, the price that investors were willing to pay for $1 of dividends jumped from $19 to $34, engendering a +85% increase in valuation, for a positive contribution to return of +6.3% annually. During the latter decade, the price of $1 of dividends fell from $34 to $19, a -44% decrease in valuation, for a negative contribution to return of -5.6% annually.

One of the ironies of this comparison is that the dividend growth rate—the second component of total return—was almost as large in the tin decade (+5.1% per year) as in the golden decade (+6.3% per year). While both of these ten-year growth rates are higher than the long-term decade average of +4.8%, even if you had known the dividend growth rates in advance, it would not have been much help to you in deciding whether or not to invest in stocks.

The first component of stock returns—the dividend yield at the start of each decade—should be of special importance to the investor, because it alone is known in advance. Long-term investors would be wise to give the current dividend yield significant weight in their appraisal of the total returns they expect from stocks since, in the long run, it has comprised nearly one-half of the average total return on stocks (average initial yield of 4.7%; average decade return of +10.5%).

In considering stock returns, then, what is most important to the truly long-term investor is corporate dividends—their yield when they are purchased and their subsequent growth. But short-term investors—those with a time horizon as short as one year or even as long as a decade—must concern themselves with not only the current yield and the future growth of dividends but also the valuation the marketplace may set for these dividends at some point in the future. The price paid for $1 of dividends varies widely over interim periods, but over the very long run has tended to return to its average level of about $24.

Over the modern history of the financial markets (going back to 1926), the average annual return of +10.3% for stocks was by far the highest of any of the three major financial asset classes. While past results offer no assurances for equity returns in an inevitably uncertain future, the superior relative results of investing in equities—in nearly every decade spanning a full century—suggest that stocks should represent a major element of your investment program.

TOTAL RETURNS ON BONDS

In this section, I use a 20-year U.S. government bond as my benchmark. This approach is to a degree simplistic since this bond has a higher credit quality than other bonds. But the long-term data appear sound and the returns are fairly representative of the bond market as a whole. Since 1926, the *annual* return on U.S. government bonds has averaged +4.8%. As was the case with stocks, however, this figure conceals at least as much as it reveals, for the average return on bonds has varied sharply from one decade to the next. Figure 1–4 shows the returns on U.S. government bonds for each of the 58 decades during the 1926–92 period.

You can see that the variations in the decade-long average returns were substantial. During the worst decade (1949–59), the only one with a negative return, bonds provided an annual return of −0.1%. In the best decade (1981–91), the return was +15.6%. From the decade ending in 1950 through to the decade ending in 1974, the average return on bonds never reached +3% annually. Beginning with the decade ending in 1985, the average annual return was +9% or higher. This sea change in the level of

FIGURE 1-4
Long-Term Government Bond Returns (Decades Ended 1935-92)

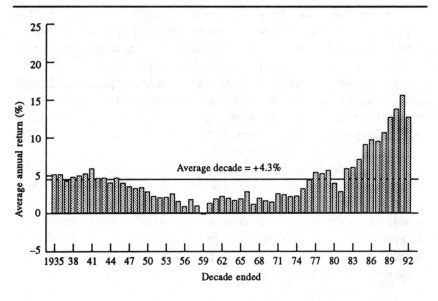

interest rates, driven in part by changes in expectations about the level of inflation, is one of the more remarkable events of modern financial history.

As in the case of stocks, the total return on bonds comprises three principal elements:

1. Initial yield.
2. Reinvestment rate.
3. Impact of rate change.

The first of these three factors is the ultimate fundamental. The initial interest rate consistently has been by far the major determinant of the future returns on bonds. It is reasonable, for example, to assume that a U.S. government bond with an 8% coupon will achieve an annual total return of +8% if held to its 20-year maturity.

This observation, however, is not always correct. Only if the semiannual interest coupon is reinvested at the same interest rate of 8% will the cumulative return equate to +8% annually. If the reinvestment rate is much higher over the term of the investment, the return will be commensurately enhanced; if it is much lower, the return will be commensurately

TABLE 1-3
20-Year Government Bond (8% coupon, $10,000 Initial Investment)

	Reinvestment Rate		
	6%	*8%*	*10%*
Value at maturity	$10,000	$10,000	$10,000
Cumulative interest coupon	16,000	16,000	16,000
Reinvestment effect	14,200	22,000	32,300
Total value	$40,200	$48,000	$58,300

reduced. Table 1-3 shows the importance of this reinvestment factor. It considers a $10,000 initial investment in a long-term bond with a maturity of 20 years, assuming a lower reinvestment rate (6%), an unchanged reinvestment rate (8%), and a higher reinvestment rate (10%).

As you can see, an instantaneous increase in rates to 10% raises the final value of the 8% coupon bond from $48,000 to $58,300. More than half of this final value is accounted for solely by the reinvestment effect, a factor so often ignored in the calculation of bond returns. At a 6% reinvestment rate, the accumulation total of $40,200 is only 85% of the accumulation achieved at the 8% reinvestment level.

Even these figures are invalid unless the bond is held until its maturity. The third component of bond returns is the impact of a change in interest rates on a bond's market price when it is valued prior to its maturity. An instantaneous increase in rates from 8% to 10% would reduce the market value of a 20-year bond with an 8% coupon from $10,000 to $8,300 (a 17% decline). An instantaneous drop from 8% to 6% would increase the bond's value from $10,000 to $12,300 (a 23% increase). Barring a default, such a paper loss or gain would be gradually reduced and finally eliminated as the bond approached its maturity date.

Changes of these dimensions in interest rates do not take place overnight. And the rate at which interest coupons are reinvested varies over a large number of intervals (i.e., 40 semiannual reinvestment dates for a 20-year bond). With all of this averaging, the combined impact of reinvestment rates and changes in the general level of interest rates has only rarely been the dominant force in explaining bond returns over any ten-year period.

TABLE 1-4
Components of Bond Returns

	Golden decade 1981–91	Tin decade 1971–81	Average decade 1926–92
Initial yield	+13.3%	+6.0%	+4.5%
Reinvestment rate	−2.6	+2.4	+0.6
Impact of change in rates	+4.9	−5.6	−0.8
Average annual total return	+15.6%	+2.8%	+4.3%

Table 1–4 presents the components of return on long-term U.S. government bonds in the average decade during the 1926–92 period and in two dramatically contrasting interim decades. Note that our golden decade of 1981–91 is the same for bonds as for stocks. However, for contrast we have selected as the tin decade the ten years ending in 1981, when interest rates rose to their highest levels in U.S. history.

These three examples reinforce the elementary nature of bond investing: the initial yield is the primary determinant of long-term bond returns. In fact, on average it has explained more than 80% of the total return in each of the 58 individual decades and virtually the entire return of the decade average. During the tin decade, the initial yield was pulled down by the sharp rise in rates from 6.0% to 13.3%, with some of the resultant principal loss offset by rising investment rates. In the golden decade, the reverse was true. A high initial yield gave way to a sharply lower yield at the end of the period, resulting in a dramatic increase in principal. This increase was only partially offset by declining reinvestment rates.

To express it in the same terms as in the previous section on stocks, the price paid for $1 of interest is the critical factor in bond returns. Figure 1–5 shows the price paid for $1 of interest on a long-term U.S. government bond during the 1926–92 period. The wide swings in the price paid for $1 of interest are simply a manifestation of wide swings in interest rates. The $50 price is equivalent to a 2.0% yield; the $8 price is equivalent to a 12.5% yield. The long-run annual average is $26, or a yield of 3.8%, a bit below the 4.5% average yield at the beginning of each decade.

The price-interest ratio shown in Figure 1–5 is for a long-term bond. The ratio is often very different for bonds of shorter maturities. (This

FIGURE 1-5
Price of $1 of Interest (1926-92)

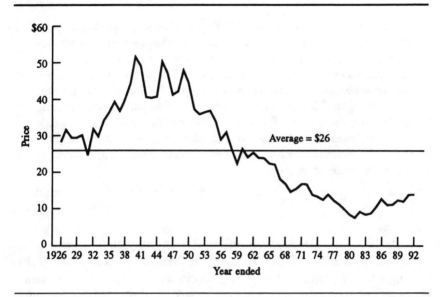

TABLE 1-5
A Shifting Yield Curve

	December 1988		December 1992	
Government bond	Interest rate	Price of $1 of interest	Interest rate	Price of $1 of interest
Short-term	9.2%	$11	5.1%	$20
Intermediate-term	9.2	11	6.1	16
Long-term	9.2	11	7.3	14

factor is known as the term structure of interest rates.) In 1988, for example, the yield curve was virtually flat; by the end of 1992 it had become the steepest in U.S. history. Table 1-5 illustrates the shift and shows how quickly the yield curve can change. As it does, your decisions about the composition of your bond portfolio may change as well.

CAVEAT EMPTOR: *Historical Evidence, or Hysterical?*

We now know two incontrovertible statistical facts: (1) since 1926, the annual total return on U.S. government bonds has averaged +4.8% per year and (2) the initial yield on bonds is the major influence on their subsequent long-term return. We can conclude that, even though the annual return on long-term bonds has averaged +4.8% over modern financial history, the 7.3% yield on long-term U.S. Treasury bonds at the end of 1992 was likely to be a far better indicator of future returns. Although many investment professionals continue to use past bond returns to guide their asset allocation decisions, at least in this case historical evidence is hysterical evidence in disguise.

Since 1926 the average return of +4.8% annually on long-term U.S. government bonds has fallen far short of the average return on stocks (+10.3%). The premium for owning stocks averaged +5.5% per year. However, the premium return averaged +6.1% through 1981 but only +1.8% thereafter, suggesting that the earlier premium may have been abnormally large. So the long-term outlook for bonds relative to stocks may well be more favorable in the 1990s than it was in the past.

TOTAL RETURNS ON CASH RESERVES

Of the three basic financial asset classes, the total return on cash reserves is the simplest to analyze. You need not be concerned about market volatility, income growth, or reinvestment rates. Your only consideration should be the current rate of interest available on cash reserves. In this analysis, I shall use the 90-day U.S. T-bill, which has provided a long-term annual total return of +3.7%.

Essentially, your return on a U.S. Treasury bill is set on the day that it is purchased. If the T-bill is held to its maturity three months later, the return has only one component: interest income. In substance, T-bills, unlike stocks and corporate bonds, incur neither principal risk nor credit risk. In this simplified comparison, they can be thought of as a haven (albeit one that promises lower returns) in which to shelter your assets

FIGURE 1–6
U.S. Treasury Bill Returns (Decades Ended 1935–92)

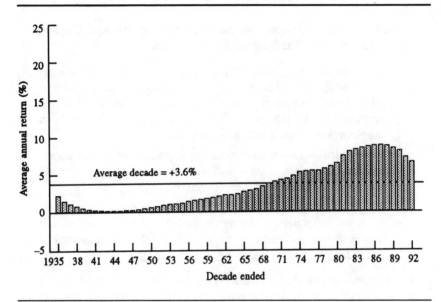

TABLE 1–6
U.S. Treasury Bill Returns

	Golden decade 1977–87	Tin decade 1932–42	Average decade 1926–92
Average annual total return	+9.2%	+0.1%	+3.6%

from principal volatility. Figure 1–6 shows the historical returns earned on U.S. Treasury bills in each decade during the 192b–92 period.

Again, the variations in return over the decades are substantial, with yields running in the 1% range during most of the decades ending in the late 1930s through the mid-1950s (when inflation was not a significant factor), only to spring up to the 6% to 9% level in the 1970s and 1980s (when inflation was considerably more prevalent). Table 1–6 shows the returns for a golden decade and a tin decade as well as the long-term decade average.

CAVEAT EMPTOR: *Regression to the Mean(s)*

There is a powerful tendency for the total returns on financial assets to regress to the mean. The question is, which mean?

- Common stock returns tend to regress to the average historical long-term rate of return. That is because, in the long run, they are determined largely by dividend yields and dividend growth, which in turn are based on the returns on capital earned by corporations in an ever-competitive economic environment.

- Bond returns—short-term, intermediate-term, and long-term alike—tend to regress, not to the historical norm, but to the interest yield prevailing at the time your investment is made.

- Bill returns tend to take on a life of their own, because their rates are reset so frequently. During the post-World War II period, bill returns show some tendency to regress to a real return (the nominal return less the rate of inflation) in the 1% range.

For all types of assets, the concept of regression to the mean is fundamental to understanding the financial markets. However, it should be used, not casually, but thoughtfully.

It is ironic that the Treasury bill rate in 1992—which averaged about 3.5%—so closely reflects the long-term decade average that lies between two remarkable extremes: the low rates associated with the Great Depression, World War II, and postwar federal monetary policies, and the high rates associated with the unprecedented price inflation of the late 1970s and early 1980s. In the abstract, we can conclude only that short-term rates are variable and that any given level of rates will persist for an indeterminate period.

THE MAGIC OF COMPOUNDING FOR TODAY'S INVESTOR

Both the data for some 120 years of investing and the data for the modern era (since 1926) confirm that, among the three asset classes, stocks have consistently provided the highest returns, long-term bonds the second

TABLE 1-7
Capital Accumulations (Annual Rates of Return)

Years invested	Initial Investment of $25,000				
	4%	6%	8%	10%	12%
1	$26,000	$ 26,500	$ 27,000	$ 27,500	$ 28,000
5	30,400	33,500	36,700	40,300	44,100
10	37,000	44,800	54,000	64,800	77,600
15	45,000	59,900	79,300	104,400	136,800
20	54,800	80,200	116,500	168,200	241,200
25	66,600	107,300	171,200	270,900	425,000

Years invested	Annual Investment of $1,000				
	4%	6%	8%	10%	12%
1	$ 1,040	$ 1,060	$ 1,080	$ 1,100	$ 1,120
5	5,600	6,000	6,300	6,700	7,100
10	12,500	14,000	15,600	17,500	19,700
15	20,800	24,700	29,300	35,000	41,800
20	31,000	39,000	49,400	63,000	80,700
25	43,300	58,200	79,000	108,200	149,300

highest, and cash reserves the lowest. Stocks have achieved their winning margin as the U.S. economy has grown and as corporate earnings and dividends have grown apace. The evidence seems compelling that, if maximum total return is your sole objective—irrespective of risk and volatility—common stocks should be your investment of choice.

While we have been dealing with the magic of compounding over periods of awesome length, it is important to realize that the same principles apply to shorter time frames that are more relevant to today's investors working to accumulate assets for their own financial futures. Table 1-7 provides a working range for considering potential capital accumulations at various (fixed) rates of return over periods up to 25 years. The accumulations are shown in two ways: (1) based on a capital investment of $25,000 at the start of the period and (2) based on regular investments of $1,000 at the start of each year during the 25-year period for a total investment of $25,000.

CAVEAT EMPTOR: *Compounding Income or Spending It?*

In this first chapter, I have used the concept of compound total returns—reinvesting all income—to illustrate the rewards of investing. To state the obvious, however, you may not be in a position to compound the income portion of your return. Rather, you may need income to meet your every-day living expenses, especially if you are in your retirement years. The difference in return achieved by investors who accumulate assets by rein-vesting their income, as compared to their counterparts who receive all of their dividends in cash, is dramatic. For example, consider an invest-ment of $10,000 in the stock market during the 25-year period ended December 31, 1992.

- If you were in the distribution phase of your life cycle, spending your income and letting your capital appreciate, you would have received cash dividends totaling $16,800 and watched the value of your $10,000 investment grow to $45,200, a combined value of $62,000.

- If you were in the accumulation phase of your life cycle and rein-vested all your income dividends, the value of your reinvested in-come would have reached $77,200 and the total value of your $10,000 investment would have grown to $122,300.

In both cases, the stock market provided an identical annual return of +13.1%. Yet the difference between the two accumulations—$62,000 versus $122,300—is awesome. It is accounted for solely by the magic of compounding. This example clearly affirms that the role of price apprecia-tion in determining total return diminishes as we move from the short run to the long run. Conversely, the role of income in determining total return escalates dramatically over time. The difference between spending income and compounding income reflects the different risks assumed by the distri-bution phase investor and the accumulation phase investor. I shall deal in more detail with this difference in the next chapter.

In my view, the most compelling message of Table 1-7 is the extraordi-nary difference in capital accumulation that occurs with seemingly trivial differences in annual rate of return. A mere two-percentage-point increase in rate of return (from +8% to +10%) increases the value of the outright investment of $25,000 from $171,200 to $270,900 over 25 years. Another two-percentage-point increase, to +12%, takes the final value to $425,000. Moving the expected return from +8% to +12%, then, would increase your final capital accumulation over the 25-year period by nearly two and one-half times, a staggering difference indeed. Even after ten years, an increase in return from +8% to +12% increases the final value from $54,000 to $77,600—an enhancement of $23,600, or more than 40%. So the length of time that an investment is made, in conjunction with the rate of return that it earns, ultimately determines your wealth accumulation.

Table 1-7 also expresses the importance of beginning to build your asset base *today*, versus postponing your investment until tomorrow. If you earned an annual rate of return of +10% on an outright investment of $25,000, in ten years your account would be worth $64,800. In 20 years your account would be worth $168,200. By the same token, putting $1,000 to work each year for ten years would result in a final value of $17,500. But by doing so for 20 years you would reach $63,000.

The accumulations, of course, would become stupendous if you simply raised the hypothetical rates of return to +15% or more. But it would be extremely unwise even to imply that such returns represent realistic financial goals. In the long run, any sustained return over +12% should probably be considered found money.

SUMMARY

Long-term investors ignore at their peril the principles manifested in Table 1-7. The clear message of this chapter is to maximize your capital by earning the highest returns you can over the longest period possible. Compound interest indeed may be the greatest mathematical discovery of all time for the investor seeking maximum reward. However, risk is every bit as central as reward in the establishment of your investment portfolio, so you must carefully consider what risks you are prepared to assume. Chapter 2 will analyze the risks of investing.

Chapter Two

The Risks of Investing
Do What You Will, Capital Is at Hazard

In 1830, Justice Samuel Putnam of Massachusetts wrote the words that were to become the foundation of the prudent man rule:

> Do what you will, the capital is at hazard. . . . all that can be required of a trustee to invest is that he shall conduct himself faithfully and exercise a sound discretion. He is to observe how men of prudence, discretion, and intelligence manage their own affairs, not in regard to speculation, but in regard to the permanent disposition of their funds, considering the probable income, as well as the probable safety of the capital to be invested.

This message is equally valid today. Manage your affairs with prudence, intelligence, and discretion. Do not speculate. Consider probable income as well as probable safety of capital. Recognize that there is no avoiding risk of one kind or another. For instance, holding cash—or hiding it in the proverbial mattress—at best assures no earnings on your capital and at worst exposes it to erosion by inflation. So the question is: What kinds of risks are you prepared to take? This chapter provides you with the background to answer that question by discussing the two major categories of financial risk. First is the inescapable risk of price inflation, which applies equally to all classes of financial assets. Second are the risks to principal and to income, which can be controlled to a large degree by your choices among the three primary financial asset classes.

THE RISK OF INFLATION

Today, investors generally accept price inflation as a fact of life. As rising prices reduce the purchasing power of the dollar, they reduce commensu-

TABLE 2-1
The Financial Markets—Average Annual Total Returns (December 31, 1871, to December 31, 1992)

	Nominal return	Inflation rate	Real return
Common stocks	+8.8%	−2.3%	+6.5%
Long-term bonds	+4.6	−2.3	+2.3
Cash reserves	+4.2	−2.3	+1.9

rately the nominal (or stated) returns earned on financial assets. The term *real return* is used to describe the nominal rate of return reduced by the rate of inflation.

Real return is more than just a statistic. It is central to your financial security. If price inflation is at the 5% level, for example, and the annual return on the capital in your savings account is +4%, you are actually *losing* purchasing power at the rate of 1% per year. If the cost of attending college is rising at the rate of 8% annually, your +10% nominal return becomes but +2% in real terms. Such a real return translates into very modest assistance in accumulating your child's college fund.

To characterize the concept of inflation risk, I shall begin with a truly long-term perspective. The studies of the returns on financial assets for the period 1872–1992 include estimates of annual inflation, restating in *real* terms the nominal returns presented in the previous chapter. Table 2–1 presents the real returns on common stocks, long-term U.S. government bonds, and short-term U.S. Treasury bills during this period.

As you can see, the average nominal return of each asset class is reduced by the same 2.3 percentage points. But the *relative* rewards of stocks are greatly enhanced since the impact of inflation on the returns garnered by each class of assets is absolute. The result is that the return on stocks rises from about twice as large as that of the other two asset classes (+8.8% vs. +4.6% and +4.2%) to about three times as large (+6.5% vs. +2.3% and +1.9%).

What these long-term aggregate statistics conceal, however, is that substantial inflation is largely a modern phenomenon. While the average annual inflation rate was 2.3% over the past 120 years, it averaged but 1.2% during the 1872–1925 period. Since 1925, it has averaged 3.1%

TABLE 2-2
The Financial Markets—Average Annual Total Returns

	Nominal return	Inflation rate	Real return
1872-1925			
Common stocks	+7.0%	−1.2%	+5.8%
Long-term bonds	+4.4	−1.2	+3.2
Cash reserves	+4.7	−1.2	+3.5
1926-92			
Common stocks	+10.3%	−3.1%	+7.2%
Long-term bonds	+4.8	−3.1	+1.7
Cash reserves	+3.7	−3.1	+0.6

(two and one-half times that level). Subdividing the full period reveals some striking differences, as shown in Table 2-2.

The table reflects a compelling consistency: common stock returns have rolled with the punches of inflation and have produced roughly similar real returns (+5.8% vs. +7.2%) in each era. But there is also a compelling inconsistency: the real returns on long-term government bonds and short-term U.S. Treasury bills provided solid competition to stocks in the first era but almost no competition after 1925. Put another way, stocks provided a +2.6% real return premium over bonds in the earlier period but a +5.5% real return premium in the latter.

Figure 2-1 shows the annual inflation rate in the U.S. since 1926. It would appear that investors were unaware of inflation risk through the 1920s, even after the post-World War I inflation. During the 1930s, inflation was virtually nonexistent because of the Depression. Even during the 1950s, inflation expectations were subdued despite the dramatic spike in inflation (which, one might hypothesize, was expected to abate) immediately after World War II. However, as inflation reached near-record levels through the 1970s and early 1980s, fixed-income investors finally began to demand returns that would compensate them for inflation risk.

Since we have already demonstrated that small differences in rates of return over time can have a tremendous impact on the final value of your investment, the message of the chart is critical. At an annual inflation rate of 3.1% (the historical average for the 1926–92 period), the value of $1.00 falls to $0.73 in a decade, to $0.53 in two decades, and to $0.39 in three decades. (In conceptual terms, if the price of an automobile rises from

FIGURE 2–1
Inflation (U.S. Consumer Price Index 1926–92)

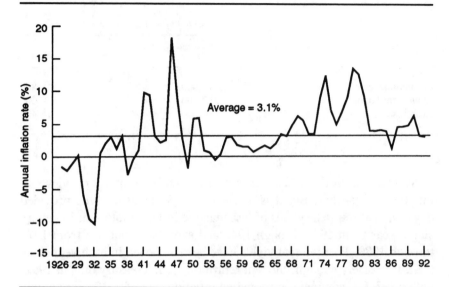

$10,000 to $13,600 over a decade, the purchasing power of $1.00 has fallen to $0.73.) So a nominal annual return of +3.1% is necessary simply to maintain the purchasing power of the original dollar. If you achieve that return—no more, no less—you are simply walking on a treadmill, making no real progress financially.

Table 2–3 illustrates the important effect of the rate of inflation on the effective purchasing power of your investment over time. It shows both the nominal value and the real value of $10,000 invested in each asset class during the period 1926–92.

If you look only at the nominal value of your investments in 1992 you would surely consider yourself wealthy. However, the stark reality is shown in the right-hand column. After adjustment for inflation, each of your investment dollars actually provides only a small fraction of its nominal purchasing power. In fact, the $7,273,800 nominal value of the stock investment falls to $918,900, one-eighth of the total. Long-term bonds also suffer a substantial reduction in their nominal value. Amazingly, if you had invested in a U.S. Treasury bill way back in 1926, you would have barely more than the original $10,000 that you started with, despite the compounding of income over nearly 70 years.

TABLE 2-3
The Financial Markets—$10,000 Initial Investment: December 31, 1925

	Final Value at December 31, 1992	
	Nominal	Real
Common stocks	$7,273,800	$918,900
Long-term bonds	237,100	30,000
Cash reserves	114,000	14,400

Speculation on the precise causes of the shifts in investors' views of inflation is just that. But it is a fact that U.S. Treasury bills provided *negative* real returns—yields of less than the inflation rate—during every single year from 1940 through 1948 and every year but one from 1973 through 1980. Positive real yields have been achieved in each year since then. Perversely enough, the real return for U.S. Treasury bills in 1992, with a +3.5% nominal return and an inflation rate of 2.9%, was barely above zero. Inflation, then, can relegate even the most conservative investments to speculative status.

It is generally accepted that stocks are more likely than bonds or bills to provide a hedge against inflation. The replacement value of corporate assets should rise with the general price level, as should corporate earnings and dividends. Nonetheless, however effectively dividends on stocks have provided an inflation hedge, the correlation of the *total returns* on stocks with the rate of inflation has been small, even over extended periods. Indeed, the evidence suggests that a causal relationship between inflation and stock returns is perceived simply because stocks have provided higher nominal returns than bonds over long periods of time. Yet there have in fact been many years, and even a few decades, in which long-term bonds and bills provided higher nominal returns than stocks and hence were the better inflation hedge.

When considering the potential effect of inflation on your investment, bear in mind that the financial markets, being highly efficient, tend to anticipate future events. Thus, the anticipated level of inflation should always be incorporated into the existing levels of interest rates and dividend yields. Of course, to further complicate matters, the anticipated level of inflation may be very different from the actual level that ensues.

CAVEAT EMPTOR: *The End of Inflation?*

As you plan for the future, you would be foolish to ignore the impact of inflation on financial assets. But you would be equally foolish to assume that inflation is an eternal fact of life. In a recent article entitled "The End of Inflation?" *The Economist* noted, "on the eve of the first world war, prices in Britain were on average no higher than at the time of the fire of London in 1666." The contrary view, of course, is that "in a democracy the people will, through their representatives, vote themselves more than they are willing to produce" (attributed to Tocqueville). That philosophy is a recipe for inflation. If it is true, inflation will be a fact of life in the U.S. for a long time. In any event, though the rate of inflation is imponderable, you would be wise to keep an open mind regarding the accuracy of any assumptions about the future rate of inflation.

The point, then, is basic: you cannot control inflation. Therefore, you should seek some protection against it. Determine which combination of financial assets is most likely to provide that protection, taking into account your own risk tolerance and your reward objectives. Through the optimal allocation of your investments among the major asset classes, that combination is within your control.

THE RISKS OF COMMON STOCKS

That reward and risk go hand in hand is a commonplace. And both the rewards and risks of investing in a diversified common stock portfolio are, as a broad generalization, higher than those of the other two asset classes. But to make that statement merely begins the discussion. So, I now turn to the risks that affect diversified portfolios of common stocks: total return risk, principal risk, and income risk.

Total Return Risk

The most widely accepted measure of the risk in any financial asset class is the volatility of its total returns. Volatility risk, quite simply, refers to the fact that a diversified portfolio will fluctuate in value and may show

---

CAVEAT EMPTOR: *Through Thick and Thin*

Volatility risk is very different from lost asset risk. The former term refers to the gains and losses in your portfolio that, as long as the holdings have not been liquidated, show up only on paper. The latter term refers to losses that have actually been realized. In this case, the risk is not that stock prices might fall and your portfolio decline in value. Rather, the risk is that a *forced* sale of your holdings may take place after the market value of your portfolio has declined below its cost. Lost asset risk, then, comes home to roost only when the portfolio is actually liquidated. If you are faced with even a remote possibility of liquidation in the near term, you must follow entirely different strategies from investors who can sustain their investment portfolios through thick and thin.

---

a loss during any interim period. However, if a diversified portfolio that is held for, say, five years achieves a satisfactory increase in value (even though it may have decreased in value during the interim), it may be said in retrospect that the investment was, for all practical purposes, safe. The distinction, then, between a safe investment program and a volatile investment program lies in the time horizon of the investor.

As shown in Figure 2-2, volatility is extremely high for common stocks when measured over one-year holding periods. Over the past 67 years, the annual total return earned by common stocks has varied from a high of +54% (1933) to a low of −43% (1931), a spread of fully 97 percentage points. There were 20 years in which common stock total returns were negative and another nine years in which their total returns fell below the long-term average of +10.3% for the full period.

As you can see in Figure 2-3, increasing the length of the period during which stocks are held tends to reduce the volatility risk reflected in Figure 2-2. While the spread in annual returns is 97 percentage points, over full decades the average annual return spread drops to 21 percentage points (a high of +20% in 1948–58 and a low of −1% in 1928–38). Over 25-year periods, the average annual total return spread falls to just nine percentage points (+15% in 1942–67 and +6% in 1928–53). It is a critical tenet that the volatility risk in common stocks is reduced as the holding period increases.

If you can afford the luxury of reinvesting dividends *and* you have a

FIGURE 2–2
Common Stocks Returns (1926–92)

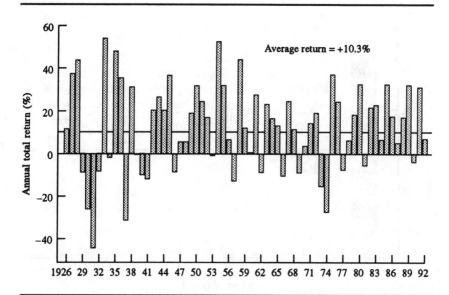

truly long-term time horizon, the total return risk of common stocks is quite tolerable. Not only does the magnitude of the disparity in returns diminish as the holding period lengthens, but the possibility of achieving a negative return decreases as well. What is more, if you also add new capital to your stock holdings regularly (or even spasmodically), in good times and bad alike, total return risk should be negligible.

It seems only logical that making many investments in the stock market at periodic intervals—known as dollar-cost averaging—will provide greater stability of return than a single all-at-once commitment. The reason is that a large single investment determines, for once and for all, the price at which you have committed your assets. By investing the same number of dollars at regular intervals over time, regardless of the market's prevailing price level, you buy more shares when stock prices are low and fewer shares when stock prices are high, virtually assuring a satisfactory average purchase price for your holdings. In addition, the regular reinvestment of dividends, year after year, irrespective of the level of stock prices, contributes still further to the effectiveness of dollar-cost averaging.

The value of dollar-cost averaging emerges clearly from a study of past

FIGURE 2–3
Range of Returns on Common Stocks (1926–92)

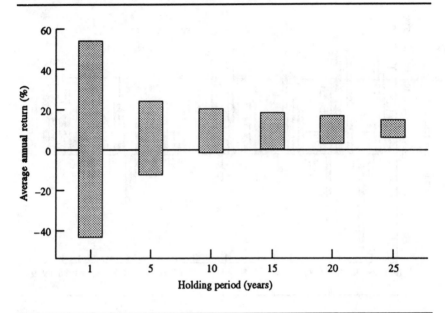

Holding period (years)

returns on stocks. Table 2–4 contrasts the best ten-year period for the stock market with the worst and illustrates how the range of returns may narrow using a program of yearly investments rather than a single lump-sum investment.

Clearly, the magic of compounding, combined with the normalizing effect of dollar-cost averaging, minimizes the volatility of investment returns. What is more, making regular annual investments of $1,000 each year rather than an all-at-once commitment would have reduced your effective average annual total return by less than one percentage point during the best decade. But it would have increased your effective average return by nearly eight percentage points during the worst decade. As far as investing in common stocks is concerned, dollar-cost averaging suggests that slow-and-steady will likely win the race.

Principal Risk

The volatility of *capital* returns, as distinct from *total* returns, is a subject given too little attention by investors. In the short run, the two risks are

TABLE 2-4
Dollar-Cost Averaging—Annual Rates of Total Return

	Initial investment of $10,000	Annual investments of $1,000
Best decade (1948–1958)	+20.1%	+19.2%
Worst decade (1928–1938)	− 0.9	+ 7.0
Range	21.0%	12.2%

similar. That is, variations in stock prices tend to overwhelm the steady dividend component of total return over periods of one or two years. But in the long run dividends, through the magic of compounding, not only become a key contributor to total return but also provide a dollar-cost averaging effect as they are regularly reinvested.

Standing on their own, principal returns on stocks vary enormously. In a worst-case example, $10,000 invested at the 1929 stock market high would have fallen to $1,400 at the market low in 1932 and would not have returned to its original value until 1954. The capital investment—measured at market value—of this unlucky investor was underwater for 25 years.

Put another way, absent the compounding of income, the principal risk of your investment increases because it reflects solely the rate of capital return. Without the income effect, the productivity of your assets is diminished disproportionately, since merely adding up returns is far less productive than compounding them through reinvestment. Table 2-5 shows the results of an investment in the stock market during an average decade in the 1926-92 time span. The top portion of the table is divided into the principal and income components of the investment. As you can see in the lower portion of the table, the final value, assuming dividends were reinvested, increases by $5,330—more than 50% of the amount initially invested.

Principal risk on common stocks is anything but an academic concept. If you are spending your current income, it is the most serious risk to which you are exposed. Unfortunately, the financial world provides virtually no information on principal risk, relying almost exclusively on total return, the compounding of capital return and reinvested income. This practice is fine if you are in the accumulation stage of your life cycle, but misleading if you are in the distribution phase of your life cycle, seeking retirement income. This phase involves yet a different kind of risk, to which I now turn.

TABLE 2-5
$10,000 Investment—Average Decade: 1926-92

	Final value
Principal value	$17,110
Income received	4,700
Total value: no reinvestment	$21,810
Total value: with reinvestment	$27,140

Income Risk

Many investors do not give much thought to income generation until after they reach retirement. Then they seek not only a reasonable level of income, but income that tends to increase steadily over time. Of our three asset classes, only common stocks—by growing their dividends—can deliver this dual objective. Of course, by investing in common stocks you assume the risk that dividends will decline during periods of recession or depression—sharply, as during the early 1930s, or more moderately, as from 1941 to 1943.

What is truly remarkable is that the record of dividend payments by U.S. corporations heavily favors rising dividends over declining dividends, almost irrespective of prevailing business conditions. Using the 1926-92 base period, annual dividends increased in 57 years, declined moderately (less than 10%) in four years, and declined by more than 10% in another five years. In one year, dividends were unchanged. On average, dividends increased at an annual rate of +4.5% since 1926, nicely exceeding the inflation rate of 3.1%, resulting in real income growth of +1.4% per year. The relationship has been particularly strong since 1950, as Figure 2-4 shows.

Barring some sort of unforeseen depression or financial catastrophe (a possibility we cannot ignore), I think it is fair to conclude that income risk in stocks is generally modest. That conclusion, sadly, is only part of the story. For it has often happened that the price paid for $1 of dividends may be so exorbitant that it could take many years for even steadily growing dividends to catch up with the equivalent total income you could earn by

FIGURE 2-4
Dividend Growth versus Inflation (1950-92)

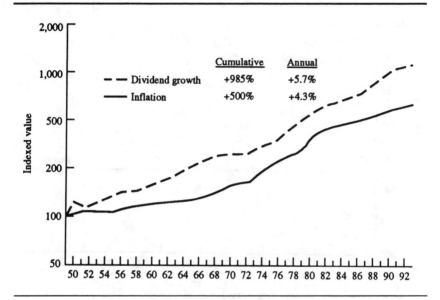

purchasing a bond. As I showed in Figure 1-3 in Chapter 1, it makes a big difference whether you pay $40 or $10 for each $1 of dividends.

Figure 2-5 compares the returns of two income-oriented investors who have a choice between investing $10,000 in (1) a diversified stock portfolio yielding 3% but with income growing at 6% annually or (2) a long-term bond yielding 7%. The investor who selects the stock portfolio receives less than half of the annual income of the bond investor at the outset. Only after 15 years does the annual dividend on the stock portfolio reach the level of the annual interest payment from the bond, and only after 26 years are the cumulative income streams of the two investments equal.

We know from Chapter 1 that the income risk in stocks is far more likely to be accounted for by paying too high a price for the dividends in the first place than by declining dividends. Unfortunately, defining what constitutes too high a price for dividends is a fallible exercise, one that must take into account not only the average historical valuations for stocks but the current valuations for other investment alternatives as well. History suggests that stocks are relatively expensive when the price paid for $1

FIGURE 2–5
Investment Income—Stocks versus Bonds

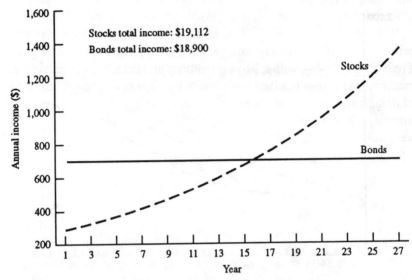

Note: 7% bond coupon; 3% initial stock yield and 6% dividend growth rate.

of dividends is above $30 (i.e., a yield of 3.3%) and relatively cheap when the price paid is less than $20 (a yield of 5%). However, stocks may well be attractive at a yield of, say, 3.5% if there are compelling reasons to assume that their dividends will increase rapidly or if yields on other classes of financial assets are relatively unattractive. In the example shown in Figure 2–5, buying a portfolio of stocks at a 3% yield rather than a bond at a 7% yield might not be a sensible investment, especially considering the incremental risk incurred in holding stocks. When stocks yield 4.5% and bonds yield 6%, that may be quite another story.

THE RISKS OF BONDS

The risks you assume by investing in bonds are remarkably complex and quite different from those you assume by investing in common stocks. It can be generalized that for bonds, total return risk tends to be significantly lower, principal risk somewhat lower, and income risk, under the best circumstances, almost infinitely lower. But, with so many sizes (maturities) and shapes (degrees of creditworthiness) of bonds available, to consider those generalizations as anything more than superficial would be potentially devastating to your financial future.

When you use specific types of bonds as benchmarks, some important principles of bond investing emerge. This section considers just two U.S. Treasury bonds, one with a 20-year maturity and the other with a five-year maturity. As a result, I deal with bonds that are essentially without risk of default and not ordinarily subject to being retired by the issuer before maturity. (I shall review credit risk and prepayment risk later in this section.)

Total Return Risk

As with common stocks, volatility is our standard measure of total return risk for bonds. In one-year holding periods measured since 1926, the total return of long-term government bonds has varied from a high of +40% (1982) to a low of −9% (1967), for a spread of 49 percentage points. While remarkably large in absolute terms, this spread is only about half the spread in one-year stock returns. There were only 18 years in which losses were incurred and 49 with gains. Figure 2–6 (see p. 38) presents the evidence.

Over full decades, the spread of average annual returns is 16 percentage points (a high of +16% in 1981–1991 and a low of 0% in 1949–59). The spread moves to 11 percentage points over 15-year periods, to nine percentage points over 20-year periods, and to seven percentage points over 25-year periods. Figure 2–7 presents this analysis. It is easy to see not only that the range of past returns on bonds narrows as the holding period lengthens but, as in the case of stocks, that there is a gradual increase in the propensity for the average total return on bonds to be positive, whatever their magnitude.

On any short-term basis, the insurmountable principle of bond returns is that rising interest rates *reduce* returns and falling interest rates *increase* returns. That said, I should quickly note that the maximum total return risk is entailed in a long-term bond; such risk is markedly reduced in a short-term bond. In both cases, however, assuming that a rate change occurs instantaneously, a dramatic change in total return takes place immediately. The reason is that the market value of a bond changes overnight with a change in interest rates. But the income component of total return

FIGURE 2–6
Long-Term Government Bond Returns (1926–92)

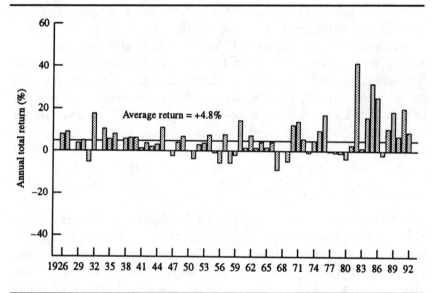

is earned over a period of years. Table 2–6 shows the immediate effect of changing interest rates on a five-year and a 20-year bond, each with a 7% coupon. The table clearly shows the sensitivity of bond total returns to interest rate changes, even as it illustrates the strong defensive character- istics of short-term bonds compared to long-term bonds.

I have presented these examples of instantaneous changes in rates of return in such large magnitudes to illustrate the potential risks of bond investing. It is highly unlikely, however, that the most extreme changes in rates would take place overnight. Since a bond's income component becomes the driving force on its total return over time, Table 2–7 shows the simple average returns for bonds over periods of one year, five years, and, for the long-term bond, 20 years, given the same instantaneous changes in rates. When sufficient time elapses for income to become a significant contributor to return, volatility risk is greatly reduced. Further, when other factors are held equal, bond returns regress to the initial interest rate as they approach maturity.

Of course, the simplified example in Table 2–7 assumes that interest income is received in cash rather than being reinvested. If you compound

FIGURE 2–7
Range of Returns on Long-Term Government Bonds (1926–92)

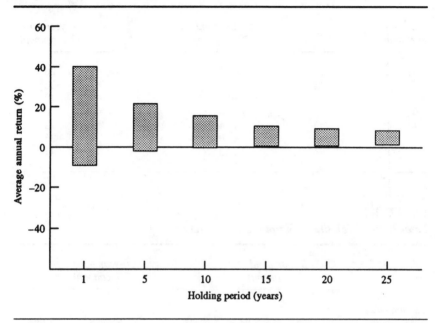

all interest by reinvesting it each year, the issue becomes more complex. Specifically, a significant reduction in total return risk occurs because changes in interest rates will have a dual but countervailing impact on your total return as the time period lengthens. When interest rates rise, bond prices decline (which *reduces* your total return), but the semiannual reinvestments of the interest income are made at higher yields (which *increases* your return). Falling interest rates have precisely the reverse effects. As the bond moves toward its maturity date and its capital and income returns interact, whether interest rates rise or fall becomes increasingly irrelevant to the total return you earn.

For example, a 20-year Treasury bond with a 7% coupon would provide a one-year total return of −8% if interest rates were to rise by two percentage points and a return of +34% on a commensurate rate decline. However, after five years the range of respective rates of return narrows to +5% and +10%. At some point, the lines cross and the gap is eliminated. Thereafter, higher rates add to return and lower rates detract. The point

TABLE 2–6
Total Return Volatility—One-Day Total Return

Instantaneous rate change	5-year bond (7% coupon)	20-year bond (7% coupon)
+3%	−12%	−26%
+2	− 8	−18
+1	− 4	−10
0	0	0
−1	+ 4	+12
−2	+ 9	+25
−3	+13	+41

TABLE 2–7
Total Return Volatility—Simple Average Returns

Instantaneous rate change	5-year bond (7% coupon)		20-year bond (7% coupon)		
	1 year	5 years	1 year	5 years	20 years
+3%	− 3%	+7%	−18%	+ 2%	+7%
+2	0	+7	−11	+ 3	+7
+1	+ 4	+7	−13	+ 5	+7
0	+ 7	+7	+ 7	+ 7	+7
−1	+11	+7	+18	+ 9	+7
−2	+14	+7	+31	+11	+7
−3	+18	+7	+47	+13	+7

of convergence is called *duration,* and it is easily measurable. In fact, the duration of a 20-year bond with 7% coupon is about eleven years, and the duration of a five-year bond with a 7% coupon is about three and one-half years.

Over long holding periods, the value to investors of higher rates versus lower rates is dramatic. As shown in Figure 2–8, a $10,000 investment in a 20-year U.S. Treasury bond with a 7% coupon would have a value (including compounded interest) of just $9,200 one year after a 2% rate increase and a value of $13,400 after a 2% rate decline. The values con-

FIGURE 2–8
Value of 7% 20-Year Treasury Bond (When Interest Rates Rise or Fall 2%)

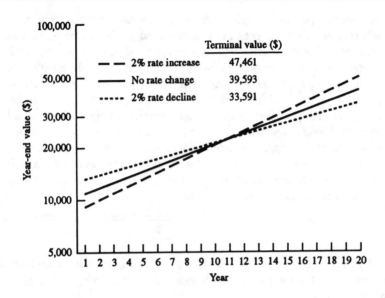

verge at $22,000 and then cross in the eleventh year. When the bond matures, the $10,000 investment has a value (including reinvested interest) of nearly $47,500 in the higher rate environment and just $33,600 in the lower rate environment—a 29% reduction in terminal value engendered by falling rates. This reversal affirms the aphorism that "it is an ill wind (indeed) that blows no good."

The main message of Figure 2–8 is that you can minimize your bond risk by selecting a duration suitable to your own investment horizon. A long-duration bond may work best if you want to lock in high income for, say, 20 years. A short-duration bond may be best if you want a higher, more durable yield than that of a U.S. Treasury bill and you are willing to accept the marginal increase in short-term volatility.

Principal Risk

When you consider solely the principal value of bonds, measured by their market prices, the risk of investing in bonds rises sharply. This increase

---

CAVEAT EMPTOR: *Understanding Duration*

Technically speaking, duration is the time period during which the investor will receive half of the present value of a bond's interest stream, plus its principal value at maturity. This is a complicated concept but one that it is not necessary to fathom. For your purposes, think of duration as the number of years at which you are indifferent to an increase or decrease in interest rates. With just a slight modification, duration is also (helpfully), the multiplier that roughly links interest rate changes with principal changes. Using a bond with a ten-year duration as an example, an instantaneous 1% rate increase would reduce its price by about 10%. For a bond with a three-year duration, the decline in its price would be only 3%. If you know the duration of a bond, you will have a good idea of the impact of a change in rates on its market value.

---

in risk is hardly surprising, given that interest coupons have accounted for nearly 85% of the total return on bonds during the average decade in the 1926–92 period.

We have already seen a good indication of principal risk in Table 2–6, which shows the overnight effect on total return of instantaneous changes in interest rates. Table 2–8 adds some information on the annual impact of these rate changes over various time periods. As you can see, changes in interest rates have zero impact on the principal value of a bond that is held to maturity. Nonetheless, large swings in interest rates, however unlikely to take place instantaneously, often take place over a relatively few years. The sensitivity of bond prices to interest rate changes creates increased principal risk with each increase in maturity. For example, Table 2–8 shows that a 3% rise in rates, from 7% to 10%, on a 20-year bond over a five-year time frame would cause a price decline that would reduce total return by −5% annually.

So far, our discussion of the principal risk on bonds has focused largely on interest rate risk—fluctuations in bond prices caused by changes in interest rates. These risks are, by definition, temporal and are eliminated when the bond matures at its stated value. But there is another kind of risk, credit risk, which may result in *permanent* impairment of principal. Credit risk is the risk that the principal of a bond will not be paid at its maturity and indeed, that interest coupons will also not be paid or will be paid at

TABLE 2-8
Principal Volatility—Average Annual Capital Return

	5-year bond (7% coupon)		20-year bond (7% coupon)		
Instantaneous rate change	Instantaneous	5 years	Instantaneous	5 years	20 years
+3%	−12%	0%	−26%	−5%	0%
+2	− 8	0	−18	−3	0
+1	− 4	0	−10	−2	0
0	0	0	0	0	0
−1	+ 4	0	+12	+2	0
−2	+ 9	0	+25	+4	0
−3	+13	0	+41	+6	0

reduced levels. In these opening chapters, to simplify, I largely ignore credit risk and consider only U.S. Treasury obligations in my examples.

As noted earlier, U.S. Treasury obligations are the safest investments in the world, with unquestioned credit quality. Bonds issued by agencies of the federal government are the next safest. High-grade municipal and corporate bonds are also quite secure. However, as we move to the lower investment-grade bonds, credit risk begins to increase. When we get to very low-grade bonds (generously called high-yield bonds but more accurately known as junk bonds), the payment of interest and principal becomes speculative. If you are seeking the yield enhancements that come from moving down the quality ladder, be aware that, at each rung, there is a corresponding increase in credit risk. As a general rule, it is unwise to assume significant credit risk; generally confine your bond holdings to those with high credit quality.

Income Risk

There is no income risk whatsoever in a U.S. Treasury bond that is held to maturity. That is to say, you can take for granted the sanctity of any commitment of the federal government to honor its debt service obligations. The value of such a guaranteed income stream, particularly if you are seeking retirement income, is substantial. All you need to do is to determine the length of time you wish to lock in this income stream, for virtually any period from two years or less to as long as 30 years.

The real risk to income in the case of the bond investor (a risk the common stock investor also faces) is simply to pay too high a price for the bonds. A low yield may be locked in for a long period of time—indeed, a near infinity to the holder of the long-term bond. Imagine your frustration if you bought a $10,000 bond at 7% and locked in a 20-year income stream of $700 annually, but within a few years found that yields had risen to 10% and you could purchase an annual income stream of $1,000 for the same amount of money (or, alternatively put, purchase the same $700 income stream for $7,000). This example is hardly extreme. Between December 1978 and January 1982, the yield on long-term U.S. government bonds climbed from 8% to 14%. Similar if less dramatic changes have occurred throughout bond market history. Of course, when rates decline, the reverse scenario happens. For instance, assuming that you hold the same 7% bond, if rates drop to 4% you will have gained a valuable benefit since your $700 annual income stream will be worth $17,500. That is 75% more than the purchase price of your bond.

It is impossible to forecast the future course of interest rates with any degree of accuracy. The best option for the bond investor who wishes to reduce risk is to do so the easy way, purchasing a range of bonds with different maturities. A good distribution might be one-third each of 5-year bonds, 10-year bonds, and 20-year bonds.

THE RISK OF U.S. TREASURY BILLS

U.S. Treasury bills are different indeed from stocks and bonds, and the analysis of their risk is straightforward. Barring the inconceivable possibility that the U.S. Treasury will not honor its obligations, there is no principal risk whatsoever in owning a Treasury bill. If you buy U.S. Treasury bills and hold them until they mature, say, 90 days later, you are assured of the return of your capital. If you purchase longer-term issues, you must rely on other investors to purchase your bonds—at a price determined in the financial marketplace—if you wish to liquidate your holdings prior to their maturity.

Total Return Risk

From a principal standpoint, U.S. Treasury bills are the ultimate haven from market uncertainty. With principal risk nonexistent, the total return

---

CAVEAT EMPTOR: *Do Not Ignore Call Risk*

When the U.S. Treasury issues a bond, it promises, in nearly all of its obligations, to pay the interest until maturity. Corporations and state and local governments are not so generous; their bonds are usually callable after a period of years (typically ten), and are thus subject to call risk. The way a call works is that, if interest rates decline, issuers may take back their bonds by repaying the debt, leaving you to replace the bonds at lower yields. If rates rise, issuers naturally allow you to hold on to your bonds. A similar if more subtle risk—prepayment risk—exists in mortgage-backed securities, such as GNMA (Government National Mortgage Association) issues. When interest rates rise, home owners with mortgages sit tight. However, when rates fall far enough to make refinancing financially attractive (taking into account any prepayment penalties and refinancing costs), many home owners prepay their debt and replace their high-interest mortgages with lower-rate mortgages. In either event, for the GNMA investor it is sort of a "heads they win, tails you lose" proposition. If you assume call risk, you should demand a compensatory increase in yield.

---

of a U.S. Treasury bill is determined entirely by the interest income it generates. Thus, total return risk and income risk on U.S. Treasury bills are identical. Given that the interest rate on bills is effectively reset every 90 days, however, income risk (and thus total return risk) is enormous— the largest for any major financial asset class. Figure 2–9 shows the annual total returns of U.S. Treasury bills during the past 67 years.

You will note two principal facts in Figure 2–9. First, U.S. Treasury bill returns were remarkably (in retrospect, almost unbelievably) low from the early 1930s through the mid-1950s. During that time they averaged less than +1% annually (before inflation). They were remarkably high from the 1970s through 1990, during which time they averaged +7.6%. Second, the yields on U.S. Treasury bills were highly volatile in many periods of notable brevity. Most recently, for example, the yield on U.S. Treasury bills dropped from 9.3% early in 1989 to 2.7% in late 1992, the lowest level since 1962.

Income Risk

Minimal principal risk, then, goes hand in hand with extraordinary income risk, and woe to the retired, income-oriented investor who holds U.S.

FIGURE 2–9
U.S. Treasury Bill Returns (1926–92)

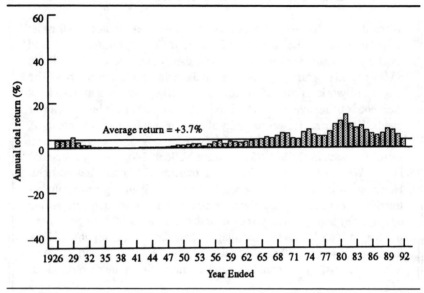

Treasury bills (or for that matter other money market instruments such as bank short-term certificates of deposit) without considering this income risk. During the 1980s, investors became accustomed to earning high returns on their cash reserves, but times have changed. It is not given to us to know when, or even if, the high returns earned on U.S. Treasury bills during the 1979–84 period (averaging +10.9% annually)—not to mention the inflation that engendered those returns—will be with us again.

SUMMARY

"Do what you will, capital is at hazard." This is a central rule of investing. Sometimes, as in the case of inflation, the hazard is beyond your control. Inflation risk, however, appears to affect each of the three major classes of financial assets pretty much equally. That is, each percentage point of inflation reduces the nominal total return for stocks, bonds, and bills alike by one percentage point. However, inflation *does* alter the relative relationships among these returns. For example, at a 3% inflation rate, a nominal stock return of +9% would be reduced to +6% and a nominal

TABLE 2-9
Investment Characteristics of Financial Assets

	Total return	Principal stability	Current yield	Income growth	Income stability
Common stocks	A	C	B	A	B
Long-term bonds	B	B	A	C	A
Cash reserves	C	A	C	NA*	C

*Not applicable; U.S. Treasury bill yields may rise or decline.

bond return of +6% would be reduced to +3%. Thus, the stock return increases from one and one-half times the bond return to two times.

There is a sensible way to balance the risks in each asset class—risks to total return, to capital, and to income—against each other. You can eliminate principal risk, or you can eliminate income risk, but you cannot eliminate both. Table 2-9 contrasts the critical investment characteristics of the three asset classes, with each instrument graded as A (best), B (average), or C (worst).

You will probably want to optimize these characteristics to meet your own investment needs, balancing the risks and rewards by owning some stocks, some bonds (probably with a range of maturities), and some bills. With this perhaps self-evident conclusion, I shall now turn to a practical discussion of mutual funds. Chapter 12 will discuss in depth the allocation of assets among the three basic classes of financial investments.

Chapter Three

Mutual Funds: Principles, Practicalities, Performance
An Idea Whose Time Has Come

"An invasion of armies can be resisted, but not an idea whose time has come." While Victor Hugo wrote those words 140 years ago, they could easily describe the power of the mutual fund idea in 1993. From an also-ran financial intermediary with assets totaling $500 million in 1940, mutual fund assets soared to $500 *billion* in 1985, and then to $1.6 *trillion* by December 31, 1992. During the brief period from 1989 to 1992, investors added to their mutual fund holdings at a rate of more than $100 billion annually—larger than the capital inflow into any other type of U.S. financial institution, including commercial banks, thrift institutions, life insurance companies, private pension funds, and the retirement funds of states and municipalities. Clearly, mutual funds have become a force to be reckoned with in the financial firmament.

A major reason for the remarkable growth in the mutual fund industry has been the diverse classes of financial assets to which its principles have been successfully applied. The first U.S. mutual fund, founded in 1924, was a common stock fund, and for the next half century the industry was dominated by equity-oriented funds, including a few balanced funds, which maintained significant holdings of bonds to moderate the volatility of the stock market. As recently as 1974, common stock funds and balanced funds represented 86% of the mutual fund industry's total assets.

Since 1974, however, there has been a stunning shift in the industry's investment emphasis. In December 1992, money market funds comprised the largest industry segment (35%), followed by bond funds (32%), stock funds (29%), and balanced funds (4%). Reflecting this diversity, Table 3-1 shows the allocation of assets among the major types of funds available at the end of 1992.

TABLE 3–1
Mutual Fund Industry (December 31, 1992)

	$ billion	Percent of total	Number of funds
Common Stock Funds			
Growth	$ 136	9%	361
Value	140	9	290
Equity income	40	2	74
Broad-based specialty	113	7	524
Concentrated specialty	34	2	183
Subtotal	$ 463	29%	1,432
Bond Funds			
Investment-grade corporate	$ 57	4%	262
Medium-grade corporate	19	1	74
High-yield corporate	33	2	78
Tax-exempt	198	12	759
Mortgage-backed	94	6	116
U.S. Treasury and government	81	5	272
Global	28	2	101
Subtotal	$ 510	32%	1,662
Money Market Funds			
Prime paper	$ 300	19%	363
Treasury and agency	159	10	292
Tax-exempt	96	6	321
Subtotal	$ 555	35%	976
Balanced Funds			
Traditional	$ 31	2%	95
Income-oriented	9	1	17
Asset allocation	14	1	85
Subtotal	$ 54	4%	197
Total Industry	$1,582	100%	4,267

Each of these fund categories represents a different combination of potential reward and potential risk. Because mutual funds are, in essence, merely financial intermediaries, they provide a convenient means of investing in the three basic financial asset classes—stocks, bonds, and cash reserves—described in the previous two chapters. So it is only one small step from investing in individual securities to investing in portfolios of securities through mutual funds.

CAVEAT EMPTOR: *The New Fund Explosion*

The explosion in the formation of new mutual funds from 1972 to 1992 carries with it two particular limitations. First, the increase in the number of bond funds from 8 in 1972 to 1,662 in 1992 means that solid long-term comparisons are difficult to come by, and considerable reliance must be placed on performance data that would otherwise be deemed statistically insufficient. Second, the increase in the number of stock funds (from 463 to 1,432) poses the same problem, but it is accentuated since this increase does not take into account the numerous funds that ceased operations during the period. In fact, nearly 100 equity funds exited the industry from 1972 to 1976 alone, reducing the number of equity offerings from 463 to 374. Most long-term performance data ignore these fund failures and evaluate only those funds that still exist today, a phenomenon called survivorship bias. Beware of ascribing too much importance to fund data that cover only a limited number of funds or ignore the assumedly poorer records of those funds that have fallen by the wayside.

FOUR BASIC PRINCIPLES

While the wide selection of mutual fund offerings has provided much of the impetus for the industry's growth during the past two decades, four time-honored principles of mutual fund investing are the core of the industry's success. These principles are (1) broad diversification, (2) professional management, (3) liquidity, and (4) convenience. They remain as valid today as they were when the first U.S. mutual fund was introduced.

The first principle of mutual fund investing is broad diversification of securities. In fact, capital market theory suggests that diversification is essential to eliminating what appears to be demonstrably unproductive risk taking in specific securities (unsystematic risk). Numerous financial studies have demonstrated that most individual investors are woefully underdiversified. Investors on average own about six stocks, which in itself is minimal diversification. But when the heavy weightings of their largest holdings are considered, most investors in individual stocks have an effective diversification of slightly less than two equally weighted holdings.

For nearly all investors, cost alone generally precludes achieving adequate diversification without using mutual funds. For instance, if you

---

CAVEAT EMPTOR: *Closed-End Funds*

This book is about mutual funds, technically known as open-end investment companies since their shares may be purchased and redeemed each day at their then-current net asset values, plus any sales charges or minus any redemption fees. It is *not* about closed-end investment companies, which make an initial public offering of shares, after which their shares trade in the marketplace at either a premium or a discount to their net asset values. Since the initial offering price of a closed-end fund includes a sales commission, the shares are inevitably issued at a premium over the assets that will actually be invested. Thereafter, diversified closed-end equity funds almost always trade at a discount. If you purchase closed-end fund shares at a premium price and then sell the shares at a discount, it would not be unusual to sacrifice as much as 20% of your capital. While financial advice should rarely include the words "never" or "always," few investors would have suffered if they had *never* purchased new offerings of diversified closed-end funds but had instead *always* purchased shares when they were available in the marketplace at a substantial discount from their net asset value.

---

had, say, $10,000 to invest, you could achieve a reasonable level of diversification by purchasing ten different stocks. However, the transaction costs incurred in buying (and ultimately selling) the stocks would be exorbitant, since many of the purchases would likely involve odd lot transactions, which typically entail much higher commission expenses. Allowing for the "drag" represented by these commission costs, it could take years for you to recoup just the costs of putting your money to work. And your level of diversification would still not be comparable to that of a typical mutual fund.

If you are investing in fixed-income securities, the diversification afforded by mutual funds should be even more important to you. In many cases, the minimum purchase amount for a typical bond transaction is $10,000. Thus, if you had just $5,000 of available capital to invest you could not purchase even one bond. In most cases, however, a $3,000 investment (or less) is sufficient to purchase shares in a mutual fund whose portfolio consists of 50 or more individual bonds. If a no-load (commission free) mutual fund is selected, the transaction may be completed at absolutely no cost. While management and administrative fees are assessed

---

CAVEAT EMPTOR: *Bushels of Chaff*

There are many "mutual-fund-like" investments available, but most have little in common with the mainstream mutual funds that provide the four advantages discussed in this chapter. While such programs usually combine the assets of many investors and employ professional managers to select portfolio investments, the investments are largely bereft of liquidity and structured primarily for their purported ability to minimize taxes. Commodity pools, tax-shelters of various types, real estate limited partnerships, and other exotic investment programs have, time and again, been tried and found wanting. Indeed, the worst ones have inflicted catastrophic losses on their investors. As a general rule, you should avoid these schemes like the plague, except in cases where (1) you are aware of the exact amount of sales charges and management costs involved, (2) they are limited to a small portion (less than 10%) of your total portfolio, and (3) you have confidence that you can select the best programs from among the many. Selecting the best is a daunting task. Shakespeare probably had the odds about right when, in *The Merchant of Venice,* he described the futility of finding "two grains of wheat hidden in two bushels of chaff."

---

each year as a percentage of your investment, a wide selection of bond funds is currently available at an annual cost of 1% or less, equal to $100 on a $10,000 investment. Considering the alternative, such charges seem relatively inconsequential.

Mutual funds provide not only diversification within a portfolio but also diversification *among* portfolios. For instance, the same $5,000 that was insufficient to purchase even one bond could, in many instances, purchase both a diversified stock mutual fund and a diversified bond mutual fund. If you are a young investor with limited finances just beginning to set aside funds for your retirement, the ability to diversify among stocks and bonds is a significant advantage.

It is impossible to overstate the critical role of diversification in an intelligent investment program. Diversification greatly reduces and can even eliminate the specific risk that comes with the ownership of just a few individual stocks and bonds. (Even a broadly diversified portfolio, however, cannot eliminate the market risk of price volatility.) Yet, with this substantial reduction in risk, there is no loss whatsoever of long-term return for investors in the aggregate. Diversification, then, is at the very heart of mutual fund investing.

The second principle of mutual fund investing is professional management. Managing an investment portfolio entails selecting and supervising the fund's holdings. The investment professionals who manage the fund must do so strictly in accordance with the fund's basic investment objectives and policies. For instance, if you invest in a particular balanced fund, you may be promised that a highly diversified list of blue chip stocks will comprise 60% to 70% of total net assets and a diversified list of high-grade bonds will comprise the remainder. The professional manager has an obligation to meet these standards under all circumstances.

Managers must also endeavor to add value over and above the returns generally provided in the financial markets in which they work, a challenging task. On the one hand, it might seem the supreme irony that, on average, the records of professional portfolio managers of mutual funds are undistinguished when compared to unmanaged averages of the returns achieved in the broad financial markets. On the other hand, since it is impossible for all managers as a group to add value *in the aggregate,* it is not at all surprising that the performance records of many professional investment advisers leave much to be desired. To say the least, the market is a tough bogey.

In the sense of rigorous financial discipline, then, professional management is the sine qua non, the absolute expectation. But in the sense of outpacing the markets, professional management does not promise you superior performance. Rather, it promises all investors hope that a particular management will outpace its peers. But only some investors will ultimately be rewarded. In sum, the collective performance record of professional managers strongly suggests that you might consider simply owning the market via an index fund, at least for a core segment of your equity portfolio.

The third principle of mutual fund investing is liquidity. Mutual fund shares may be acquired or liquidated at a moment's notice at the fund's next determined net asset value per share. What is more, there is no direct cost of market impact, wherein buying securities tends to drive prices higher and selling securities tends to push prices lower. Nor is there a charge when shares are liquidated (although in some cases a 1% redemption fee is charged and in other cases a contingent deferred sales load may be assessed).

CAVEAT EMPTOR: *Taking the Wrap*

The closest proxy for a mutual fund is a wrap account. For a single fee, you obtain the services of a professional money manager, who then invests your assets in a diversified portfolio of stocks and bonds. The brokerage commissions and advisory fees are ''wrapped'' in the overall fee. It sounds like a mutual fund, but it is not. It carries some significant baggage since it is difficult to ascertain the validity of past performance data. The choice of a manager is left to your stockbroker and, depending on the relationship between the adviser and the broker, may involve a potential conflict of interest. Most importantly, the costs involved in wrap accounts are very high. Maximum annual fees typically total 3% of assets, with reduced fees available to investors with assets of $1 million (2.5%) or $5 million (2%). Hidden execution costs may add another 0.5% or more to the fee. The original wrap account concept has now been extended by the creation of mutual fund wrap accounts. Here, the broker or adviser selects a mutual fund portfolio for the client, charging an annual fee of 1% to 1.5%. When the fund expense ratio of, say, 1% to 1.5% is added, total annual costs may be as high as 3% (excluding the transaction costs incurred by the funds themselves). The payment of any sales charges would raise the cost more. It is difficult to see how, in either kind of wrap account, you can incur such costs without eliminating any realistic chance of outperforming the market averages over the long term. In either case, you should beware of ''taking the wrap.''

Owning securities individually, of course, is also apt to provide a reasonable level of liquidity. However, mutual funds can easily be converted into cash at a fraction of the cost you would incur in selling individual stocks or bonds. More, the ability to switch easily among different investment options provides remarkable flexibility in building a diversified portfolio, especially considering the costs involved in exchanging individual securities.

For instance, if you want to exchange, say, $10,000 of stock A for $10,000 of bond B, you might pay a brokerage firm a commission of about 2% to sell the stock (after having already paid a commission to purchase the stock) and an effective commission of about 1% to buy the bond. Shifting your allocation from stocks to bonds would cost you about $300, an expense that would be repeated each time you made an exchange. But if you were to request a similar exchange from a stock mutual fund into a bond mutual fund and you were moving between funds within the same no-load family, the transaction would cost you nothing.

The fourth basic principle, that mutual fund ownership provides simplicity and convenience, begins the moment you first purchase a fund's shares. Your purchase may take place through a one-step process handled by a representative of a stock brokerage firm (broker distribution). Or you may select a multistep process in which no broker is involved (direct distribution). In this case, you call a fund sponsor toll-free, a prospectus and application are sent to you, your application and check are returned to the sponsor, and you then receive a confirmation statement showing the amount of your investment, the number of shares you purchased, and the purchase price.

The convenience of mutual fund ownership continues following the initial purchase, with such features as automatic reinvestment of dividends and capital gains distributions, tax reporting, programs for regular additional investments and for systematic withdrawals, checkwriting on money market funds, and even telephone exchanges among different funds within the same family. Finally, if you want to redeem your shares and withdraw from the fund, you can usually do so at a moment's notice with a simple phone call.

Are these four compelling advantages accompanied by any disadvantages? Of course they are.

- The mutual fund depersonalizes the relationship between the client and the adviser. If you prefer to rely on a personal adviser or stockbroker rather than an intermediary to select individual investments for you, mutual funds will prove to be unsuitable.

- Mutual funds come with a remarkable range of costs, some direct (sales charges and management fees) and some indirect (portfolio transaction costs). Taken to excess (and some are) such costs can easily overpower the advantages cited earlier.

- Through a mutual fund, you lose control over the realization of capital gains. In an individual account, you can decide precisely when to realize gains and losses and take taxes into account in making your decisions. For most mutual funds, tax consequences resulting from the sale of portfolio securities are a secondary consideration for the advisers. As a result, taxable distributions to shareholders from realized capital gains usually comprise a substantial portion of an equity fund's total return over time.

- The very growth in the diversity and number of mutual funds—there are now some 4,300 competing for your attention in the marketplace—means selecting the most appropriate funds to meet your investment objectives is an awesome challenge.

THE PRACTICALITIES OF SELECTING A FUND COMPLEX

Where does the intelligent investor begin the process of selecting mutual funds? There are three principal avenues to the purchase of fund shares.

- A stock brokerage firm or a bank will provide fund selection, asset allocation, and transaction services. Many investors require such services, although their value must ultimately be measured against the sales commissions and other costs that may be involved. You should learn whether the funds offered are those managed by the brokerage firm or bank itself or by independent mutual fund managers who use their sales networks.
- A direct distributor offers its funds to the investor without an intermediary, and provides abundant information but does not usually recommend specific funds in its complex. The direct distributor funds are available on a no- or low-commission basis, and are used by investors who believe they have sufficient financial judgment and self-reliance to make their own investment decisions. These funds, as a group, should be expected to provide the same dimension of returns as those provided by the broker-sold funds. However, since no sales commissions are paid by no-load fund investors, they enjoy a distinct financial advantage.
- An independent investment adviser will usually provide fund selection and financial planning services in return for an asset-based fee, or a sales commission, or a combination of the two. It is important to know the basis of the fee charged, as well as whether the adviser recommends load funds or no-load funds.

Nearly all major mutual funds are members of one fund complex or another. Most fund complexes comprise a large variety of funds with different objectives and policies but are managed, administered, and distributed by a single central entity (usually called a management company). The 20 largest fund complexes, for example, comprise some 800 distinct mutual funds. Once you have decided to invest in mutual funds to meet your financial objectives, your next step will likely be to decide which mutual fund complex should be the primary focus for your investment assets, so that your goals can be served at a single central nexus.

The advantages of investing with a single fund complex are numerous. They include common transaction statements in a consistent format; standardized administrative policies and procedures; up-to-date, one-stop information on the status of your holdings in the form of a combined account statement; and the ability to move easily from one type of fund to another as your investment objectives change. The principal disadvantage, of course, is that a given complex may not offer all of the funds required to match your particular investment objectives. For instance, one mutual fund complex may have the bond funds and money market funds that meet your needs but not the stock funds. Or one fund complex may offer a full complement of competitive stock, bond, and money market funds but not a particular star performer in which you are interested.

For some investors, the limitations of investing with a single complex will outweigh the administrative advantages. There is no overriding reason not to invest in funds from two complexes or even three, nor is there any reason to limit your choices merely to the major complexes. A single stand-alone fund, run by an adviser of demonstrated competence, need not be excluded from your consideration. In fact, many funds with exceptional records of long-term performance come from precisely this group.

You can, through a single account in a brokerage firm, own a variety of stock, bond, and money market funds offered by different fund sponsors. The extra cost of such a "master" mutual fund account may be worth the price if you want transaction flexibility and a single portfolio statement but you cannot decide on a single fund family. A master account may be available through a regular stockbroker with customary commission costs or through a discount broker who makes available no-load mutual funds at nominal commission rates.

In any case, you should get answers to some rudimentary questions before entrusting your assets to any single complex, or indeed to any fund. First and foremost, in my view, is the reputation of the fund sponsor. Is the firm generally known for its integrity and the quality of its service to investors? Can you trust the organization that will be acting as the trustee for your assets? These are issues that tend to be subjectively analyzed, but you can get at least a sense of the values of an organization from its

---

CAVEAT EMPTOR: *Read the Annual Report*

When you call for a prospectus, be sure to request a copy of the fund's most recent annual report to its shareholders. Review it carefully and then ask yourself a few questions. Does the report provide clear, upfront information about total return? Does it compare the fund's return with norms such as unmanaged market indexes and peer groups (groups of funds with similar policies and objectives)? Does it provide long-term as well as short-term performance comparisons? Is the chairman's letter candid and complete? Does the report discuss prevailing conditions in the financial markets in which the fund invests? Does the portfolio manager discuss the major factors affecting the fund's investment return? Believe it or not, in the mutual fund industry providing all of this information has been the exception rather than the rule. The annual report will tell you what information you can expect to receive as a shareholder.

---

shareholder reports, from the financial press, and from the many independent publications that evaluate mutual funds. In the best case, you can learn from the experience that personal advisers or friends have actually had with the firm.

The best real-world test may be to simply call the fund family on its 800 number. Ask several investment questions: "What is the yield on your U.S. Treasury money market fund?" "How should I decide in which of your stock funds to invest?" "What is the average maturity of the bonds in your long-term corporate bond portfolio?" The answers will help you to determine the knowledge, courtesy, and professionalism of the investor information staff.

One relatively easy question to answer is how long the fund sponsor has been in business. Nearly all of the large fund organizations commenced operations prior to 1950. Four decades of survival in a highly competitive industry suggest that the organization has been successfully tested. Many younger and smaller organizations may also meet your standards, but it would seem wise to evaluate their reputation with even greater care.

Once you have received responses to all of your questions—the ones I have suggested as well as any of your own—consider the services available through the fund complex. Among the principal attributes you will want to review are these:

1. *Variety of funds in the complex.* It is not enough to look only at the total number of fund offerings by an organization. You should also consider the variety of funds offered within the stock, bond, and money market categories. A complex with, say, ten stock fund offerings but only one money market fund offering and no bond fund offerings will not give you many options when it comes time to alter your asset allocations among the three asset classes.

2. *Minimum initial investment.* Fund groups typically require that you open an account in any one fund with a minimum deposit of from $1,000 to $3,000. But some fund groups allow investments of as small as $250, and a few require no minimum investment whatsoever.

3. *Number of free exchanges.* For funds that assess a sales load, there is usually no provision for free exchanges. Many no-load fund groups permit an unlimited number of free exchanges, but some limit exchanges to as few as two per year. While an unrestricted exchange privilege may be advantageous to a particular fund shareholder, remember that excessive transactions by large numbers of fund shareholders—especially market timers—are disadvantageous to the long-term shareholders remaining in the fund, since the fund itself bears the transaction costs engendered by portfolio turnover. If you are a long-term investor, be wary of funds that encourage or permit frequent exchanges.

4. *Business hours for telephone service.* Around-the clock access to account information and prices has become the industry standard, and accepting transaction instructions is moving in that direction as well. However, transactions must take place at the net asset value that is determined at the market's *next* close following the receipt of your order, either by telephone or by mail. Whether you place a telephone exchange order with the fund at 6:00 A.M. or at 3:45 P.M., it is executed at a price determined at 4:00 P.M. that day.

5. *Individual retirement accounts.* IRAs are available through virtually all fund groups but differ in the minimum investment required to open an account (usually $250 to $500 per fund) and the level of yearly maintenance fees. IRA fees typically amount to $10 per year for each fund account you hold in your IRA. In some cases they are limited to a single $10 fee for all of your IRA fund accounts, and in other cases you incur no direct IRA fees whatsoever. Of course, you should consider the total

expenses associated with your IRA investment—including not only such external fees but any applicable sales charges and the fund's expense ratio—since it is the total of all of these expenses that will determine the net return on your investment.

6. *Checkwriting on money market funds.* This service is almost universally available at no extra cost. The minimum check that may be drawn typically varies from $250 to $500. However, it is becoming more common for funds to charge separate per-transaction fees for checkwriting services.

7. *Consolidated statements.* Periodic statements that show your account transaction activity and balances in all of the funds you own in a given complex are now supplanting the practice of providing separate statements for each fund account. The consolidated portfolio statement will become the industry standard, affording particular convenience to investors who own several funds in a single complex.

This list highlights only a few of the myriad services that are available to you as a mutual fund shareholder. In the end, it is up to you to determine the relative importance of the many contributing factors—reputation of the fund sponsor, quality of service, number of fund offerings, range of service offerings and, to be sure, fund investment performance—in selecting a fund complex.

MUTUAL FUND PERFORMANCE

If the first two elements of investing in mutual funds are the basic principles and practicalities of picking a mutual fund complex, surely the final element is mutual fund performance. Indeed, many investors consider performance the sine qua non of mutual fund investing. Exactly how a given investor defines good performance is not entirely clear. For many it has generally come to mean "earning superior total returns," although the definition of superior is usually obscure. I would define good performance for a mutual fund as the delivery of total returns that are, with reasonable consistency, superior to those achieved by other mutual funds with like investment policies, objectives, and structures.

To whatever avail, total return has become the major methodology in measuring mutual fund results. In the next four chapters, I will discuss some rules for the selection of stock funds, bond funds, money market

---

CAVEAT EMPTOR: *The Clash of the Cultures*

When applied to the physical world, scientific techniques have been successfully used to determine causes and effects, helping us to predict and control our environment. This success has encouraged the idea that scientific techniques can be productively applied to all human endeavors, including investing. But investing is not a science. It is human activity that involves both emotional as well as rational behavior. Financial markets are too complex to isolate any single variable with ease, and there is no evidence that definitive predictions on short-term market fluctuations can be made with any accuracy. Intelligent investors try to separate emotion from reason and trust in reason to prevail over the long term. In this sense, they are philosophers and intellectuals rather than technicians. This difference suggests one of the great paradoxes of the mutual fund industry, which might be called the clash of the cultures. Even as it becomes increasingly clear that staying the course with your financial assets is far more productive than market timing (or even hopping from one stock fund to another), fund organizations, through modern information and communications technology, make it increasingly easy for their shareholders to engage in frequent and rapid movements of their investment assets. In his 1959 opus *The Two Cultures and the Scientific Revolution,* British author Sir C. P. Snow was not far from the mark when he contrasted "literary intellectuals at one pole—at the other scientists . . . Between the two a gulf of mutual incomprehension." If you think of long-term investment strategy as being, in a sense, for the intellectual-philosopher, and rapid-fire investment tactics as being for the scientist-technician, a financial plan founded on the former culture seems far more apt to provide the most productive long-term returns.

---

funds, and balanced funds. But first I will briefly describe the concept of total return and discuss a major refinement of that concept.

Total return is the percentage change—over a specified period of time—in a mutual fund's net asset value, with the ending net asset value adjusted to take into account the reinvestment of all income dividends and any capital gains distributions made by the fund. It is almost always calculated before the deduction of sales charges and taxes payable by the shareholder on the income dividends and capital gains distributions.

Total returns can be presented on a cumulative basis or as an average

---

CAVEAT EMPTOR: *Apples to Apples*

Comparative performance assessment is impossible unless the comparisons are being made over identical time periods and among mutual funds with similar objectives and policies. That time periods should be identical is best illustrated by the effect of the October 1987 market crash. The Standard & Poor's 500 Stock Index provided an average annual return of only +8.3% for the five-year period beginning at the market high on August 31, 1987, but a return of +15.9% for the five years beginning on December 31, 1987. Similarly, however difficult the effort, you should attempt to fine-tune comparisons by using only mutual funds that are seeking the same goals in essentially the same way. Remember to compare apples to apples when considering any fund performance statistics.

---

annual compound rate. I strongly caution you against relying solely on cumulative total returns. While the miracle of compounding indeed takes place as the holding period of your investment lengthens, it is simply impossible for most investors to easily compare cumulative total returns in a sensible way. For example, did a fund with a ten-year cumulative return of +100% earn an average annual compound return of +10%? (Answer: No. The annual return, reflecting the yearly compounding effect, was +7.2%.) Did a fund with a five-year cumulative return of +93% do better or worse than one with a ten-year cumulative return of +271%? (Answer: Their annual compound rates of return were identical, +14%.) Has a fund with a seemingly staggering gain of +1,602% over the 30 years ended December 31, 1992, been singularly successful? (Answer: The annual rate of return was +10%. During the same period, however, the stock market's annual return was +11%, for a total of +2,107%.) Be sure to focus on *annual rates* of total return rather than *cumulative* returns.

It might be useful to consider the difference between *compound* rates of return and *simple* rates of return. The former figure is derived from linking each year's return through multiplication; the latter figure is derived from adding each year's return. For example, consider a fund with annual returns of +20%, +25%, and −15% over three years. The value of an initial investment of $100 in the fund would be calculated as follows: $100 × 1.20 × 1.25 × 0.85, or $128, equivalent to an average annual compound rate of +8.3%. However, when the returns are simply added, the final value of the investment would be $130, a simple average rate of +10% annually.

To do full justice to the difference between the two methodologies, consider an investment that provides a return of +100% in the first year and −50% in the next, or vice versa. The average return would be +25% (100 − 50 ÷ 2), but the average compound return would be zero. Since the reality is that you would have seen your initial $100 double to $200, only to fall back to $100, it is clear that zero is the appropriate figure. So you should rely on what is called the geometric rate of return—which is annualized on a compound basis and will precisely reflect the total return that you would have actually received—rather than the simple arithmetic rate.

To be sure, the use of average annual compound rates of return tends to reduce sharply the apparent gaps among good performers, mediocre performers, and bad performers. But seemingly small differences in annual rates of return can result in enormous differences in total return over long periods of time. For example, a +12% rate of return from a good performer produces a +211% cumulative return over ten years. For a mediocre performer, an +11% rate produces a +184% total return. And for a poor performer, a +10% rate produces a +159% total return. Even as you use annual rates of return as your standard of choice, then, do not ignore the magic of compounding.

What is too often ignored in fund performance comparisons is how much total return is derived from capital appreciation and how much is derived from dividend income. In general terms, capital returns of stock funds (including the change in a fund's share value adjusted to take into account the reinvestment of any capital gains distributions) have been volatile, sometimes positive and sometimes negative. This volatility is muted in balanced funds, even more so in bond funds, and nonexistent in money market funds. That said, the dividend streams of stock funds and balanced funds have generally been stable, with an upward bias, while the dividends on money market funds—comprising 100% of their total returns—are notoriously volatile. Table 3–2 gives some idea of the difference between these two components of return for the major types of funds, using the 15 years ended December 31, 1992.

This table shows that considering total return in terms of its capital and income components makes it even more useful for measuring past performance. Such information is critical if you are in the distribution (income-producing) phase of your investment life cycle. But it also helps

TABLE 3-2
Components of Mutual Fund Returns (15-years ended December 31, 1992)

	Rate of Return			Contribution to Total Return	
	Total return	*Capital return*	*Income return*	*Capital*	*Income*
Stock funds	+14.6%	+11.4%	+3.2%	78%	22%
Bond funds	+ 8.8	− 0.9	+9.7	−10	110
Money market funds	+ 8.7	0.0	+8.7	0	100
Balanced funds	+13.2	+ 6.0	+7.2	45	55

to compare major investment styles if you are in the accumulation (investment and reinvestment) phase. For example, there is a substantial difference in the contribution of income to the total returns of various types of equity funds that has important implications for investors with long-term growth objectives.

SUMMARY

The proverbial Topsy said, "I 'spect I growed. Don't think nobody ever made me." The same thing cannot be said about the mutual fund industry. The industry has grown because of its elemental principles, applied first to stock funds and balanced funds, and then to bond funds, and finally to money market funds. Not only have industry assets soared to $1.6 trillion, but the number of funds available to investors has reached the staggering total of 4,300. The selection of individual funds by investors has become a demanding task, which I shall address in the chapters that follow.

II

MUTUAL FUND SELECTION

P art II provides some new perspectives on the challenges and opportunities involved in selecting common stock funds, bond funds, money market funds, and balanced funds, and offers statistical evidence of the difficulty—or the ease—of making intelligent fund selections.

The first four chapters in this section introduce a number of evaluation criteria by which you can assess a fund's past returns, potential risks, and actual costs. They also introduce several important statistical concepts. The fifth chapter describes some readily available sources of mutual fund information and warns about the misinformation that abounds.

Chapter Four

How to Select a Common Stock Mutual Fund
Let's Look at the Record

Time and again during the presidential election campaign of 1928, Alfred E. Smith, the Democratic candidate, said, "Let's look at the record." The phrase became part of our political language. In the mutual fund field, too, investors say "Let's look at the record." It is an important, if potentially fallible, step in the fund selection process. In this chapter, I shall first examine the major types of common stock funds and the ways to distinguish them. Next I will turn to the structural investment characteristics of stock funds. I will conclude by looking at the record and discussing the role of past fund returns in the selection process.

This chapter considers common stocks as a distinct asset class. There is no presumption that you have yet decided what portion of your total investment portfolio should be represented by common stock mutual funds. The allocation of dollars among the three primary classes of financial assets is an entirely different decision with its own unique considerations, and I will address it in Chapters 12 and 13.

Deciding which particular common stock funds to invest in is a challenge. Today there are some 1,400 common stock mutual funds. They tend to adhere to investment policies and objectives generally in line with broad strategic definitions. I divide common stock funds into five basic classifications, and indicate the number of funds in each category.

1. *Growth funds (361)* seek long-term capital appreciation, with dividend income more or less incidental.

2. *Value funds (290)* seek a combination of growth and income, often focusing on stocks with above-average yields and below-average price-earnings ratios.

3. *Equity income funds (74)* seek to provide a major portion of to-

---

CAVEAT EMPTOR: *Mainstream Funds*

The most critical determinant of the performance of an equity mutual fund is the performance of the stock market as a whole. On average, the market explains about 85% of the total return of most growth, value, and equity income funds. I call funds that meet that standard *mainstream* funds and those with substantially less market correlation *differentiated* funds. For example, the return on the U.S. stock market (as measured by the Standard & Poor's 500 Stock Index), in and of itself, explains about 70% of the return of small capitalization funds, about 60% of the return of specialty funds, only about 40% of the return of international funds, and 0% of the return of gold funds. The distinction between highly diversified mainstream funds and less diversified differentiated funds is useful. However, note that, by reason of their particular investment objectives and policies, some growth and value funds provide limited diversification and fit well within the differentiated category.

---

tal return through income and invest in stocks with yields that are generally well above average.

4. *Broad-based specialty funds (524)* focus on the major market subsectors, such as aggressive growth stocks (135), small company stocks (152), and international or global stocks (237).

5. *Concentrated specialty funds (183)* invest in the stocks of a single industry, such as health care, public utilities, or gold mines.

It is no mean task to decide in which of these five stock groups to invest, to say nothing of the myriad choices within each group. Further, even investors with a long-run focus often invest with more concern for a fund's record of past performance than the appropriateness of its investment objective. While you should always read the prospectus to determine a fund's investment objective, too many stock funds set forth their objectives so broadly that it is almost impossible to discern anything specific. For example, "we will do our best to earn you the highest possible return" is an objective as meritorious as it is meaningless.

In general, you have two basic strategies from which to choose in seeking the holy grail of superior long-term performance. The first is to select a mainstream stock fund in either the growth or the value category

TABLE 4-1
Growth Funds versus Value Funds (20 Years Ended December 31, 1992)

	Average Annual Rate of Return	
5-year periods (inclusive)	Growth funds	Value funds
1973–77	− 2.9%	+ 1.7%
1978–82	+19.1	+15.9
1983–87	+11.0	+13.5
1988–92	+14.7	+13.6
Total period 1973–92	+10.1%	+11.0%

and hope for marginal superiority, with some level of consistency, over stocks in the aggregate. This plan, implicitly adopted by most fund shareholders, provides the broadest level of diversification. The second strategy is to select a differentiated fund in either the growth or value category, or a specialty fund whose returns and risks will vary significantly from the market as a whole. In either case, you should be aware of the extra risk assumed in accepting a lower (sometimes much lower) level of diversification. Put another way, the potential rewards of owning a mutual fund that might rank among the top 10% of all funds during a given interval are usually accompanied by the risks of owning a fund that might rank in the bottom 10%. Or, as it has been said, "many that are first shall be last, and the last shall be first."

The primary mainstream funds, as I noted, include growth funds and value funds. In practice, there is a soft distinction between these two stock fund classes. While their short-term returns have varied from one period to another, their long-term returns have been fairly similar, as Table 4-1 shows. Admittedly, looking at five-year aggregates blurs much of the distinction between the returns of these two stock fund categories. But on a year-by-year basis over an extended period, a slow cyclical pattern emerges in which first one type of fund leads the market, then the other. The upper part of Figure 4-1 shows the cumulative returns of both types of funds over the past 20 years; the lower shows the *relative* returns achieved by each fund type over the period. When the line is rising, growth funds are leading. When the line is falling, value funds are leading.

FIGURE 4–1
Growth Funds versus Value Funds

Cumulative Returns 1973–92

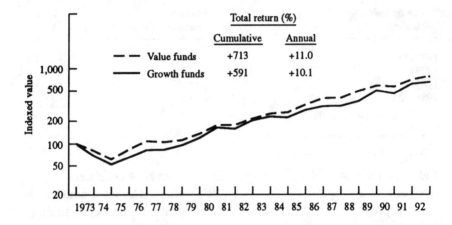

Ratio of Cumulative Returns 1973–92

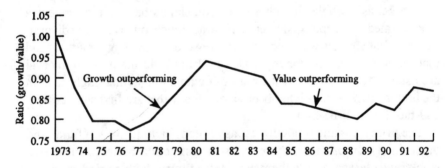

Note that value funds had their day from the end of 1972 to the end of 1976, received their comeuppance from 1977 to 1980, only to resume dominance through the end of 1988. The message of the chart, it seems to me, is that there are few profits—and lots of problems—in trying to predict the relative performance of these two investment styles.

Some further difficulty in distinguishing between these two basic types of funds is manifested in their portfolio holdings. Table 4–2 compares ten equity holdings (ranked in terms of percentage of assets) that comprise a

TABLE 4-2
Rank of Equity Holdings (December 31, 1992)

	Growth funds	Value funds
Philip Morris	1	1
FNMA	2	5
Merck	3	4
PepsiCo	8	16
Pfizer	11	19
American International Group	13	13
Royal Dutch	16	6
General Electric	18	2
Bristol-Myers Squibb	20	12
IBM	21	7

substantial portion of the portfolios of both value funds and growth funds. The portfolio parallelism begins with Philip Morris, the largest holding in each fund group, but it hardly ends there. The overlap between the two columns confirms that the real-world similarities between the typical growth fund and the typical value fund are far greater than the differences. This process of mongrelization seems to have developed over the past decade. It means that the accepted broad definitions of equity fund categories are considerably less useful than each individual fund's specific investment characteristics.

Equity income funds represent a third type of mainstream offering. They can be considered close sisters to value funds, with a tilt toward current income. Such funds entail a more conservative approach to equity fund investing, but their returns are heavily influenced by the general level of interest rates. The broad-based specialty funds, on the other hand, represent a more zealous investment approach that entails higher price volatility than the mainstream funds. For instance, aggressive growth funds seek maximum capital appreciation as a primary objective. They frequently pursue this objective through the fairly active buying and selling of securities, resulting in high levels of portfolio turnover. The small company funds, on the other hand, focus their investments in stocks with relatively small market capitalizations and often emphasize more speculative emerging companies.

Small company stocks have, over the long term, outperformed their larger capitalization cousins, which dominate the typical growth and value

FIGURE 4–2
Small Cap versus Large Cap Stocks (20 Years Ended December 31, 1992)

Cumulative Returns 1973–92

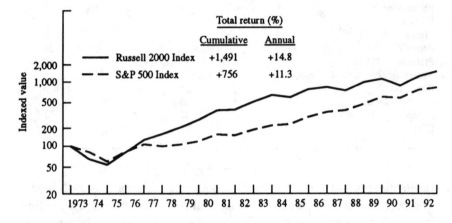

Ratio of Cumulative Returns 1973–92

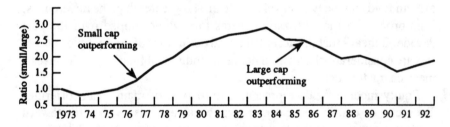

fund portfolios. However, there have been protracted periods when large company stocks performed better. The upper chart in Figure 4–2 shows the cumulative performance of small stocks (Russell 2000 Index) and large stocks (S&P 500 Index) over the 20-year period ended December 31, 1992. The lower chart shows the relationship between the returns of the two stock groups. When the line is rising, small company stocks are outperforming large company stocks; when the line is declining, the reverse is true. While small cap stocks provided higher returns over the full period, their dominance was achieved prior to 1984. Since then, large cap stocks have been by far the better performers.

TABLE 4–3

Components of Total Return (15 Years Ended December 31, 1992)

Fund type	Income return	Capital return*	Total return	Income as percent of total return
Equity income	+6.2%	+ 7.8%	+14.0%	44%
Value	+4.3	+ 9.4	+13.7	31
Growth	+2.7	+12.9	+15.6	17
Small company	+1.8	+14.3	+16.1	11
Aggressive growth	+1.2	+12.7	+13.9	9

*Includes increases in net asset value plus reinvested capital gains distributions.

Each equity fund type has particular investment characteristics. In evaluating each, be aware of two important distinctions. First, while the total returns of each stock fund type are often comparable over extended periods, the equity income and value funds have tended to carry lower risk (less price volatility) than have the growth, aggressive growth, and small company funds. Second, there is a difference in the *character* of returns among these fund types. Specifically, dividend income comprises a higher proportion of total return for equity income and value funds than for the other three fund types. Dividend income tends to be stable and durable over time. Capital growth is more volatile and spasmodic. This is an important distinction as you select a stock fund.

Table 4–3 gives some idea of the marked difference in the composition of total returns among the primary equity fund types, using the past 15 years as an example. The table shows that, while the long-term total returns of these five stock fund types were remarkably similar over the 15-year period, the composition of those returns was strikingly disparate. Clearly, if you are in the accumulation phase of your life cycle—unconcerned with generating current income from your investments and interested in minimizing taxable income—you may well prefer a growth fund over an equity income fund. Conversely, if you are in the distribution phase of your life cycle, you may prefer an equity income fund or a value fund. By evaluating the composition of total returns, you can select the most appropriate type of stock fund and then proceed to make specific fund comparisons within that group of funds. Evaluating past returns in this manner provides a logical framework in which to make rational investment decisions.

There is another type of common stock mutual fund, the international fund. This term has come to describe funds investing entirely outside the U.S. Thus far, I have virtually ignored international funds mainly because they entail unique risks that are not relevant to the investor in domestic common stock funds. The rationale for investing in international funds is that they should provide an ancillary level of diversification to your portfolio. Since the prices of foreign stocks often move in different directions, at different times, and in different dimensions than the prices of U.S. stocks, their inclusion in a diversified portfolio tends to reduce its short-term price volatility.

Compelling arguments have been promulgated to support the notion that investing in foreign stocks will improve your cumulative total return while reducing the volatility of your annual return. However, I am skeptical that international funds will add substantial value for the long-term investor. In my view, there is no inherent reason to believe that the major bourses outside of the United States will provide either higher or lower returns than the U.S. stock market. The so-called emerging markets such as Malaysia, Thailand, Mexico, and the like may offer the opportunity for relatively higher growth, but only at considerably higher risk. When the total returns in foreign markets are converted from local currency to U.S. dollars (which is ultimately the only currency that matters to the U.S. investor), returns become much more variable, reflecting the wide fluctuations in the value of the U.S. dollar versus foreign currencies. This currency risk means that a weakening U.S. dollar will enhance the returns earned by U.S. investors in international markets and a strong dollar will reduce their returns.

In Figure 4–3, the upper graph compares the returns achieved in the U.S. stock market since 1973 with those achieved in foreign markets in the aggregate, measured in both local currency terms and U.S. dollar terms. The lower graph reflects the relationship between foreign market returns (measured in local currency terms) and U.S. market returns. The benchmark for the foreign markets is the unmanaged Morgan Stanley Capital International Europe, Australia, and Far East Index (referred to as EAFE).

The upper chart shows that, measured in local currency, the U.S. market was a much better performer than the foreign markets in the aggregate, achieving an average annual return of +11.3% versus +9.9% for foreign stocks. However, the general weakness of the U.S. dollar increased foreign stock returns for the U.S. investor to +12.1% annually. In the lower

FIGURE 4–3
U.S. versus Foreign Markets

Cumulative Returns 1973–92

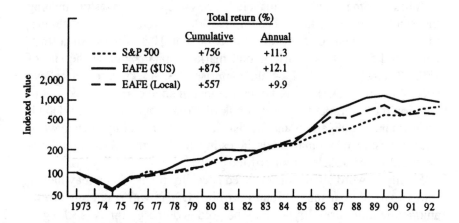

Ratio of Cumulative Returns 1973–92

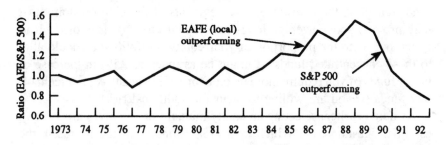

chart, you can see that the foreign markets were relatively strong performers during most of the period from 1983 to 1988 but have lagged the U.S. market by a significant margin since then.

The fact that currency fluctuations have had a positive impact on the returns earned by U.S. investors in foreign markets over the full period does not mean that you should ignore currency risk. For example, from 1979 to 1984, foreign markets enjoyed a gain of +166% measured in local currencies, but a gain of just +75% in U.S. dollar terms. In my view, despite the currency reward illustrated in the upper chart in Figure 4–3, the best assumption you can make is that currency fluctuations will have a limited impact, either positive or negative, on the long-term returns earned by your foreign investments. If that is the case, you should evaluate your international fund holdings just as you would your U.S. fund holdings, in terms of their fundamental value.

It has become popular in financial circles to speak of investors owning the "entire world market." The implied added diversification would justify a commitment of 57% of equities to non-U.S. stocks, since they comprised 57% of the world's total market capitalization at the end of 1992. The remaining 43% would comprise U.S. stocks. I do not believe such a posture makes sense. Given the incremental currency risk, not to mention the addition of sovereign risk (the risk that a nation will default on its financial obligations and the risk of political instability or even war), your exposure to mutual funds investing in foreign stocks should not exceed 20% of your equity portfolio.

Finally, a word about concentrated specialty funds. Some may have a role as part of your mutual fund portfolio. Others will not. In my view, among the more useful types may be gold and energy funds (seeking to provide a hedge against inflation), utility funds (seeking to provide a higher level of income than equity income funds), and technology and health care funds (enabling the investor to own segments of the U.S. economy that may provide above-average long-term capital growth). It is difficult to generalize as to the proportion of your equity portfolio you should allot to these concentrated funds. It might be as much as 25% in the case of utility funds (if you require more income) or 10% in health care or technology funds (if you are willing to incur the additional risk).

As noted earlier, selecting an equity mutual fund revolves around two essential questions: (1) Which mainstream fund(s) should represent the core portion of your investment portfolio? and (2) Which differentiated fund(s), if any, should represent the marginal portion of your investment portfolio? To address these questions, I shall first discuss mutual fund structural characteristics and then provide some standards for evaluating past mutual fund performance.

STRUCTURAL CHARACTERISTICS

Too many investors select a common stock fund based solely on its past performance record. The record provided by the fund sponsor is usually

---

CAVEAT EMPTOR: *The Rise and Fall and Rise of the Sector Funds*

Sector funds, designed for trading back and forth in the securities of a particular industry (such as automobiles, oils, or chemicals), were a mainstay of the mutual fund industry during the 1930s and 1940s. The idea was for investors to jump from one industry to the next as each danced through its inevitable market cycle of leadership and followership. But investors insisted on buying the industries whose stock prices had recently risen the most. Thus, investments were often made at the peak of the industry's performance, only to be liquidated in the subsequent valley. So the concept failed to serve investors well, and it was given a decent and well-deserved burial in the late 1950s. Sector funds returned in 1981, and the same pattern has predictably re-emerged: investment near the peak, liquidation near the trough. I am not going to discuss these funds in great detail since such factors as a fund's size, age, and the tenure of its portfolio manager are usually irrelevant compared to the overpowering factor of the relative strength of its industry group in the marketplace. Mutual fund investors should own sector funds only for a specific purpose and only for a small portion of their equity assets. Mutual fund speculators should enjoy them to their hearts' content, providing that they do not mind the burden of sales charges, high expense ratios, and the transactions costs engendered both by surging cash inflows and outflows and by truly awesome rates of portfolio turnover (200% per year is not uncommon).

---

a chronicle of championship results for one or more of its funds, carefully selected and accompanied by braggadocio about being the top-performing fund for some particular period. Reports by the financial press typically lionize the portfolio managers who had the ''best'' records (i.e., achieved the largest gains) during the previous quarter or year or even longer. This myopic focus on past performance is not helpful. It is a flawed and counterproductive way to select a mutual fund.

There is, however, a place for the evaluation of past performance in the fund selection process. But it should come only *after* a review of the fund's principal structural characteristics. Before turning to the romance of performance evaluation, I shall examine some key structural characteristics of common stock funds. While these points are broad generalizations with many exceptions, they are still worthy of consideration.

Size of Fund

As a general rule, you should probably avoid funds with assets of less than $50 million simply because of the relatively higher expenses associated with small funds, along with the possibility that a small fund may not survive or may undergo a change in objectives in the search for greater acceptance in the marketplace. However, you might make an exception for a small fund that is part of a larger complex—say, $500 million or more in aggregate assets—or is managed by a large advisory firm. In both cases, the management should have the resources to manage the fund's affairs with reasonable efficiency.

On the other hand, if you are seeking an exceptional return—and are prepared to assume exceptional risk—you may wish to exclude funds with more than $1 billion of assets. This is not to say returns on larger funds will fall short of returns on smaller funds in the aggregate, for there is no evidence of this. Rather, it suggests that regression to the mean—a strong tendency for the gap between a fund with exceptional past returns and its peers to narrow—is a fact of life. Whether through asset growth or other factors, over time a fund's return tends to move toward the average.

Age of Fund

In most cases, a fund should prove its merit over a period of at least five to ten years. There are notable exceptions. A new fund introduced by an established investment management firm and modeled on its traditional investment philosophy should be considered. Another exception may be a new fund with specific investment objectives and characteristics that is part of a large complex. For example, if a fund complex offers a new balanced fund—and has provided good returns on its stock and bond funds over time—there would seem to be little hazard. Also, the inauguration of an index fund (and we shall see many of these in the coming years) poses few potential problems. But to invest in *any* fund without considering its heritage seems foolish.

Tenure of Portfolio Manager

Find out whether a portfolio manager has run the fund for a few months, a few years, or a few decades, and give this information whatever weight you deem appropriate. That said, many fine equity funds are run by teams of managers, with the advisory firm as an organization putting its corporate stamp on the funds' strategies and their implementation. Because of this diversity, such funds tend to be classic mainstream funds, and the tenure of a single manager should be relatively inconsequential.

Even when funds have individual portfolio managers, performance in a particular period can be due to much more—or less—than the manager's skill. For instance, a manager may be less important than the research and analytical support he receives. Or a manager may grow, or shrink, in capability. It is not unknown for a new manager to do better than a successful predecessor. A market environment in which a manager has been able to shine brightly may be replaced by a very different environment that does not favor the manager's investment style. Finally, good luck (always a factor in shaping fund returns) may turn to bad, and vice versa. Tenure is but one factor for you to consider. When managers change, a wait-and-see policy is usually appropriate.

Cost of Ownership

Chapter 10 is devoted to the extraordinary impact of costs on a fund's return. While cost may be less important in a stock fund than in a bond fund, balanced fund, or money market fund, you should always take into account front-end sales charges, redemption charges, and expense ratios. These costs are too often overlooked by investors. The cost factor may have seemed insignificant during the golden decade of the 1980s, when the stock market provided an average annual return of +17.6%. But if the market return in the 1990s is in the +10% range, costs will consume a much larger percentage of your return. It is worth emphasizing that, since market indexes exist only on paper, they are completely free of costs and so overstate the returns actually earned by real-world investors.

Portfolio Characteristics

Among the most important of the many factors that you should understand in a basic evaluation of an equity mutual fund are cash position, portfolio concentration, market capitalization, and portfolio turnover.

Cash position. What percentage of the portfolio is held in cash reserves? Has the percentage varied? Has the cash position been effective in adding stability during market declines while not unduly retarding growth during market rises? Since there is no evidence stock managers have had any success in raising cash at market tops, nor in investing cash at market bottoms, with rare exceptions cash reserves should play only a limited role in an equity fund (say, 5% of the portfolio's total net assets). It does not seem sensible to pay high advisory fees for the privilege of owning the residual cash reserves held by most stock funds. Years ago, cash was supposedly held as a liquidity reserve to meet a possible run of redemptions on fund shares. Today the futures markets readily and inexpensively permit funds to remain effectively fully exposed to the stock market, while maintaining cash reserves for possible redemptions.

Portfolio concentration. It is not enough to know how many stocks a fund owns, because many of them may represent a small percentage of net assets and have little impact on the fund's overall performance. The better test is the proportion of total assets the fund holds in its largest positions. One good measure is to check the fund's ten largest holdings. In the more concentrated funds, the ten largest holdings may comprise up to 50% of the portfolio; in the less concentrated funds, they may comprise as little as 15%. As a general rule, the greater the portfolio concentration, the greater the opportunity for the fund to provide differentiated performance. (The differentiation may be positive or negative.) It is also worthwhile to note the industry concentrations in a fund's portfolio as a further measure of its level of diversification.

Market capitalization. A fund's market capitalization will indicate whether the fund emphasizes the stocks of blue-chip companies with large market capitalizations, emerging companies with small capitalizations, or something in between. You should know the difference. The average weighted market capitalization of the common stocks owned by equity funds may range from more than $15 billion to less than $500 million. An average market capitalization in the range of $5 billion to $8 billion is typical for a mainstream stock fund. There is no right or wrong average market capitalization. It is simply a good measure of a fund's investment emphasis and, to some degree, the risks that it assumes. Over the long term, surprises, while they occur in all types of stocks, are less likely among the large blue-chip issues. (However, surprises among the blue chips have been rife in the early 1990s.)

Portfolio turnover. Turnover—the purchase and sale of securities in a fund's portfolio—is too often ignored by investors. But it is an important indicator of a fund's fundamental investment strategy. Low turnover tends to indicate a longer-term investment orientation, high turnover the reverse. Turnover has a significant influence on two aspects of investment performance: (1) the cost of managing the fund and (2) the realization of capital gains. Other things being equal, the higher the portfolio turnover, the higher the fund's transaction costs, and the higher the proportion of total return represented by realized (and thus taxable) capital gains. Both factors lower the return to the investor. I shall cover costs in more detail in Chapter 10 and taxes in Chapter 11.

Portfolio Statistics

In comparing total returns among funds, it is critical to always compare like with like. The three concepts of ExMark, Beta, and gross dividend yield may seem a bit complex, but you will want to understand them. Taken in combination, these statistical measures have proven to be a solid basis for comparing funds that are similar in their investment approaches. They help to ensure that a fund's record is judged only against those of other comparable funds.

ExMark. I have coined this expression to define the extent to which a mutual fund's return is *Ex*plained by a particular financial *Mark*et. The usual designation for this concept is *R-squared*, a term that defines the relationship between a fund's return and some market index (for U.S. stocks, typically the S&P 500). While you will not find the term *ExMark* used elsewhere, it seems to me the term *R-squared* is too arcane.

For a typical mainstream equity fund, the ExMark runs from 80% to 90%, meaning that an exceedingly high proportion of its total return is explained by the performance of the overall stock market. Only the remaining 20% to 10% of return is explained by some combination of (1) the fund's basic strategy and (2) the tactics and investment selections of the fund's portfolio manager. An ExMark below 80% indicates significantly less predictability of relative performance. A figure of 95% or above means that a fund's return has been shaped predominantly by the action of the stock market itself. Such a fund may be a "closet" index fund, charging high advisory fees but providing little opportunity to add value over and above the market's return. An index fund, the return of which is entirely explained by the action of the stock market, would of course carry an ExMark of 100%.

CAVEAT EMPTOR: *The Return of Halley's Comet*

The application of general mathematical concepts such as R-squared (here, ExMark), Beta, and Alpha to the measurement of investment performance began in the late 1960s. That they were not especially well-received was indicated by this news story covering my discussion of these ideas at a mutual fund conference in 1971.

> John C. Bogle, with the help of several floppy charts, made a presentation on performance. It was very interesting for those of a mathematical turn of mind, those who track the outer nebulae, and those who figure the reappearance dates of Halley's Comet.

A lot has happened to performance measurement since, but even after more than two decades these concepts have failed to emerge from the realm of the arcane. Since they provide valuable information, however, the intelligent investor will want to understand and utilize them.

Beta. A Beta is a measure of risk that, when applied to investment portfolios (as distinct from individual stocks), provides useful statistical information. It indicates a fund's past price volatility relative to a particular stock market index. The term *Beta,* widely used by professional investors and academics, may seem esoteric. But I believe it will gain gradual, if grudging, acceptance by individual investors. Most mainstream equity funds have Betas in the range of .85 to 1.05 (fairly close to the 1.00 Beta represented by the market in the aggregate). Especially conservative stock funds may register Betas as low as .75, meaning that in a -10% market decline, their values might be expected to fall -7.5%. Aggressive funds with Betas of 1.25 might see their values fall by -12.5%. The same general dimension of relative volatility also prevails in rising markets. Conditions in each market cycle differ markedly, and Beta should be regarded only as a rough proxy for your volatility expectations.

Gross dividend yield. The gross dividend yield is a significant indicator of mutual fund investment characteristics. Among stock funds, gross yields tend to be higher, for example, in value-oriented funds and lower in growth funds, hardly an unexpected result. However, most fund statistical services present yield improperly for comparative purposes. The reported net yield is *after* fund expenses, while a fund's investment

---

CAVEAT EMPTOR: *Ignore Alpha*

Many fund evaluation services place heavy reliance on *Alpha,* a term denoting the purported superiority or inferiority of a fund's results. Alpha adjusts the fund's total return for the risk it has assumed, as measured by Beta. Positive Alpha is good, so the argument goes; negative Alpha is bad. But Alphas are volatile and can swiftly move from positive to negative. In my view, Alpha, because of its unpredictable and backward-looking nature is a counterproductive measure. I believe Alpha is a flawed measure of what to expect from a fund and should generally be ignored. On the other hand, ExMarks and Betas of most mature funds with stable investment objectives and policies tend to remain stationary even over decades, making these two concepts far more reliable and useful.

---

characteristics are reflected by its gross yield *before* expenses. The dramatic difference is seen in the hypothetical illustration in Table 4–4.

As you can see, the net yields of the two funds are precisely the same. But the 4.0% gross yield of the value fund is fully 60% higher than the 2.5% gross yield of the growth fund. This range is about what might be expected in a marketplace in which the average yield is 3.2%. Clearly, the gross yield is the more reliable differentiator of a fund's investment philosophy.

Taking these three significant evaluation statistics together, Table 4–5 shows how they work in differentiating the particular stock fund types. The mainstream funds—growth, value, and equity income—demonstrate predictably higher average ExMarks, a manifestation of their similarity to the stock market as a whole. The small company funds, on the other hand, have much higher Betas and much lower gross yields. In all, the table establishes a comparative framework in which to assess the principal investment characteristics of the various stock fund groups.

Since there are variations in investment characteristics even among funds with the same investment objective, closer evaluation is required if you prefer to fine-tune the analysis. For example, if the value fund in which you are interested has a lower ExMark, a lower Beta, and a higher gross yield than the average for its group, fair comparison requires that you select a subset (or peer group) from among funds with investment characteristics that are more similar. Two examples may suffice to make this point, as shown in Table 4–6.

TABLE 4-4
Yield Comparison

	Value fund A	*Growth fund B*
Gross yield	4.0%	2.5%
Expenses	2.0	0.5
Net yield	2.0%	2.0%

TABLE 4-5
Portfolio Statistics Analysis (December 31, 1992)

Classification	ExMark	Beta	Gross yield
Growth funds	83%	1.01	2.3%
Value funds	87	0.87	3.7
Equity income funds	87	0.76	5.0
Aggressive growth funds	68	1.19	2.4
Small company funds	69	1.16	1.5
International funds	38	0.65	3.0
Gold funds	0	0.00	2.6
Standard & Poor's 500 Index	100	1.00	2.8

TABLE 4-6
Portfolio Statistics Analysis (December 31, 1992)

	ExMark	Beta	Gross yield	*Annual return five years ended December 31, 1992*
Selected value fund	78%	0.70	4.2%	+13.4%
Peer group average	84	0.69	4.4	+12.7
Value fund average	87	0.87	3.7	+13.6
Selected growth fund	91	1.19	1.2	+16.0
Peer group average	90	1.13	1.6	+16.4
Growth fund average	83	1.01	2.3	+14.7

Let's consider this table in two segments. The selected value fund appears to have provided a subpar return (+13.4% versus +13.6%). But the fund had less of its return explained by the market, took substantially less risk, and earned a higher income yield than its objective group. When compared to a peer group with comparable risk characteristics, the fund was actually a superior performer (+13.4% versus +12.7%). The selected growth fund, on the other hand, is clearly a winner when compared to its broad objective group. But, compared to a peer group of growth funds that also have been more diversified, assumed higher risk and earned somewhat lower yields, it is actually a slightly below-average performer.

These portfolio statistics, however scientific they may appear, should not be considered precise evaluators of differences among funds. Henry Clay was right when he warned "statistics are no substitute for judgment." But these three factors, taken together, substantially narrow the parameters in which to evaluate a fund's relative performance. Thus, they provide useful information.

To perform the sort of analysis outlined in this section, you will need to gather all of the data I have discussed. Facts on fund asset size, age, manager tenure, and cost are readily available through prospectuses and major financial publications. While information on portfolio characteristics and portfolio statistics is more difficult to obtain, several statistical services provide it. Chapter 8 offers a full discussion of the sources and uses of mutual fund statistics and information.

In the final analysis, I cannot emphasize enough the importance of fairness (and common sense) in assuring that you compare only funds that have *similar* investment policies and characteristics. Sensible performance comparisons can be made only after establishing that fairness. Even then, as I shall now show, selecting equity funds on the basis of past performance is likely to be a futile effort on your part and virtually certain to be a futile effort for fund investors in the aggregate.

EVALUATING PAST PERFORMANCE

No matter how many cautions are expressed about picking mutual funds simply on the basis of their past performance, most investors still do exactly that. It seems so easy. Yet the record is crystal clear that past performance success is rarely the precursor of future success. Here are a few guidelines about what I mean by past performance and how to evaluate it.

To begin, evaluate the composition of a fund's return to determine if it will meet your needs for either income generation, capital growth, or some combination of the two. From that point, consider the fund's total returns in the aggregate. Since long periods of time are more meaningful in evaluating fund performance than short periods, it clearly is more relevant to observe a fund's returns over a decade than over a year.

As the time frame lengthens, it is critical that you observe not only the fund's average return over a period of years but also its performance from one year to the next to make sure there is some thread of consistency in annual returns. Consider two hypothetical funds in the same peer group: both have achieved identical +12% annual rates of return versus +11% for their peer group. Yet one has outpaced the group by +1% every year. (Such consistency, of course, does not occur in the real world.) The other underperformed by −1% in eight of the ten years but outperformed by +10% in two of the years. (This kind of inconsistency is anything but rare, especially among smaller or more specialized funds.) You should be wary of attributing too much meaning to the past returns in which top performance is concentrated in just a few short periods.

With that thought in mind, let's look at the record. Time and again, it has been demonstrated that the relative return achieved by an equity mutual fund yesterday has virtually no material predictive value for tomorrow. While you may intuitively suspect that this is the case, it is subject to testing in the laboratory of fund performance. The basic level of analysis is simply this: consider the actual past records of all broad-based general equity mutual funds, pick out the top 20 in a given period, and then observe the actual future relative returns they achieve. Let's begin on the short-term level. How did the one-year champions perform during the subsequent year?

To minimize the possibility of randomness in the one-year data, I compared fund rankings for each year in the past decade (i.e., where the top 20 mutual fund performers of 1982 ranked in 1983, and so on to where the top 20 of 1991 ranked in 1992). For simplicity, I then averaged the ten periods. Table 4–7 presents the results. Here are some of the significant conclusions:

- A top 20 fund's performance in one year has no systematic relationship to its ranking in the subsequent year. (A glance at Table 4–7 demonstrates this randomness.)
- A typical top 20 fund provided a phenomenal return of +42.3%

CAVEAT EMPTOR: *What's Past Is (Not) Prologue . . .*

Marketers of mutual funds have a fairly easy time achieving—and then bragging about—returns that mark their funds as "#1." Here is the strategy: Select a fund that ranks first in any class of funds with similar objectives and asset size (say, growth funds with current assets over $500 million) over any specified period (the past quarter or year or even 25 years). Advertise it as #1. When the ranking subsequently drops (and it will), select another fund, in another class or another time period (or both), and advertise *it* as #1. While these comparisons are ridiculous when taken over a period as short as a single quarter, they are even more misleading when taken over the long term. A fund identified by its sponsor as #1 for 25 years may be ranked last for the immediately preceding five years. These promotions provide simplistic information that is easily manipulated and has absolutely *no predictive value*. Even their marketers, if directly confronted, cannot deny the accuracy of this assertion. Similar rankings published in the financial press lack the fund sponsor's bias and are completely objective. However, these rankings are also utterly without predictive value, and you should give them credence only as interesting historical artifacts. Despite Antonio's assurance in *The Tempest*, beware of assuming that "what's past is prologue." It is not.

---

in its leadership year, more than three times the all-fund average of +13.3%. In the second year, its return averaged +17.6%, compared to the all-fund average of +13.1%. (If this margin could be sustained by the fund in subsequent years, its performance would be outstanding.)

- Funds in the top 20 in a given year have, on average, ranked 284 of 681 funds in the subsequent year. While better than mere chance—which would suggest an average rank of 341—it can be described as regressing to the mean.

Perhaps surprisingly, these general conclusions seem to be affirmed over longer holding periods. In our ten-year study (1972–82 versus 1982–92), the rankings were only marginally helpful. The average member of the top 20 provided a premium annual return of +8.3% (+17.3% versus +9.0% for the all-fund average) in the first decade. But the margin dropped to +1.2% (+14.3% versus +13.1%) in the subsequent decade. The evidence, as shown in Table 4–8, is really quite striking:

TABLE 4–7
One-Year Rank Order of Top 20 Equity Funds (1982–92)

First year rank	Average rank in subsequent year	First year rank	Average rank in subsequent year
1	100	11	310
2	383	12	262
3	231	13	271
4	343	14	207
5	358	15	271
6	239	16	287
7	220	17	332
8	417	18	348
9	242	19	310
10	330	20	226

Average rank of top 20 in subsequent year = 284
Average number of funds = 681

Concentrated specialty and international funds excluded.

TABLE 4–8
Ten-Year Rank Order of Top 20 Equity Funds

Rank 1972–82	Rank 1982–92	Rank 1972–82	Rank 1982–92
1	128	11	222
2	34	12	5
3	148	13	118
4	220	14	228
5	16	15	205
6	2	16	78
7	199	17	209
8	15	18	237
9	177	19	119
10	245	20	242

Average rank of top 20 in subsequent decade = 142
Number of funds = 309

Concentrated specialty and international funds excluded.

- The average rank of the top 20 funds in the first decade fell to 142 of 309 funds in the second. While that is a slightly higher rank than the median rank of 155 that would be achieved at random, the difference is almost certainly statistical noise.

CAVEAT EMPTOR: *The All-Star Team*

Some real-world idea of the difficulty of picking the best fund managers may be gained from the experience of a clever concept introduced in 1986. The concept was to form an investment company that would be managed by all-star portfolio managers, selected on the basis of their past performance records. These managers, it was suggested, would manage the fund to fame and its shareholders to fortune. Alas, from the fund's offering in October 1986 through the close of 1992, the expected performance advantage of the all-star managers was conspicuous only by its absence. During this period, the unmanaged S&P 500 provided an average annual total return of +13.9%, about one percentage point ahead of the fund's average return of +12.8%. It is as if a randomly selected team of average high school and college football payers had beaten the National Football League's All-Star team by a 14–13 score.

- Only four of the top 20 funds in the first period remained in the top 20 in the second.
- To add insult to injury, while the average total return of the top 20 funds during the second decade (+14.3%) was above the all-fund average (+13.1%), it fell well short of the return of +16.2% on the unmanaged S&P 500 Index.

In short, even when examined from the vantage of a long time period, investing in the winners of the past, solely in terms of highest relative return and irrespective of investment objective, does not appear to increase your chances of selecting the winners of the future.

This "bet on the winner" analysis, involving equity funds of all stripes, is simplistic. But the same general conclusions are affirmed when we take the analysis to a more sensible level. Table 4–9 compares the rankings of growth and value funds—essentially mainstream funds—by quartile for the decade ended December 31, 1987, with their rankings over the subsequent five-year period. I have used a slightly different time frame, grouped funds by quartiles rather than by rank, and limited my analysis to mainstream funds with generally comparable investment characteristics.

There were 176 such funds in operation throughout the entire period, and I examined the results of the funds in each quartile during both periods. I wanted to discover whether the rankings of the 44 funds in each quartile

TABLE 4–9
Performance of Growth and Value Funds by Quartiles

	1987–92 Ranking				Five-Year Average		
	First quartile	Second quartile	Third quartile	Fourth quartile	Gross return (%)	Expense ratio (%)	Net return (%)
First quartile	14	10	12	8	15.9	0.9	15.0
Second quartile	8	13	11	12	14.8	0.9	13.9
Third quartile	13	12	10	9	15.5	1.0	14.5
Fourth quartile	9	9	11	15	14.6	1.7	12.9

1977–87 Ranking

during the first period would predict their quartile rankings during the second period. Table 4–9 shows that performance predictability was virtually nonexistent. A completely random distribution of returns—an exercise in coin flipping, for example—would have placed about 11 funds in each box. With four exceptions, each of the 16 boxes had between 9 and 13 entrants.

In fairness, a very slight bias appears toward both first-quartile funds and fourth-quartile funds repeating their performance. The odds, rather than being the expected three out of four against a repeat, were "only" about two out of three at each extreme. Are these odds worth betting on? Probably not, for several reasons:

1. The difference in returns is generally small. The average net return on the ten-year first-quartile funds, for example, was +15.0% during the subsequent five-year period, compared to +13.9% for the second quartile funds and +14.5% for the third. That, too, looks a lot like statistical noise.

2. In terms of average return, the fourth-quartile funds appear to have remained poor performers. However, while the net returns of these funds were inferior, their gross returns (before being dragged down by inordinately high expenses) were about aver-

age. This discrepancy shows the tendency of the returns earned by fund portfolios to regress to the mean, while the expense ratios of the fund portfolios do not.

3. On a gross return basis, the five-year results achieved in each quartile were remarkably similar. The first and third quartile funds were equal, for all intents and purposes, as were the second and fourth. Ironically, if you believe past ranking is an intelligent method of predicting future relative returns, you should not limit your selections to funds in the first quartile; the third-quartile funds provided nearly identical opportunities.

4. The unmanaged S&P 500 Index provided a return of +15.9% for the five-year period. This was better even than the average net return for the first-quartile funds and arguably achieved with much better odds.

This test poses a question: Does comparing relative returns among generally similar funds over extended periods suggest skilled portfolio managers can be identified in advance? The answer seems clear: No. Even if evaluations of the past fairly compare only mainstream equity funds, and even if extended measurement periods are used, the record suggests that past performance has virtually no predictive value.

Of course, the test in Table 4–9 was based only on a theoretical, what-if analysis. But the conclusion that it is no easy task to preselect a top-performing equity fund is also demonstrated by a more sophisticated real-world test. Rather than simply picking the top performers in retrospect, let's actually select *in advance* what we might logically expect to be better fund performers, taking into account their total return over at least ten years, their relative performance in both rising and falling markets, and their continuity of portfolio management over at least seven years.

What I just described is the process of selecting funds for the *Forbes* Honor Roll. It is an eminently sensible and fair system of equity fund selection and has been consistently prepared by the magazine each year since 1974. It encompasses a diverse group of equity funds and an extended time period for evaluation.

How have the Honor Roll selections performed over time? Let's suppose you read the Honor Roll listing each year and purchase (or hold) an equal amount in each fund on the list, eliminating funds as they were dropped from the list. Such an approach avoids the inevitable bias of back-testing (massaging past numbers until they produce the desired result, or as is sometimes said, "applying different tortures to the data until it finally confesses").

CAVEAT EMPTOR: *Coming Down to Earth*

I noted earlier that regression to the mean is a critically important concept for investors to understand. In the stock market, it means that returns substantially above or below long-term norms are likely to subsequently move down, or up, toward the norm. The same principle applies in equity fund performance. The fund shown below exceeded the returns of the stock market by an average of 20 percentage points a year during the first seven years of the selected 14-year period. But it provided an average margin of only three percentage points during the second seven years. While this margin is indeed healthy, the lessening of superiority shown in the example provides a good illustration of a fund's performance "coming down to earth." It is also a reminder that no fund can consistently sustain exceptionally high relative returns.

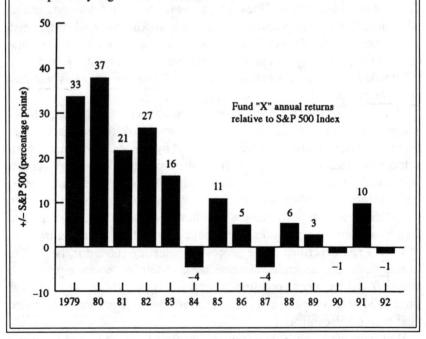

Let's now examine (1) whether the Honor Roll selections as a group provided better returns than other comparable funds and (2) whether they provided better returns than the stock market as a whole. The results are not especially encouraging to those who believe that what's past is prologue. The performance of the Honor Roll funds fell short of both standards. Table 4–10 shows the summary figures.

TABLE 4–10
Honor Roll Analysis (1974–92)

	Average annual return	Cumulative return	Final value of initial investment of $10,000
Honor roll funds	+11.2%	+650%	$ 75,000
Average equity fund	+12.5	+843	94,300
Total stock market*	+13.1	+936	103,600

*Wilshire 5000 Index

FIGURE 4–4
Relative Performance of the Honor Roll (1974–92)

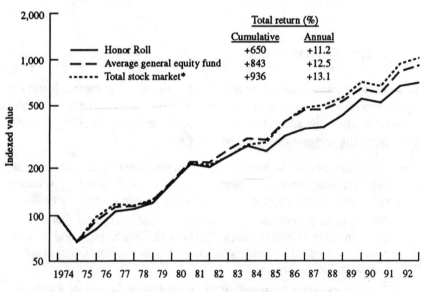

*Wilshire 5000 Index (adjusted for annual expenses of 0.20%)

   The net result is that returns on equity mutual funds—whether selected carefully or aggregated—have fallen short of those of the total stock market during the Honor Roll's history. Cumulatively, through compounding, the initial $10,000 investment grew to $75,000 for the Honor Roll funds, $94,300 for the average equity fund, and $103,600 for the market index. As a whole, this maximum difference in return of $28,600 is equal to 290% of the amount initially invested. Figure 4–4 shows the cumulative results.

A few words about costs: (1) The Honor Roll performance data have been adjusted to take into account any sales charges that would have been incurred on the annual fund purchases. (2) The average equity fund performance data have been reduced by an estimated sales charge of 4% paid only on the initial purchase. (3) The stock market return includes no sales charges but has been reduced by 0.2% annually to reflect expected real-world operating costs. If sales charges were ignored (although there is no reason for doing so), the return of the Honor Roll funds and the average equity fund would have been +13.0% and +12.8%, respectively.

The Honor Roll example makes it clear that picking the winners, even with thoughtfulness and judgment, is far too often a fruitless exercise. Another of Alfred E. Smith's memorable phrases might have been used to describe the hazards of placing too much reliance on a fund's past performance: "No matter how thin you slice it, it's still baloney."

SUMMARY

The previous comments represent a tough, demanding approach toward equity fund comparison and an acknowledgment that even the most careful analysis provides no assurance of success. Nonetheless, decide you must. The following suggestions may be helpful:

- Invest principally in broadly based mainstream funds; diversification is usually widest in these funds. If current income is a major requirement, give special consideration to equity income funds.

- Select funds by comparing their investment characteristics with those in their objective category (growth, value, etc.) and with a peer group of other funds you may be considering. Comparing like with like is critical.

- Give important consideration to the technical factors of ExMark, Beta, and gross yield. Also consider the age and size of a fund, its portfolio turnover rate and, to the appropriate degree, the tenure of its portfolio manager.

- Consider carefully the cost of acquiring and holding the fund's shares (respectively, sales loads and expense ratios). In an unpredictable world, cost may be the only predictable element of fund performance.

- Focus primarily on a fund's returns for the previous ten years or,

---

CAVEAT EMPTOR: *The Madness of Crowds*

It is not possible to fix the precise time when the idea of capturing extraordinary performance through mutual funds became a popular delusion. But, sometime during the period from 1965 to 1968, retrospectively known as the go-go years, this madness took hold. During these four years, a small group of stock funds with performance records "too good to be true" (and that was how it turned out) became the driving force in the mutual fund industry, just as the sector funds had been in the pre-World War II era. With the stock market up +39% cumulatively during those four years, the returns of the six major go-go funds *averaged* +214%. Their assets rose from $40 million to $2.3 billion. The return to reality came promptly, with a −36% drop in value for the funds in 1969–70 (when the stock market dipped only −5%). A brief revival for the go-go funds in 1971 was quickly aborted, and then the 1973–74 crash ensued. On average, these six go-go funds dropped in value −64% during the period 1969–74. Their assets collapsed to $660 million as a result of falling asset values accentuated by massive redemptions of shares. (In fairness, during the same period the stock market declined by −19%, a healthy reminder of the risk of picking the winner by hindsight, and also of the risk that exists in stocks as a group.) Since the lion's share of the new money flowed into the go-go funds after the high returns and departed near the market lows, rare was the investor—if there was one—who avoided severe capital losses. The go-go era "came and went," one more illustration of the aptness of the title of Charles MacKay's book on the history of speculation, *Extraordinary Popular Delusions and the Madness of Crowds.*

---

for a newer fund, its lifetime. Note year-to-year variations in returns relative to competitors.

- Avoid funds at the top of the performance deck with hot recent records. Particularly avoid funds that are bragging about it or whose managers are lionized in the press. Hot funds never fail to cool off (i.e., to regress toward the mean).

- Avoid as well funds that are persistently at the bottom of the performance deck. Success doesn't persist, but there is fragmentary evidence that failure, in part because of inordinately high expenses, does.

- Limit narrowly based funds (such as international and small company funds) to perhaps 20% of your equity assets in the aggregate. Do not try to beat the market by engaging in short-term trading among sector funds.

If following these rules of common stock mutual fund selection seems overly analytical, tedious, and time-consuming—and, based upon the record of the past, uncertain of success—there is a simpler way. It is called owning the entire market, and I shall discuss it in Chapter 9.

Chapter Five

How to Select a Bond Mutual Fund
Attention Must Be Paid

The growth of bond mutual funds is one of the most remarkable aspects of the soaring popularity of mutual funds. Bond fund assets have grown from just $4 billion in 1970, representing 9% of total mutual fund assets, to $510 billion at the end of 1992, representing 32% of total fund assets. This increase represents a compound growth rate of +25% annually. In contrast, equity fund assets have expanded at a rate of just +12% annually over the same period—less than half of the bond fund growth rate. To borrow a line from *Death of a Salesman*, "attention must be paid" to bond funds. This chapter will pay precisely that attention, beginning with a brief overview of the different types of bond funds available. Then I shall discuss the structural investment characteristics (especially quality, maturity, and cost) of bond funds. Finally, I will propose a remarkably simple framework for selecting a particular bond mutual fund for inclusion in your investment portfolio.

It is paradoxical that, considering the enormous amount of attention newspapers and magazines give to equity mutual funds and their portfolio managers, the types of stock funds are by no means as diverse as those of bond funds. As we saw in Chapter 4, stock funds largely comprise some combination of five major investment sectors: growth, value, equity income, broad-based specialty, and concentrated specialty. But bond funds have two levels of comparison. First, there are three major maturity levels: short-term, intermediate-term, and long-term. Second, there are eight distinctly different major investment sectors: U.S. government, mortgage-backed, investment-grade corporate, medium-grade corporate, high-yield (junk) corporate, investment-grade municipal, high-yield municipal, and global. As a result, there are 24 potential bond fund sectors,

TABLE 5-1
Bond Fund Sectors—Number of Funds (December 31, 1992)

	U.S. government	Mortgage- backed	Investment- grade corporate	Medium- grade corporate	High- Yield corporate	Investment- grade municipal	High- yield municipal	Global	Total
Short-term	69	52	73	2	–	20	–	48	264
Intermediate-term	49	64	64	–	78	41	–	–	296
Long-term	154	–	125	72	–	670	28	53	1,102
Total	272	116	262	74	78	731	28	101	1,662

of which 17 are occupied by existing mutual funds. Table 5-1 shows the number of funds available in each sector.

In the major common stock fund sectors, the evidence illustrates a remarkable overlap between the portfolios of funds with supposedly distinct investment objectives. For example, both value funds and growth funds hold many of the same stocks. In general, however, each type of bond fund has its own distinctive characteristics. For instance, there are 69 short-term U.S. government bond funds available to investors. Each holds, for the most part, a homogeneous portfolio invested in securities of the U.S. Treasury and federal government agencies, and maintains an average maturity generally ranging from two to four years. As you move down the quality ladder and up the maturity ladder, differences in portfolio composition among bond mutual funds with supposedly similar investment objectives become more prevalent. Among high-yield bond funds, the distinctions are truly striking. (This chapter focuses on the investment-grade bond fund sectors; a separate section at the end deals specifically with the high-yield sector.) In any event, you can compare bond funds within each sector shown in Table 5-1 with a high level of confidence that you are comparing apples with apples.

If the thought of selecting one or more bond funds from among 17 separate bond categories comprising approximately 1,700 fund offerings seems daunting, all I can say is, it is. But the fund selection process does not need to be as onerous as these numbers suggest. The fundamental issue is how to reduce this universe of funds to a more manageable size.

To begin, ask yourself why you want to purchase a bond fund in the first place. Are you saving to build capital for your retirement? Then you

---

CAVEAT EMPTOR: *A Bond Fund Is Not a Bond*

When you purchase a 20-year U.S. Treasury bond, its price sensitivity to changes in interest rates decreases as the bond moves closer to its maturity date (i.e., your principal risk declines each year that you hold the bond). A U.S. Treasury bond *fund*, on the other hand, maintains a more or less fixed average maturity, so you are always exposed to a given level of principal risk—no matter how long you hold the bond fund. If you are a conservative investor who has adequate assets, interested only in maintaining a fixed stream of interest income payments, it might be wise to purchase a Treasury bond instead of a Treasury bond fund. In doing so, you will own a long-term bond that gradually becomes a short-term bond, while the bond fund will retain its long-term characteristics. This principle holds true with short-term bonds, though the divergences in income and principal value are less striking. It is important to recognize the distinction between the substantially fixed maturity of a bond fund and the steadily declining maturity of a bond.

---

might want to limit your analysis to longer-term bond funds in the hope of earning the relatively higher returns they have typically provided. Do you want a relatively steady and durable stream of monthly interest payments to supplement your income during your retirement? Some combination of long-term and intermediate-term bonds might be the most appropriate alternative. Are you moving out of a certificate of deposit to attain a higher yield offered by a bond mutual fund? A short-term bond fund may be the best choice. These questions will help you determine whether the maturity and quality characteristics of a bond fund fit your financial goals. Whatever your reason for purchasing a bond fund, give careful consideration to the incremental risks involved in lengthening your maturity horizon.

Asking these kinds of questions will force you to consider the crucial investment characteristics of a bond fund before you consider its past performance. The past performance of a particular bond fund relative to the performance of all bond funds as a group has little value as a precursor of the future. But there is, as I shall show later, a substantial amount of predictive strength if a bond fund is compared with other funds having similar structural and portfolio characteristics. So investors must first consider the specific portfolio characteristics that will determine whether a particular bond fund suits their investment objectives. I will begin this analysis by evaluating the broad structural characteristics common to all mutual funds and then those characteristics unique to bond funds.

STRUCTURAL CHARACTERISTICS

Age and Size of Fund

Because bond funds tend to have explicitly stated investment policies and objectives, there's little reason not to invest in a fund with a limited track record. The asset level of a bond fund will probably not have any correlative relationship to its future performance as long as it has assets of at least $50 million and can therefore garner reasonable economies of scale. Nevertheless, given an established fund with a reputable management firm and another with similar objectives offered by an untested firm, the former would be the more prudent choice.

In the case of new fund "products," make no exception for the lack of a track record. Government-plus bond funds come quickly to mind. Offered as a way to dramatically increase yield by including capital returns with income returns, these funds soon lost capital, and interest income dwindled. This was a major industry black mark. More recently, adjustable rate mortgage funds and short-term global income funds have been offered as safe alternatives to money market funds, only to experience unexpected declines in their net asset values and their dividends. Without the framework for evaluating the potential vulnerabilities of such funds and the new financial instruments they comprise, you would be wise to wait on the sidelines for several years before committing your assets.

Tenure of Portfolio Manager

Investors seem to feel more confident about investing in a fund when they believe the portfolio manager responsible for its past returns will continue to be responsible for its future returns. The skill and tenure of a professional portfolio manager are important considerations when evaluating stock funds, but may be less important in evaluating bond funds. Nonetheless, bond funds must be managed by experienced, competent, and diligent professional advisers. Active portfolio management, of course, will enhance the relative returns of some bond funds, but will reduce the returns of others. In most cases, you should look beyond the skills of a particular manager. The most significant determinants of a bond fund's relative return are (1) its investment objectives and policies, especially its specified quality and maturity standards, and (2) its operating costs.

Relative Yields

All else being equal, investors seeking to maximize income should naturally seek out the fund with the highest current SEC yield. (This is the advertised yield calculation prescribed by the Securities and Exchange Commission.) But looking at relative yields in a vacuum is a perilous strategy; there are many ways of calculating fund yields (to say nothing of enhancing them) to facilitate comparative analysis. For example, bond fund yields may be calculated on a current yield basis (income as a percentage of the fund's current market value) or on a yield-to-maturity basis (amortizing any premiums and discounts over the life of the bonds). You have a right to know both of these yields.

To clarify, if a bond fund owns a portfolio of five-year maturity bonds selling, on average, at a price of $105 (a 5% premium), the current yield of the portfolio, assuming a 6% coupon, is 5.7%. However, the yield to maturity is 4.9%, because principal will decline by about 1% annually as the premium bonds approach their maturity dates, at which time only their face values will be paid. If you are concerned *only* with current income, you can ignore a bond fund's yield to maturity, since premiums or discounts will not affect the fund's monthly income distribution. But the higher income returns tend to be offset—dollar for dollar—by lower capital returns. If your focus is on total return, the message is clear: do not weigh current stated yield too heavily.

Municipal bond funds have invested particularly heavily in high-coupon bonds, largely issued during the high-interest-rate environment of the early to mid-1980s. When interest coupons are well in excess of current market interest rates (as during 1992), and when the ten years of call protection expire, such bonds are almost certain to be called back by their issuers. They will be replaced inevitably with bonds providing much lower yields, and the dividends paid on municipal bond funds owning high-coupon bonds will decline.

In a low-interest-rate environment, there is a temptation for bond funds to maximize their stated yields by owning premium bonds with high cou-

---

CAVEAT EMPTOR: *Prepayment Risk*

Perhaps nowhere is the complexity of yield calculations more evident than in mortgage-backed obligations. Calculating a yield to maturity for Government National Mortgage Association (GNMA) securities, for example, requires making assumptions about mortgage prepayments under existing market conditions. GNMA funds emphasizing mortgages with high-interest coupons run a far greater risk of accelerating prepayments than funds emphasizing low-coupon mortgages. The pricing of each GNMA obligation requires yet another assumption, the so-called speed rate of prepayments. Even small changes in the speed rate affect the value of GNMA obligations. Complex as all of this may sound, the wise GNMA investor should know these data. Average coupon data for GNMA funds are provided by some statistical services, but prepayment assumptions are available only from the fund's investment adviser. These issues are even more complex when collateralized mortgage obligations (CMOs) are held in a bond fund's portfolio. In any event, prepayments can dramatically alter the dividends of funds holding mortgage-backed securities, so you should obtain this important information.

---

pons and by making heavy commitments to mortgage obligations. While these practices cry out for full disclosure, for now it is largely left to investors to uncover them. When a bond fund reaches for yield in this way, it is converting capital return to income return, which may well impair principal. Be cautious of a fund whose gross (pre-expense) yield significantly exceeds market norms. If a fund's gross yield is well above the norm, ask some hard questions of the fund's sponsor.

Cost of Fund Ownership

You should always know the expense ratio of a bond fund before investing. While some stock funds, some of the time, have provided premium performance despite prodigious costs, most bond funds, most of the time, have failed to do so. The reason is that, within the major sectors, bond funds operate under comparable quality and average maturity standards. U.S. Treasury bond funds, for example, all have identical and unmatched credit quality and are segmented into sectors with clearly identified average maturities. All insured municipal funds are rated AAA, and so on.

CAVEAT EMPTOR: *Loads Reduce Yields*

Sales loads of one type or another are assessed on 726 of the 1,662 bond funds in Table 5-1. Front-end loads immediately reduce the principal value of your investment, resulting in a significant reduction in yield. A yield of 6.0% in a no-load fund would be reduced, all else held equal, to 5.7% in a fund with a 5% sales commission—if the fund's shares were held to infinity. Spreading the load over five years would reduce the 6.0% yield to 5.0%. If the shares were held only one year, the effective yield would drop to less than 1%. Sales charges are often hidden by the assessment of "contingent deferred sales loads." In this case, the fund does not charge a front-end load, but if you exit in the first year there is a 5% load penalty, which gradually drops to zero by the sixth year. You also may pay another 1% each year in asset-based sales charges (0.75%) and service fees (0.25%). However hidden this combined charge, over five years it has the same impact as a 5% front-end sales load. Further, the annual sales charge may continue over subsequent years and the annual service fee may continue into infinity. The sales load should be a critical factor in choosing between bond funds with comparable quality, maturity, and expense ratios. Some bond funds (unbelievably) assess yet another sales charge when shareholders reinvest their dividends, which can reduce yield by another 0.3%. Avoid them like the plague!

Bond funds within each investment objective differ most importantly in their total costs—expense ratio plus any sales charge. The expense ratio, of course, represents the amount taken by the fund's management from the *gross* interest income earned by the fund, before distribution of the *net* interest income to the fund's shareholders. Therefore, a lower-cost bond fund will likely provide a superior return relative to its higher-cost counterpart. With the wide variety of funds available in each category, it does not make sense to own one with annual expenses of 1% or 2% (or more), which would reduce an 8% gross yield to 7% or 6%. In my view, even annual expenses much over 50 basis points (0.50%) seem patently rich. In any event, you must, without fail, be aware of what portion of your income is consumed by fund expenses.

Table 5-2 shows the impact of costs on the yields received by investors in three funds. Each fund has the same credit quality and maturity (hence the same risk), and earns the same annual gross yield, 7%. As you can

TABLE 5–2
Impact of Costs on Bond Fund Yields

	Type of Fund		
	Low-cost (no-load)	High-cost (no-load)	High-cost (5% sales load)
Gross yield	7.0%	7.0%	7.0%
Expense ratio	−0.4	−1.5	−1.5
Net yield	6.6%	5.5%	5.5%
Impact of 5% sales load	0.0	0.0	−0.5*
Net yield after sales load	6.6%	5.5%	5.0%

*Assumed ten-year holding period.

see, the low-cost, no-load fund in the example provides 32% more income than the high-cost, load fund. If the latter fund also carries a sales charge on reinvested dividends, its effective yield would drop another 0.3%, to 4.7%. Then, the income advantage of the low-cost, no-load fund would be 40%. Translated into dollars and assuming an investment of $10,000, that is the difference between income of $660 per year and $470 per year. Since risk is held constant in these examples, the disparity in income is extraordinary.

The expense ratio differentials shown in the table are by no means extreme. Indeed, 20% of all bond funds have annual expense ratios below 0.40% and 20% have expense ratios above 1.50%. The range is about 0.25% to 2.25%, or a spread of 2.0%. Since the spread shown in Table 5–2 is only about half that amount (1.1%), you can see that this example substantially understates the importance of expenses.

Portfolio Characteristics

At the very heart of evaluating bond funds is an intelligent appraisal of such portfolio characteristics as quality, maturity, and the use of derivative instruments.

Quality rating. Investors should carefully consider not only the average quality of a bond fund's portfolio but the *distribution* of the individual security ratings as well. I have never seen a corporate bond fund advertisement that addresses the issue of quality. Most bond funds do not report their quality structure in their prospectuses, nor do they provide the credit ratings of current portfolio holdings in regular reports to shareholders. But such ratings are readily available, published by Moody's Investors Services, Standard & Poor's Corporation, and others. A general familiarity with the concept of credit ratings might be helpful.

1. Bonds issued by the U.S. Treasury and most federal agencies are deemed completely secure in every respect. While it is unconventional, I have used the rating AAA+ to describe such obligations.

2. The AAA rating means unquestioned credit quality. Only a few blue-chip corporations and municipalities (as well as insured municipal bonds) carry this rating.

3. The AA and A ratings are assigned to highly secure corporate and municipal bonds.

4. BBB is the lowest investment-grade rating. It means solid creditworthiness, but with moderate risk.

5. BB is the rating of the highest-quality bonds in the noninvestment-grade grouping, often called junk bonds.

6. Bonds rated B or C are of low quality, with significant questions about the payment of annual interest and the return of principal at maturity.

7. D quality indicates the highest degree of uncertainty with respect to the payments of interest and principal.

8. The quality of unrated bonds may range from A to D. In evaluating bond funds, as a general rule it is best to treat them as speculative.

Since each drop in quality entails a commensurate increase in yield, gaining extra yield is relatively easy, but only by assuming higher credit risk. Many so-called investment-grade bond funds are reaching out for yield, in part to offset their higher expenses. However, when fund expenses and any sales charges are taken into account, purchasing the lower-quality portfolio does not always translate into higher income to the investor. Table 5–3 presents three examples of this anomaly.

1. The relatively higher-quality, short-term corporate bond fund held a portfolio comprising just 15% of assets in bonds rated BBB or below, while the relatively lower-quality fund invested fully 35% of its assets

TABLE 5-3
Bond Fund Yields—Impact of Quality and Expenses (December 31, 1992)

	Short-term corporate bond fund		National municipal bond fund		California municipal bond fund	
	High quality	Medium quality	High quality	Medium quality	High quality	Medium quality
Gross yield	7.7%	7.9%	6.7%	8.0%	6.1%	7.2%
Expenses	−0.3	−0.6	−0.2	−2.1	−0.2	−1.9*
Net yield	7.4%	7.3%	6.5%	5.9%	5.9%	5.3%

*Includes expense ratio of 1.4% and 5% sales load amortized over ten years.

in that category. Yet the lower-quality fund—given its high expenses—provided a marginally lower yield.

2. The two long-term national municipal bond fund portfolios were rated, respectively, 98% and 64% A or above. However, given its astronomical expense ratio, the lower-quality fund provided a net yield of only 5.9%, versus 6.5% for the higher-quality fund.

3. The portfolio of one California state municipal bond fund was rated 31% BBB and below; the other comprised 100% AAA *insured* municipal bonds (especially important in an earthquake-prone state). But the insured fund provided a net yield of 5.9%, compared with 5.3% (including a hefty sales charge) for the uninsured fund. Just imagine being paid 0.6%—a 11% premium—for buying an insurance policy.

These examples raise a question about whether you should *ever* purchase a lower-quality bond fund that incurs a much higher expense ratio than a higher-quality bond fund with a comparable maturity. If one bond fund has a gross yield 1% higher than another, and an expense ratio that is also 1% higher, both will deliver the same *net* yield. Over time, the spread between a long-term U.S. Treasury bond and a long-term BBB industrial bond has averaged about 1%. The higher expense ratio means you are paying for a Treasury bond but receiving in return a medium-grade industrial bond. It is not a sensible transaction.

Average maturity. As we saw in Chapter 2, interest rate risk simply means that changes in the level of interest rates are necessarily

TABLE 5–4
Price Volatility of Bond Mutual Funds

| | December 31, 1992 | | Impact of Change in Yield on Net Asset Value | | | |
| | | | Higher rate | | Lower rate | |
Government issue	Maturity	Yield	+2%	+1%	−1%	−2%
Bills	90 days	3.1%	0%	0%	0%	0%
Short-term bonds	2 ½ years	4.8	−4	−2	+2	+5
Intermediate-term bonds	10 years	6.7	−13	−7	+7	+16
GNMAs	9 years	6.8	−11	−5	+4	+7
Long-term bonds	20 years	7.3	−18	−10	+11	+25

Estimated price changes exclude interest income. GNMA price changes include an estimate of prepayment risk.

accompanied by commensurate changes in the value of your bond fund investment. Since the magnitude of the change in principal that accompanies a change in interest rates is determined by a bond's duration—which is largely controlled by the bond coupon and the number of years it must be held until maturity—investors who ignore a bond portfolio's average maturity do so at their peril.

The interim price fluctuations in the bond market can be every bit as frightening as those in the stock market. If you do not have the constitution to stomach constant fluctuations in your principal, you will want to steer clear of the longer-term bond funds and focus on the shorter-term offerings. If you have a longer-term investment horizon, you can presumably afford to ignore the price fluctuations in a long-term bond fund and enjoy the higher coupon. Table 5–4 shows the yields on December 31, 1992, for five different U.S. Treasury-guaranteed fixed-income securities and their expected sensitivity to interest changes of 1% and 2%.

Clearly, you can gain a significant yield increase by lengthening maturity, but only with heightened principal volatility. To improve your yield, you might be best served by extending your maturity modestly and committing only part of your assets to longer-term bond funds. In an uncertain world, compromise is a good basis for allocating your assets.

Of course, a myopic focus on principal risk might be costly in the long run, since shorter-term fixed-income investments expose you to considerable *income* risk. Specifically, while a 90-day U.S. Treasury bill has no principal risk, its annualized yield quickly plummeted from more than 9% in 1989 to less than 3% in 1992, to the distress of investors accustomed to receiving substantial interest payments to supplement their retirement income. A fund's average maturity is a two-way street, and you should consider this portfolio characteristic in the light of the length of time you expect to hold your investment. Again, for most investors, intermediate-term bond funds or a combination of long-term and short-term bond funds will probably be appropriate.

Use of derivatives. In a simpler age, it was reasonable to assume that, with maturity held constant, the higher the quality of a bond fund, the lower its risk. However, with the development of complex and exotic derivative instruments, even obligations issued by the U.S. Treasury and the federal agencies have, in subtle ways, become very risky. The easiest illustration of the current use of derivatives is the development of the zero coupon U.S. Treasury bond, which separates the stream of semiannual interest payments from the face value at maturity. Each resulting security is known as a Treasury strip and carries special risks for its holders. If the conventional ownership of a bond and its interest coupon has a duration of, say, 12 years, the price of the bond will rise or fall about 12% for each 1% decrease or increase in interest rates. That in itself is significant principal risk. But the ownership of a 30-year principal-only bond would entail a duration of 30 years, with principal value rising and falling fully 30% with each 1% change in interest rates. (You may recall from Chapter 2 that duration is the multiplier that roughly links interest rate changes with principal changes.)

This heightened risk in U.S. Treasury strip investing may also exist in CMOs, which are essentially federal agency securities representing pools of residential mortgages, except that they can be far more complex. A CMO is separated into numerous individual pieces, some of which are principal only, some income only, and some a combination of the two in varying proportions. These instruments can be much more or much less sensitive to interest rate risk and prepayment risk (especially unanticipated prepayment risk) than conventional mortgage obligations.

Bond funds, especially short-term bond funds, have been known to enhance their stated yields by owning CMOs, sometimes at the expense

---

CAVEAT EMPTOR: *Locking In Return—And Risk*

Zero coupon bonds, for the long-term buy-and-hold investor who wants to have a fixed amount of capital on a certain future date, can be said to carry no risk whatsoever to total return. If your goal is to have, say, $50,000 in capital in 20 years, you could buy a 7.5% U.S. Treasury "zero" with a 20-year maturity for about $9,600. In substance, the trade-off escalates volatility risk but eliminates reinvestment risk, since the final value is locked in at the rate prevailing at the time of purchase. There are some mutual funds that invest in zero coupon bonds with preset maturities; however, their costs reduce the returns on the underlying bonds. Thus, a U.S. Treasury zero coupon bond is apt to be a better alternative than a corresponding bond fund.

---

of their capital. But the complexity of CMOs makes it difficult for most investors to measure their risk. At one extreme, principal is highly volatile; at the other, income is highly susceptible to decline. In my view, investors who do not fully understand CMOs should avoid bond funds that place significant reliance on CMOs that carry the highest inherent risks.

Tax Implications

Chapter 11 presents an in-depth analysis of the effect of income taxes on investment performance, but it seems appropriate to consider here the implications of selecting a tax-exempt bond fund rather than a taxable one. Specifically, interest payments on municipal bonds are generally free from federal income taxation, and bonds of a particular state are usually free of that state's taxes as well. As a result, since financial markets are highly efficient, municipal bonds provide lower yields than taxable bonds. Investors, then, must calculate which alternative produces the most after-tax income.

For example, assume that an investment-grade corporate bond fund with a 10-year average maturity yields 8% and a comparably rated munici-pal bond fund yields 6%. Since the latter yield is 25% lower, the municipal bond fund represents approximately fair value only to those investors paying a marginal federal tax rate in excess of 25%. (That is, an 8% yield reduced by 25% equals 6%). While the arithmetic of this comparison is

CAVEAT EMPTOR: *Swapping Principal for Income*

The intelligent investor must take the trouble to look beyond current yields in evaluating short-term bond funds. Today yields can be enhanced, not only by the traditional steps of reducing quality and lengthening maturity, but also by using derivative instruments and CMOs that provide more income return, usually at the expense of capital return. The table shows two apparently similar AA bond funds, both with average maturities of three years. Fund B, however, generated 26% more gross income than Fund A. Despite an expense ratio more than double that of Fund A, Fund B provided 20% more net income return. In this case, it achieved an illusory advantage by holding 16% positions in both GNMA securities and derivative instruments. As interest rates fell during 1992, the piper was paid and the investor's capital in Fund B was impaired. The total return achieved by the lower-yielding Fund A was 33% higher than that of Fund B. Moral: Yields on short-term bond funds are not always what they seem.

Short-Term Bond Funds *(12 months ended December 31, 1992)*

	Fund A	Fund B
Gross income return	+6.9%	+8.7%
Expense ratio	−0.3	−0.8
Net income return	+6.6%	+7.9%
Capital return	+0.6	−2.5
Total Return	+7.2%	+5.4%

simple enough, it would be foolish to only consider yield and ignore such factors as quality, call protection, and cost. You should also be aware that tax-exempt and taxable bond funds alike may periodically realize capital gains as bonds are sold for more than their purchase prices. (Such gains are taxable to fund shareholders.) This is most likely to occur following significant declines in interest rates.

The structural characteristics just described should provide a useful framework for evaluating the appropriateness of various types of bond funds for your investment program. But once you have determined the characteristics of bond funds that fit your risk/reward profile—after carefully considering credit quality and length of maturity—be thorough in your individual fund selections. At the very least, compare like with like and pay close attention to total fund expenses. Ultimately, you must decide on the category of bond fund in which to invest and, within that category, which particular bond fund is likely to provide the highest relative return. It is to this topic that I now turn.

EVALUATING PAST PERFORMANCE

If looking at the past absolute returns of common stock funds is a futile method of forecasting their future total returns, it is equally futile in the case of bond funds. As we saw in Chapter 1, the annual total returns on stocks have tended to regress toward a long-term mean of +10.3%, reflecting the fundamental dividend yields and dividend growth that American corporations have provided for their shareholders. However, while returns for long-term U.S. government bonds have averaged +4.8% annually since 1926, this figure reveals nothing substantial about what you may expect from bonds in the years ahead.

From the 1980s through the early 1990s, as I noted earlier, nominal bond returns were quite generous compared with historical norms. For example, the return on 20-year government bonds, which had averaged +3.1% annually during 1926–79, increased fourfold, to +12.2% during 1980–92. This dramatic example makes it obvious that past bond returns have not been a reliable indicator of the future. By far the best single indicator of potential future bond returns is the current interest coupon.

Some of the performance measurement techniques I applied to common stock funds should be applied to bond funds as well. For instance, average annual rates of return rather than cumulative figures should be the rule for making basic performance comparisons among different types of bond funds. However, rather than the ten-year evaluation period used for stock funds, an evaluation period of as little as five years or so may be sufficient for bond funds. Bond funds holding to the same maturity and quality standards are affected quite similarly by market conditions (i.e., fluctuations in the general level of interest rates). This shorter period of evaluation is also pragmatic, given that relatively few bond funds have been in existence for as long as a decade.

The logical place to begin analyzing performance characteristics of bond funds is with the composition of their total returns over an extended

TABLE 5-5
Corporate Bond Funds (Six Years Ended December 31, 1992)

	Average Annual Returns		
	Income return	*Capital return*	*Total return*
Short-term			
First four years	+7.7%'	−0.4%	+7.4%
Last two years	+6.5	+1.7	+8.2
Total	+7.4%	+0.3%	+7.7%
Intermediate-term			
First four years	+9.0%	−1.8%	+7.2%
Last two years	+8.1	+2.7	+10.8
Total	+8.7%	−0.3%	+8.4%
Long-term			
First four years	+9.2%	−2.3%	+6.9%
Last two years	+8.5	+3.9	+12.4
Total	+9.0%	−0.3%	+8.7%

period. As I noted in Chapter 3, during the 15 years ended December 31, 1992, income accounted for only about 25% of the total return on stock funds, but accounted for 110% (the capital return was marginally negative) of the total return on bond funds. Essentially the same relationship prevailed during the six years ended December 31, 1992, a period I selected for analysis since it includes both rising and declining interest rates, with little net change on balance.

The data in Table 5-5 show conclusively that, for the full period, the income component utterly dominated the capital component of bond fund returns, no matter what length of maturity was involved. This result strongly suggests that all types of bond funds should be prized primarily for their income returns and not for their capital returns. As you would expect, income returns increased as the portfolio maturities of the funds lengthened, from short, to intermediate, to long. The higher levels of income earned over the full period by the longer-term bond funds (levels well above what historic norms would suggest) appear to be achieved at virtually no additional risk to the investor's capital. But this seemingly negligible risk was largely the result of the nature of the bond market during this particular six-year period. Interest rates at the end of the period were little changed from their beginning levels. A closer examination of the data reflects the fact that the full period masks significant interim principal volatility. As suggested in Table 5-5, rates increased during the first four years, but declined during the final two years.

This table highlights four important points about the total returns garnered by bond funds. (1) Over the full six-year period, the capital component of return in each maturity level had only a modest effect on total return. (2) In the first period, when interest rates rose, the capital component of return was negative; in the second, when interest rates declined, it was strongly positive. (3) Volatility of capital return increased sharply as the focus moved from shorter-term to longer-term bond funds. (4) The longer the fund's maturity, the greater the income component of its return.

Although past absolute returns of bond funds are a flawed predictor of future returns, there is a fairly easy way to predict future relative returns. Since net income (after all fund expenses) is the driving force in shaping bond fund performance, expenses should explain most of the difference in relative returns among funds with similar investment objectives and policies. I have tested this theory against actual experience. Instead of using a long-term test, however, I have chosen a seemingly brief period of three years. Only 71 bond funds have ten full years of performance history, and many subcategories of bond funds did not exist a decade ago. A three-year period enables me to expand the analysis to include 256 bond funds. By carefully separating the bond funds based on the market sector in which they invest, any possible bias from the impact of changes in the general level of interest rates is substantially eliminated.

After separating the bond funds into their major quality and maturity categories, I considered their annualized investment returns in terms of their expense ratios. Funds with annual expense ratios of less than 0.50% were placed in the lowest-cost group, funds with ratios above 1.50% were placed in the highest-cost group. Between these two groups were two additional groups with ratios of 0.50% to 1.00% and of 1.01% to 1.50%.

As shown in Table 5-6, this test provides a remarkably effective basis for determining superior performers among bond funds. The results of the test are dramatic. In every case and in every category, the superior funds could have been systematically identified based solely on their lower expense ratios. At the extremes in each group (with the exception of short-term corporate bond funds, where no higher-cost funds existed), the lowest-cost funds outpaced the highest-cost funds by between +1.0% and

TABLE 5–6

Bond Funds—Annual Returns by Expense Level (Three Years Ended December 31, 1992)

| Category | Average return | Funds with Expense Ratios | | | | Added return of low cost over high |
		Less than 0.50%	0.50% to 1.00%	1.01% to 1.50%	Greater than 1.50%	
Government						
Long-term	9.6%	10.6%	10.3%	9.4%	8.5%	+2.1%
Short-term	8.8	9.1	8.7	NA	8.1	+1.0
GNMA	10.5	11.0	10.5	9.9	9.8	+1.2
Corporate						
Long-term high-grade	10.2	10.6	10.1	10.0	8.4	+2.2
Long-term medium-grade	10.6	12.2	10.6	10.5	10.0	+2.2
Short-term high-grade	8.4	8.5	8.3	NA	NA	NA
Municipal						
Long-term AAA	8.8	9.6	9.1	8.1	7.8	+1.8
Long-term AA	8.9	9.6	9.1	8.2	7.8	+1.8
Long-term A	9.0	9.8	9.0	8.6	7.6	+2.2

+2.2% annually. The average enhancement in return was +1.8% per year.

This +1.8% advantage in return for the lowest-cost funds over the highest-cost funds has extremely important implications. With the magic of compounding, an increase in annual return from, say, +7.0% to +8.8% would increase the accumulated capital value of an initial investment of $10,000 in a bond fund from $19,700 to $23,200 over a decade, a gain of +18%. When related to the initial investment of $10,000, this additional $3,500 of total return—equal to 35% of the initial investment—approaches the awesome.

For investors in the distribution phase of their life cycle, the results are also dramatic. A $10,000 investment yielding 6.0% after expenses would provide $600 of income each year; a $10,000 investment yielding 7.8%

after expenses would provide $780 of annual income. This 30% increase in income can be achieved by the investor without incurring any extra volatility or quality risk.

The reason the enhanced returns are so predictable is perhaps self-evident. When bond funds have closely specified quality and maturity standards, they tend to earn similar gross yields. Their net return is differentiated simply by their expenses relative to other comparable funds. Since net income is the overwhelming component of bond fund returns, the advantage of a low-cost fund is potent. Further, there is no evidence that particular portfolio managers can provide substantial and sustainable capital appreciation over a full interest-rate cycle. Thus capital returns differ only modestly and tend to regress to the mean. It is *net* income return that drives the equation, and net income is heavily influenced by costs. Since costs do not regress to the mean, a powerful correlation exists between bond fund returns and bond fund costs.

This is not to say that investors who have confidence in their ability to select a bond fund should not seek out the most competent portfolio managers. But the evidence is compelling that the search for such managers should focus on bond funds in the lower-cost range. Moreover, the search should focus on no-load bond funds, since sales loads further reduce returns. For example, in a 7% interest rate environment, a no-load bond fund with an expense ratio of 0.5% would provide a yield of +6.5%. A no-load bond fund with an expense ratio of 1.5% would provide a yield of +5.5%. But this yield would be reduced to +4.5% if the fund also assessed a 5% sales charge, spread over a five-year period. This adjustment would leave the high-cost, load bond fund with a yield 31% below that of the low-cost, no-load bond fund.

A CLOSER LOOK AT HIGH-YIELD BOND FUNDS

High-yield bond funds (commonly referred to as junk bond funds) were excluded from my earlier analysis for two reasons. (1) Unlike the other bond fund categories I have discussed, they exhibit substantial variations in quality; some carry average quality ratings as high as BB+ and others carry average ratings as low as C or less. (2) Substantial rewards may be earned by high-yield bond funds whose managers select the "best" bonds, just as substantial penalties may be suffered by funds whose managers select the "worst" bonds. In this sense, high-yield bond funds are analo-

TABLE 5-7
High-Yield Bond Funds—Average Annual Total Returns (Six Years Ended December 31, 1992)

	Income return	Capital return	Total return
First four years	+12.2%	−11.7%	+0.5%
Last two years	+12.4	+15.5	+27.9
Full six years	+12.2%	−3.3%	+8.9%

gous to common stock funds. Performance variations may be large; cost, while important, will play a less defining role.

In 1982, the high-yield bond sector represented just a fraction of total corporate bond issuance and was composed primarily of "fallen angels," bonds that had been high-quality securities before their issuers encountered difficulties in their business operations. Following the junk bond boom of the 1980s, the value of the high-yield bond market reached $230 billion by the end of 1992, more than one-fourth of the value of the total corporate bond market. Given this weighting, such funds cannot be ignored.

As the high-yield bond market developed, it became less of a haven for fallen angel bonds and more of a market for highly leveraged new bond issues designed primarily to finance corporate restructurings. Under these circumstances, bonds usually represented a very high proportion of a corporation's capital structure, with limited cash flow available to meet interest and principal payments. This heightened credit risk marks junk bonds as quite different from investment-grade bonds, much more volatile and highly sensitive to corporate and economic conditions. To illustrate the dramatic price fluctuations in the junk bond sector of the bond market, Table 5-7 returns to the six-year period I discussed earlier in this chapter divided into two distinct segments.

The table dramatizes the substantial capital volatility of high-yield bond funds. High-yield bond prices reached their peak in 1986, just prior to the period shown, and then went into a four-year period of retreat as the economy slowed and many junk-bond interest coupons were slashed. The annual capital return of −11.7% during these four years resulted in a cumulative loss of −39% in value. Even the high income return was barely sufficient to compensate for this principal risk, leaving average annual returns at a mere +0.5% over four full years.

TABLE 5-8
High-Yield Bond Funds versus Investment-Grade Bond Funds—Average Annual Total Returns (Six Years Ended December 31, 1992)

First Four Years	
High-yield bond funds	+0.5%
Investment-grade bond funds	+7.2
Last Two Years	
High-yield bond funds	+27.9%
Investment-grade bond funds	+10.8
Full Six Years	
High-yield bond funds	+8.9%
Investment-grade bond funds	+8.4

As is often the case in the investment world, the tables turned abruptly. Junk bonds staged a recovery during 1991–92, with a cumulative increase in value of 33%. This increase translates into an annual capital return of +15.5%. Combining this annual capital return with the income return of +12.4% brought the two-year total return to +27.9% per year.

Investors must decide for themselves whether the additional principal risk starkly illustrated in Table 5-7 will be compensated in the future by the higher income component provided by junk bond funds relative to investment-grade bond funds. As shown in Table 5-8, junk bonds provided an average annual total return of +8.9% during the six-year period, compared to +8.4% for intermediate-term bond funds of investment-grade quality. (Most junk bond funds are of intermediate maturity.) At least during this period, the compensation for the extra risk appears to have been inadequate.

When comparing high-yield bond funds with investment-grade bond funds, these three points emerge. (1) Yields are much higher for junk bond funds. (2) Total returns for junk bond funds are considerably more volatile from one period to the next. (3) Principal risk is much higher for junk bond funds largely because substantial credit risk is involved. If you select a high-yield bond fund you should be aware that at least some of the income premium will be eroded by capital penalty.

Although a six-year period may be regarded as an inadequate basis for evaluating the risk premium on junk bond funds, I have used it for consistency with the period selected for investment-grade bond funds.

Results for the 15 years ended December 31, 1992, echo my conclusions. During this period, the average annual total return for each bond fund type was identical, at +10.0%. While junk bond funds may provide higher current income to meet day-to-day living expenses, they are likely to do so only with a potential sacrifice of principal.

Even if you understand the speculative nature of junk bond funds and are willing to accept the considerable risks they entail, your weighting in these funds should be held to a modest portion (say, no more than 20%) of a fully diversified portfolio of stocks and bonds. Junk bond funds are not for investors who cannot stomach both the inevitable fluctuations in the market value of junk bonds and the possible deterioration of their high initial income.

SUMMARY

It is easy to see that selections among the 17 current bond fund sectors shown in Table 5–1 will vary substantially from one investor to another, depending on each investor's income requirements, tolerance for interest rate risk, willingness to assume quality risk, expected holding period, and marginal tax bracket. That is a lot to consider, but perhaps this summary will help you.

- Consider the impact of income yield and principal change on to-tal return in light of how long you expect to own your bond fund investment. While a rise in interest rates has a negative *short-term* impact on bond prices, it has a positive *long-term* impact on bond returns if interest payments can be reinvested at higher (more attractive) rates on a sustained basis.

- Determine how much risk—to both principal and income—you are willing to accept in terms of average maturity. Ask the fund's sponsor about the duration of the fund's portfolio so you can measure its sensitivity to interest rates.

- Examine closely a bond fund's expense ratio before investing. It is highly probable that when maturity and quality are held con-stant, lower costs will result in higher returns and vice versa.

- Know the yield sacrifice involved when the bond fund carries a sales load and make sure that there are compensating advantages, rare though they appear to be.

- Consider credit quality very carefully. Principal will fluctuate as interest rates move up and down, but money in a defaulted bond is gone forever.

- Never purchase a bond fund with a lower-rated portfolio and a relatively high expense ratio, when a fund with a higher-rated portfolio and a relatively low expense ratio provides an equal or even higher yield.

- Ignore advertisements that point to high yields ("the highest-yielding short-term bond fund!") if they do not disclose the quality, maturity, coupon structure, and other relevant portfolio characteristics of the fund.

- Be particularly careful of short-term bond funds that may be enhancing income by artificial means, often at the expense of capital.

- Compare like with like. A comparison between two bond funds with different quality ratings and different average maturities is a futile exercise, unless you give appropriate weight to these structural differences.

In the end, as you consider the plethora of bond funds from which investment selections may be made, you will likely conclude that bond fund relative returns can be predictably enhanced by one of only two primary factors: (1) assuming higher risk by holding bonds of longer average maturity and/or lower investment quality and (2) lower expense ratios. Once you have decided on the maturity and quality sectors that meet your needs, select from among the lower-cost funds rather than the higher-cost funds. If attention is paid to this simple strategy, the outcome is almost certain to be productive.

Chapter Six

How to Select a Money Market Fund
A Penny Saved

"A penny saved is a penny earned," said Benjamin Franklin two centuries ago. What he meant, I think, is that any amount of money, no matter how small, is worth saving. And there is no better place in the mutual fund industry to achieve a modest but meaningful improvement in return—without extra risk—than by the careful selection of a money market mutual fund from among the 976 such funds available at the end of 1992. If Ben Franklin were alive, he would surely approve of not only the simplicity of the money market fund investment concept but the ease of saving a few more pennies through a wise fund selection.

The first money market funds came into existence in 1971 with a basic concept: The fund would hold only short-term financial instruments such as U.S. Treasury bills, bank certificates of deposit (CDs), and commercial paper (the short-term IOUs of large U.S. corporations). The concept was also creative: The fund would have a stated (but not guaranteed) net asset value of $1.00 per share, accrue dividends on a daily basis, and offer checkwriting privileges, all at a time when interest rates on bank savings accounts were fixed at levels well below those that money market funds could obtain. The money market fund opened the door for the average investor to enjoy the higher short-term rates of return previously available only to large institutions and wealthy individuals.

Acceptance among investors of this new class of mutual fund was virtually instantaneous. In 1980, assets invested in money market funds reached $74 billion, fully 56% of total mutual fund industry net assets of $133 billion. While that percentage declined to 35% at year-end 1992, assets of money market funds totaled a massive $555 billion, more than the assets

TABLE 6–1
Money Market Mutual Funds (December 31, 1992)

Fund type	Number of funds
Taxable	
Prime instruments*	363
Federal agency notes	160
U.S. Treasury bills	132
Total taxable	655
Tax-Exempt	
National municipal	169
Single-state municipal	152
Total tax-exempt	321
Grand total	976

*Commercial paper, certificates of deposit, and Eurodollar deposits.

of the entire mutual fund industry in 1985. That figure represents a truly staggering responsibility for the fund sponsors.

As shown in Table 6–1, 976 money market funds are available to individual investors (some funds are available only to institutions) in five categories separated by credit quality or by taxability. But all money market funds have the same basic structural characteristics.

First, money market funds of all types provide the most price stability and the most yield variability over time (i.e., the lowest principal risk and the highest income risk). In that sense, their investment characteristics closely resemble U.S. Treasury bills, whose rewards and risks were discussed in the first two chapters. Second, the money market fund is the only class of mutual fund whose total return in every period comprises 100% income return. Unlike stock and bond funds, it offers no opportunity for capital return.

Money market funds have existed during a turbulent period for interest rates. At the beginning of 1972, short-term interest rates were relatively low, running about 4% on CDs. Rates then soared to the 12% level in 1974, fell back to 5% by 1976, and, incredibly, topped 15% on a number of occasions from the start of 1980 to mid-1982. Rates then settled into

FIGURE 6-1
Three-Month Certificates of Deposit—Quarterly Yields (1972-92)

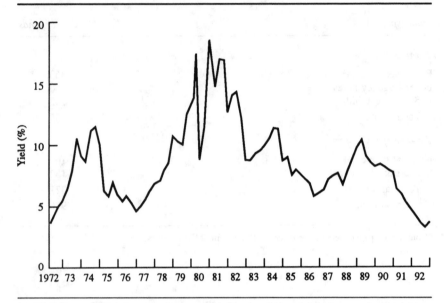

a range of about 6% to 10% through mid-1991, trailing off to less than
3.5% by the end of 1992. Figure 6-1 presents the picture.

My analysis of money market funds will focus on three principal factors:
(1) the quality of the fund's portfolio, (2) the yield it generates, and (3)
the amount the yield is reduced by the fund's operating expenses. In
combination, these factors determine virtually the entire return generated
by each money market fund. While this may seem obvious today, it was
not so long ago that money market funds employed any number of "strategies" to give the impression of relatively superior earning power.

Prior to June 1991, for instance, it was possible for money market
mutual funds to offer higher yields than their competitors by holding large
positions in lower-rated—and therefore more risky—commercial paper or
by extending their average maturities beyond the typical 30-day to 90-day
range for the average money fund. This situation made it difficult for
investors to determine the degree to which higher risk, in the form of lower
quality and/or longer maturity, accounted for the relatively higher yield
of one money market fund versus another.

But when the SEC published new standards for the management of

---

CAVEAT EMPTOR: *Is What You See What You Get?*

In an effort to avoid hamstringing portfolio managers, the SEC definition requires that "highest grade" be based on ratings by two of five nationally recognized statistical rating services. The most prominent of these rating services are Standard & Poor's Corporation (highest rating of A1) and Moody's Investors Services (highest rating of P1). However, some money market funds, bent on obtaining higher yields, accept ratings from the remaining services, whose standards are often less stringent. You should get the facts on portfolio quality ratings from the fund's sponsor. It does not make sense to select money market mutual funds investing in these marginally lower credits, especially if their higher yields are offset by higher expense ratios. In the case of money market portfolio ratings, what you see is not always what you get.

---

money market mutual funds in 1991, the fund manager's decision tree was considerably pruned. The SEC now requires that a money market fund invest at least 95% of its assets in bank certificates of deposit and commercial paper of the highest grade. The SEC also limits the average maturity of a money market fund to 90 days or less. As a result of these constraints on credit risk and interest rate risk, money market funds have become a more homogeneous investment class.

It would theoretically be possible for the portfolio manager of a money market fund to make marginal shifts to the portfolio's maturity structure to add value to its return. For example, the manager might hold a portfolio with a ten-day maturity when interest rates were low and expected to rise and a 90-day maturity when rates were high and expected to fall. Given the inherent fallibility of interest rate forecasts, however, this degree of risk taking is rare. Most money market portfolios maintain average maturities between 40 and 75 days. Moving between these limited extremes simply has not generated significant, sustained extra returns.

In its simplest form, a money market fund invests in the short-term securities of the so-called money market, generally the safest and most stable securities available. However, a shareholder's investment in a money market mutual fund is *not* insured, while the typical bank savings account or certificate of deposit is insured up to $100,000 in principal value by the Federal Deposit Insurance Corporation (FDIC), a federal agency.

FIGURE 6-2
Money Market Mutual Funds versus MMDAs—7-Day Yields (1983-92)

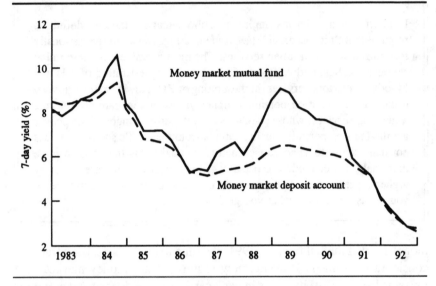

The costs associated with money market funds are substantially lower than those associated with bank savings accounts, in part because banks must pay insurance premiums to the FDIC, in part because banks generally incur the greater operational costs associated with accounts having small dollar balances and high checking volumes, and in part because banks tend to maintain a vast brick and mortar distribution system. The lower operating expenses of money market funds have resulted in higher yields relative to bank money market deposit accounts (MMDAs) since bank interest rates were deregulated beginning in 1982. Figure 6-2 illustrates the yield comparison.

STRUCTURAL CHARACTERISTICS

Despite the recent SEC-imposed investment restrictions, the structural characteristics of the money market portfolio remain a primary consideration in selecting a fund. First and foremost, your evaluation of money market funds should begin by comparing yields, since yield will ultimately determine the return on a money market fund. But there is considerably

---

CAVEAT EMPTOR: *A Money Market Fund Is* Not *a Bank Account*

The investment options of money market fund managers are now heavily regulated. But no amount of regulation can ensure that one or more of the issuers of bank or commercial instruments held by a fund might be unable to meet their obligations for interest and principal payments. While U.S. T-bills are "money good," no regulation can completely reduce the possibility that a rapid upward spike in interest rates could temporarily depress the net asset value of a money fund with a maturity stretched to the 90-day limit. Under either of these circumstances, a money fund's net asset value could fall below the sacrosanct $1.00 per share for an extended (in the first case) or brief (in the second case) period of time. However remote that risk, it *always* exists. Indeed, this marginal risk to principal is one reason money market funds have, with remarkable consistency, provided higher returns than most short-term certificates of deposit.

---

more to the analysis of money market funds. How a fund's yield is attained is also of paramount importance. The most salient factors you should consider before investing in a money market mutual fund are its management, portfolio quality, and cost of ownership.

Management

While it is virtually impossible for professional money market fund managers to significantly differentiate their performance on the basis of security selections and average maturity, it requires considerable skill simply to run the complex daily investment activities of the fund. This skill is usually a given among the large and mid-size money market funds. In smaller funds, investigate this issue before you invest.

Portfolio Quality

Important differences in quality exist among the three basic types of taxable money funds, investing respectively in (1) U.S. T-bills, (2) federal agency notes, and (3) corporate and bank instruments. U.S. Treasury money market funds, which hold solely "full faith and credit" obligations with the explicit backing of the Treasury, entail the highest quality available.

TABLE 6–2
Money Market Fund Yields (December 31, 1992)

Money market fund	Percentage of assets rated A1/P1*	Gross yield	Expense ratio	Net yield
Higher quality	100%	3.53%	0.30%	3.23%
Lower quality	90	3.61	0.72	2.89

*Standard & Poor's and Moody's ratings only.

It could be argued that such funds provide greater safety than bank CDs, since the FDIC, an agency of the U.S. government, carries only the implicit backing of the U.S. Treasury. Federal money market funds, which hold largely obligations of the major government agencies, are a close second in quality, since agency obligations are generally regarded as implicitly backed by the U.S. Treasury. Prime money market funds carry neither an express nor an implicit credit guarantee. The conservative investor should consider only those prime funds whose portfolios consist entirely of issues that receive the highest quality ratings from the most prominent rating agencies.

Differences in credit risk are small among the prime money market funds, but they do exist. Table 6–2 shows the quality ratings for two popular money market funds. Although the lower-quality fund generated a higher *gross* yield than the higher-quality fund, the expenses of the lower-quality fund more than offset its higher gross yield, so its net yield is more than 10% lower than that of the higher-quality fund.

Should you have any concern about the credit quality of your prime money market fund's portfolio holdings, it is a simple matter to exchange into a Treasury or federal money fund. If there is any sacrifice in yield (and as we note later, there need not be any), it will be more than offset by an enhancement of your peace of mind.

Cost of Fund Ownership

The cost of ownership is the most powerful force in differentiating the net yields of money funds. Therefore, the expense ratio can tell you at a glance approximately how much of a fund's comparative net yield advantage or disadvantage arises from a lower or higher fee structure. Any remaining

TABLE 6-3
U.S. Treasury Money Market Funds (December 31, 1992)

Money fund	Annualized gross yield	Expense ratio	Annualized net yield
A	3.22%	0.30%	2.92%
B	3.17	0.37	2.80
C	3.23	0.46	2.77
D	3.19	0.55	2.64
E	3.31	0.65	2.66
F	3.36	0.85	2.51

difference is accounted for by either marginally higher (or lower) quality standards or by stretching average maturity to the available limit. Table 6-3 illustrates this point, using U.S. Treasury money market funds as an example since their credit quality is uniform. The table shows the remarkable disparity in net yields (after expenses) among six selected U.S. Treasury money market funds, in contrast with the virtual parity among their gross yields (before expenses). Fund A earns 3.22%, deducts expenses of 0.30%, and provides a net yield of 2.92% to the investor. Fund F earns slightly more (3.36%) but after the deduction of a 0.85% expense ratio, its net yield is only 2.51%. A yield increase of more than 15% can be garnered effortlessly by selecting a low-cost money fund.

There are enormous differences in the costs incurred by money market funds, with expense ratios ranging from about 0.30% up to 2.0% annually. As a result, if the gross yield of a fund was, say, 4.0%, management fees and operating costs could consume anywhere from one-thirteenth to more than half the interest income received by the fund.

Fee waivers. Sometimes the yield you see advertised for a money market fund may be the yield you get, but not for very long. Several mutual fund complexes have created new money market funds that appear at the outset to have higher yields than their older sister funds. Nearly always, the main reason for this yield advantage is that the manager waives its fees and absorbs the expenses on the new fund for a temporary (and often indeterminate) period of time.

In this manner, the new fund can offer a higher yield in order to attract assets from especially yield-sensitive investors. This strategy is usually accompanied by a massive marketing campaign. Ironically, this extrava-

---

CAVEAT EMPTOR: *Hidden Yields*

The published yield tabulations that appear in the newspapers and investment letters rarely include the very highest-cost (and therefore the lowest-yielding) money market funds, presumably because their sponsors are too embarrassed to provide the figures. A good rule of thumb: Do not own a money fund whose yield is not published.

---

gant spending to attract shareholders to the new lower-cost fund is arguably paid for by the shareholders of the older, higher-cost sister fund. A typical practice is to waive all expenses charged to the fund for one or two years and then gently (in hopes that shareholders won't notice) ease the expenses upward, all the while guaranteeing that costs will not exceed a relatively low level for several more years.

Leaving aside the marketing hype and dubious ethics involved in such a campaign, there is absolutely no reason an investor should not consider purchasing such a fund, so long as the expenses are being waived and the yield is significantly higher than those of other similar funds. However, as the fees are added and the relative yield drops—and it will drop—the massive advertising campaign that accompanied the fund's introduction will fade away. You can be confident an advertising campaign of similar magnitude will not be instituted to inform you that the fees are creeping back in. So consider such funds only if you are prepared to monitor their yields on at least a monthly basis. When the yield superiority vanishes, you will want to move your assets to a fund with durably low costs.

Relating Return to Risk

Skeptical as you should be about investments that claim to deliver more return with less risk, this free-lunch phenomenon may easily be achieved in the money market field, given the wide variations in expense ratios. Many lower-cost U.S. Treasury money funds have provided yields in excess of higher-cost prime money funds. Amazingly enough, at the end of 1992 the five highest-yielding funds investing solely in U.S. Treasury bills provided greater yields than 199 of the 222 largest prime money funds available to individual investors. Shareholders in 90% of these prime money market funds could have increased their yields while

FIGURE 6-3
Taxable versus Municipal Money Market Funds—After-Tax 7-Day Yields

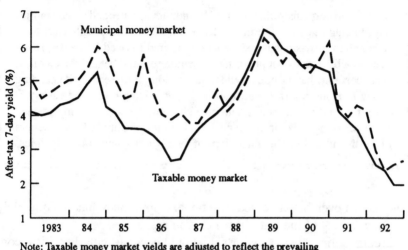

Note: Taxable money market yields are adjusted to reflect the prevailing
maximum marginal tax rate.

reducing their risk. For many investors, this astonishing dichotomy is even more extreme, since income from U.S. Treasury obligations is exempt from state and local taxes in every state, except Pennslyvania, that imposes an income tax.

Tax-Exempt versus Taxable Money Market Funds

As with bond funds, for investors in the highest marginal tax bracket the yields on tax-exempt money market funds very often provide higher after-tax returns than their taxable counterparts. So you should carefully study the relationship between taxable and tax-exempt yields as it applies to your own circumstances. Figure 6-3 compares the yields on MIG-1 notes (Moody's rating for the highest-quality municipal paper available) over the past ten years to those of taxable money market instruments, adjusted for the highest federal tax rate then prevailing. During this period, the relationship has consistently favored tax-exempt funds for investors taxed at the maximum marginal rate. This chart does not consider state and local taxes. If you live in a state with a relatively high state tax rate,

---

CAVEAT EMPTOR: *Floating Rates*

Many short-term instruments issued by individual states and municipalities pay floating rates and are in substance long-term issues with short-term redemption provisions based on letters of credit issued by banks. However, if a bank does not honor its obligation to stand behind the credit, it is conceivable that the bond could trade as a long-term security demanding a long-term interest rate. The low coupon would thus command a substantially reduced price. You should consider only those tax-exempt money funds that emphasize instruments with both top-quality issuers of letters of credit and underlying obligations of the highest-quality municipalities.

---

you may be even better served by a tax-exempt money fund holding only the instruments of the state in which you reside.

Credit quality, always important, should be a particularly critical consideration in your selection of a tax-exempt money market fund—especially single-state money funds where the highest-grade issues may be in limited supply or available only at lower yields, a great temptation for the fund to compromise on quality. The primary risk for state-specific investments, of course, is the highly concentrated and relatively undiversified credit risk. In most states, the various agencies that issue municipal instruments are affected, for better or worse, by the same regional economic climate. The result is that the credit ratings of municipal bonds within a given state may be correlated with one another, so that even a "diversified" portfolio carries implicitly greater risk. Insist on knowing the quality structure of a state money fund's portfolio, and accept no less than an average rating of MIG-1 by Moody's Investors Services. Also, be aware of any unusual portfolio concentration, such as in particular types of bonds (e.g., hospital bonds) or in limited geographic regions.

EVALUATING PAST PERFORMANCE

My earlier evaluation of equity funds strongly suggested that future relative performance could not be accurately forecast for two primary reasons: (1) past performance was an unreliable indicator and (2) the relative returns

TABLE 6–4
Prime Money Market Funds—Average Total Return and Expense Ratio
(December 31, 1992)

Expense ratio range	Number of funds	Average expense ratio	Average 1992 total return
Below 0.40%	12	0.24%	3.76%
0.40%–0.49%	9	0.45	3.61
0.50%–0.59%	39	0.54	3.45
0.60%–0.69%	36	0.65	3.41
0.70%–0.79%	40	0.75	3.30
0.80%–0.89%	31	0.84	3.14
0.90%–0.99%	20	0.95	3.07
1.00%–1.09%	18	1.02	2.99
1.10% and above	16	1.24	2.81

Only funds in existence for at least two years were included.

achieved by individual equity funds had a strong tendency to regress to the average return of all equity funds. On the other hand, my evaluation of bond funds strongly suggested that future relative performance among similar types of funds within specific parameters could be forecast with considerable accuracy, not on the basis of past performance but on the basis of known operating costs and sales loads.

What is suggested in the forecasting of bond fund returns is a near certainty in the forecasting of money market fund returns. I have shown that relative gross returns are virtually identical within each type of money fund and that net returns are therefore driven almost exclusively by fund costs. Since costs are a known quantity, as long as they remain constant forecasts of relative future returns on money market funds based on relative past returns will be highly reliable.

A simple example will make this point forcefully. In Table 6–4, you can see the direct relationship between money market fund expense ratios and their returns. The two figures move in virtual lockstep, a relationship that is remarkably consistent. At the extremes, the spread between the yield of the highest-yielding group (3.76%) and the lowest-yielding group (2.81%) is 0.95%. The difference in expenses, at 1.00%, is virtually identical. By the simple expedient of using expenses to determine your money fund selection, you could have achieved a yield increase of 34%.

A LOT MORE PENNIES

For investors who want what money market funds have to offer—generous yields compared to most bank account alternatives and instant liquidity at a price virtually certain to remain at $1.00 per share—it is relatively easy to select a money market fund that will provide top performance compared with its peers.

However, before deciding on any money market fund, you should carefully consider the extent to which you actually need liquid reserves in your investment program (as distinct from your savings and transaction account balances). If you are willing to assume a slightly higher volatility risk, you can quite easily earn, not just "a few more pennies," but a lot more pennies.

You can achieve this modest goal simply by investing in a short-term bond fund (with a typical average maturity of two to four years) rather than in a money market fund (typical maturity of one to three months). The yields on short-term bond funds have usually been one to one and one-half percentage points higher than on money market funds. At the end of 1992, with the average short-term investment-grade bond fund yield at 5.2% compared with 2.8% for the average money market fund, the spread was 2.4 percentage points.

The only negative is that, unlike the money market fund, the short-term bond fund will experience moderate fluctuations in its net asset value as interest rates rise and fall. How significant is this volatility risk? The average short-term investment-grade bond fund has experienced just one quarter of negative total return (−0.06% in the fourth quarter of 1992) during the 1982–92 decade. To compensate for this marginal risk to principal, and under the particular market conditions that existed during this decade, the total return for the typical short-term bond fund averaged +9.0% annually over the ten years ended December 31, 1992, compared with +7.1% annually for the average money market fund. Figure 6–4 illustrates the cumulative results of the two fund types.

In considering the risks and rewards of short-term bond funds, you should be aware of three important facts: (1) While interest rates indeed fluctuate, the odds of a rise are probably about the same as the odds of a fall; in the longer run, nearly all of the return on a short-term bond fund

FIGURE 6–4

Short-Term Investment-Grade Bond Funds versus Money Market Funds—
Cumulative Returns (1983–92)

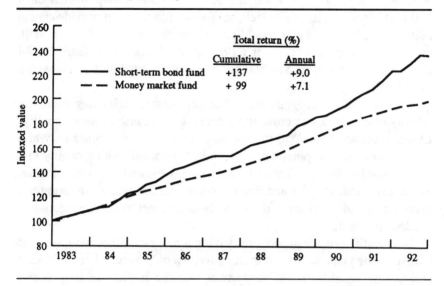

will likely be determined by its yield, as is the case with money market funds. (2) No credit risk need be assumed, since many funds investing solely in short-term U.S. Treasury bonds are available. (3) As in the case of money market funds, cost is the primary determinant of the relative returns of comparable short-term bond funds.

In my view, too many investors think of short-term bond funds in the same way they think of long-term bond funds, as highly volatile and interest-rate sensitive. In fact, there is almost infinitely less volatility risk in short-term bond funds. Investors also tend to overestimate their need for instant liquidity. These two factors have kept short-term bond funds from the investment recognition they merit. The intelligent investor will want to give them that recognition.

SUMMARY

A penny saved in expenses is indeed a penny earned in net spendable income. And, with the magic of compounding, those pennies turn into dollars, hundreds of dollars, even thousands of dollars over time. For example, in an environment of 5% short-term interest rates, the highest-cost group of funds shown in Table 6–4 should earn a net return of about +3.8%, compared to +4.8% for the lowest-cost group. Based on a $10,000 initial investment in each, the former funds would provide annual income of $380; the latter would provide annual income of $480. With their returns compounded over a decade, the highest-cost funds would achieve a final value of $14,500 and the lowest-cost funds a final value of $16,000.

It is essential to recognize the difference between achieving this extra return because of lower costs and achieving it because of lower quality. Lower costs are "free" to the investor. Lower quality comes only at a price: an increase in potential credit risk. Compromising on quality in a money market fund, whether taxable or tax-exempt, is unacceptable. While extra risk may be justified in seeking higher returns in long-term investments, in short-term reserves, held to meet contingencies when needed, it is not.

The most important aspect of selecting a money market fund, then, is to investigate yield quotations thoroughly, but only hand in hand with cost and quality considerations. Remember that the higher-yielding money funds are not necessarily of lower quality, nor are lower-yielding money funds, by any means, necessarily of higher quality. Remember also that, as previously waived expenses are assimilated into a higher-yielding money fund, the fund will quickly lose its yield advantage and quietly retreat into the pack. In the final analysis, when quality and length of maturity are held constant, costs alone will differentiate the winners from the losers. There is no reason why you should not always find yourself in a winning money market fund.

Chapter Seven

How to Select a Balanced Mutual Fund
The Golden Mean

"Whoever cultivates the golden mean avoids both the poverty of a hovel and the envy of a palace." When the Roman poet Horace wrote those words back in the year 23 B.C., he was hardly thinking about the principles of investing that were to prove themselves 2,000 years later. But the golden mean is an apt description of the modern balanced mutual fund.

In a sense, the balanced mutual fund is the ultimate fund, the ideal manifestation of the fund concept. Combining a stock component, a bond component, and a money market component, the balanced fund is a complete investment program in a single portfolio. The equity portion of the balanced fund should be evaluated based on the standards applicable to equity funds and the bond portion on the standards applicable to bond funds. (Since most balanced funds maintain modest cash reserve positions, the standards applicable to money market funds are not especially significant.) I shall first review these standards to provide a starting point for more detailed evaluation. Once these structural elements have been considered, I will turn to the past returns achieved by individual balanced funds relative to those of their peers.

The first balanced funds were founded during the late 1920s and remained a major component of the mutual fund industry until the mid-1960s, before losing much of their allure during the go-go years, when their conservative policies made them look passé. They provided disappointing returns relative to equity mutual funds through 1981, as their bond holdings constituted a major drag on performance during this period of sharply rising interest rates. But from 1982 through the early 1990s, when bond returns approached those achieved by stocks, balanced mutual funds came back into their own, with the number of equity-oriented (tradi-

---

CAVEAT EMPTOR: *Taxable Bonds Only*

Despite their obvious advantages of conservative investing and asset allocation, balanced funds do have at least one drawback: their bond component consists entirely of *taxable* bonds. Investors for whom tax-exempt interest provides a significant increment in after-tax returns will want to make their own balanced portfolio by holding a widely diversified, high-quality mainstream stock fund and a municipal bond fund (or funds) of appropriate maturity. For investors for whom taxable income provides the higher net return and investors in tax-deferred retirement plans, the balanced funds described in this chapter remain attractive investment options.

---

tional) balanced funds rising from 23 to 87. This renaissance was remarkable, and the assets of such funds totaled $30 billion at the end of 1992, representing 2% of the assets of the entire mutual fund industry. When the assets of equity-oriented balanced funds are combined with the assets of their relatives of more recent years—income-oriented balanced funds and asset allocation funds—total balanced fund assets reach $54 billion, about 4% of industry assets.

This small share of mutual fund assets is surprising, since the balanced mutual fund can solve the dilemma investors face as they struggle with the concept of sensibly investing their assets. Nearly all traditional balanced funds have broadly based equity portfolios (apt to be more similar to those of value funds than those of growth funds) and, with a few exceptions, tend not to compromise on the quality of their bond portfolios. The primary decision to make is which of the three major types of balanced funds listed below meet your needs.

1. *The equity-oriented balanced fund* normally maintains about 55% to 65% of net assets in a broad spectrum of equities, with most of the remainder in investment-grade bonds. (Cash reserves are typically about 5% of assets.) This traditional balanced fund usually does not make major departures from its specified investment allocation range. It might be described as a fund that provides a balanced emphasis on current income, reasonable capital growth, and conservation of capital.

2. *The income-oriented balanced fund* is similar to the traditional equity-oriented balanced fund but invests a much lower percent-

age of total assets in stocks. Usually some 20% to 35% of assets are allocated to equities, approximately the reciprocal of the equity-oriented balanced fund allocation. The equity portion of the income-oriented balanced fund usually provides a relatively higher dividend yield, most often by placing a heavy emphasis on public utility stocks. (This means the total portfolio is quite sensitive to changes in interest rates.) For such a fund, current income is the first goal and capital conservation the second, with capital growth ranking a clear third.

3. *The asset allocation fund,* unlike the other two types of balanced funds, makes substantial changes in its stock/bond ratio depending on its portfolio manager's view of the relative outlooks for the stock and bond markets. Most of these funds have not been tested under fire and are therefore unproven. Further, they differ significantly from one another in their approach to asset allocation. Some of them can be described as conservative, not too far from the traditional equity-oriented balanced funds, and some as aggressive, taking risks that exceed those of many mainstream equity funds. At their best, asset allocation funds endeavor to capture a solid share of stock gains in bull markets, while avoiding being fully exposed to stock declines in bear markets. It is a challenging objective.

In balanced funds of all types, you relinquish the asset allocation decision and delegate it to the fund adviser. In both the traditional equity-oriented and the newer income-oriented balanced fund, what you see is what you get—a stable equity ratio (either higher or lower) and an orientation toward income. In the asset allocation fund, what you see and what you get are much less clear, and the answer may vary substantially from one fund to the next. The investor, therefore, has some basic decisions to make in the selection process.

STRUCTURAL CHARACTERISTICS

As is the case when evaluating equity funds and bond funds, you should review the structural characteristics of balanced funds before turning to their records of past performance. However, the relative returns of balanced funds have experienced much less variation than the returns for equity funds, so selection—at least with the traditional balanced funds—is easier. As I shall show, the long-term performance of balanced funds

---

CAVEAT EMPTOR: *Asset Allocation or Market Timing?*

About half of today's asset allocation funds were founded *after* the great crash of the stock market in October 1987. Some techniques for allocation had worked well before the crash and in its aftermath, and it was only a matter of time until the mutual fund industry took notice. Their recent history is far too short to pass reliable judgment on their results. (Some varieties were tested during the 1940s and 1950s; they failed.) Today's asset allocation funds require careful analysis before selection. The more conservative asset allocation funds are characterized by (1) moderate and gradual changes in their stock/bond ratios, generally remaining in a ratio of 30/70 to 70/30; (2) stock/bond ratio changes that are based on quantitative disciplines that assess relative fundamental valuations in the stock and bond markets; and (3) the use of basic market-index-oriented portfolios. The more aggressive funds, probably fairly described as market-timing funds, are quite the reverse. They are characterized by (1) wide, precipitate swings in equity exposure (from 0/100 to 100/0); (2) stock/bond ratio changes based largely on intuitive judgment, often influenced by technical factors and by optimism or pessimism; and (3) the use of actively managed equity portfolios with relatively unpredictable characteristics. In the abstract, you might consider the conservative asset allocation fund for a fairly large portion—perhaps as much as 25%—of your total mutual fund portfolio. For the fund making allocations based on market timing, 10% of your portfolio should probably be the maximum. As we gain experience with asset allocation funds and as new types are formed, these limitations may change. But the more conservative asset allocation funds seem destined to play a larger role in investors' portfolios as the critical importance of asset allocation becomes better understood.

---

is much more intimately linked to structural characteristics than to management capability.

Nearly all of the concepts that were applied to stock funds in Chapter 4 and bond funds in Chapter 5 also apply to the equity and bond portions of the balanced funds. Note, however, that asset size, age of fund, and tenure of portfolio manager may be less important, given the fact that most balanced funds follow objectives and policies that are quite clearly articulated. Further, portfolio characteristics—cash reserves position, portfolio concentration, market capitalization of the stock portfolio, quality ratings and average maturity of the bond portfolio, and portfolio turn-over—are usually more consistent among balanced funds than among stock and bond funds. The similarities are greater than the differences. While you should review these subordinate factors before selecting a balanced fund, the dominant differentiating factors are portfolio balance, bond char-acteristics, cost of ownership, and portfolio statistics.

Portfolio balance. There are two important aspects of this issue. (1) To what extent does the balanced fund vary its allocation among stocks, bonds, and cash reserves? (2) What weight is given to current income, as distinct from total return? There are no right or wrong answers to these questions. They should serve to focus your attention on just what strategy you wish to pursue.

Bond characteristics. The bond portfolios of balanced funds are generally of investment-grade quality (rated BBB and above). A quality rat-ing below that level should be avoided in a conservative fund. Even among the investment-grade categories, you should differentiate between, say an all-BBB portfolio and one with an average rating of A or AA. The bond portfolios of most balanced funds carry average maturities in the ten-year range; evaluate carefully any substantial deviation from that range.

Cost of ownership. The importance of cost—the total expenses incurred by the investor—increases as the differentiating characteristics of the funds in a group decrease. So cost is relatively more important in a balanced fund than in a stock fund. Note that the average annual expense ratios of the three types of balanced funds are substantial: 1.2% for the equity-oriented funds, 1.0% for the income-oriented funds, and a hefty 1.5% for the asset allocation funds. Especially if you have an income objective, focus the selection process on funds with lower costs. For example, if two similarly constructed balanced funds have an identical gross yield of 5.0%, the one with an expense ratio of 1.5% would yield 3.5%, while the one with an expense ratio of 0.5% would yield 4.5%. A 30% difference in net income should not, to say the least, be trivialized.

Portfolio statistics. Returning to the three concepts I discussed in Chapter 4 for making fair comparisons among stock funds, Table 7–1 examines how these portfolio characteristics differ among the three types of balanced funds, using the S&P 500 Index as the baseline.

TABLE 7-1
Portfolio Statistics Analysis—Balanced Funds (December 31, 1992)

Balanced fund	ExMark	Beta	Gross yield
Equity-oriented	87%	0.64	5.1%
Income-oriented	65	0.42	7.1
Asset allocation	75	0.53	4.8
S&P 500 Index	100%	1.00	2.8%

Each column in this table is important. (1) The equity-oriented balanced funds have lower ExMarks than the stock market index because of their greater emphasis on value stocks versus growth stocks. The income-oriented funds have the lowest ExMarks by virtue of their concentration in public utility stocks. (2) The lower Betas for the balanced funds as a group reflect their substantial bond positions, reducing stock market risk, as would be expected. As a result of their lower equity exposure, volatility in the balanced funds is from 30% to 60% less than that demonstrated by stocks as a group. (3) The gross yields on balanced funds are about two to two and one-half times the yield for stocks as a group.

The variations in these portfolio characteristics from one fund to another tend to be narrower in the case of traditional and income-oriented balanced funds and wider in the case of the asset allocation funds. Table 7-2, using representative funds that differ from the category norms, makes the point. Nonetheless, as the table illustrates, there are significant variations in the ExMarks, Betas, and gross yields within each group. As a generalization, in the inherently more conservative arena of balanced fund investing, it seems wise to avoid those funds at the extremes of the ranges.

To reiterate from Chapter 4, I cannot emphasize enough the importance of fairness (and common sense) in assuring that you compare only funds that have *similar* investment policies and characteristics. Sensible performance comparisons can be made only after establishing that fairness.

EVALUATING PAST PERFORMANCE

After repeating my caution against picking stock funds simply on the basis of past performance, I would add that the same concepts of performance measurement I applied to common stock funds should be applied to bal-

TABLE 7-2
Variations in Portfolio Characteristics of Balanced Funds

Balanced category	ExMark	Beta	Gross yield
Average equity-oriented fund	87%	0.64	5.1%
Conservative fund	92	0.57	6.2
Aggressive fund	84	0.81	4.4
Average income-oriented fund	65%	0.42	7.1%
Conservative fund	80	0.39	6.2
Aggressive fund	58	0.48	7.4
Average asset allocation fund	75%	0.53	4.8%
Conservative fund	93	0.52	5.3
Aggressive fund	55	0.94	3.5

anced funds as well. In particular, total returns should be evaluated not in terms of cumulative aggregates but rather in terms of average annual rates. I would again emphasize the importance of dividing return into its income and capital components. Table 7-3 compares the returns among the different types of balanced funds for the past 15 years with common stocks in the aggregate. Compared to historical norms, this was an exceptionally strong period for total returns on both stocks and bonds.

Table 7-3 illustrates the same elementary point that we demonstrated with respect to common stock mutual funds. The two basic types of balanced funds have experienced substantial disparities in the contributions to their total returns from investment income and capital growth. Both types of balanced funds, as it happened, provided similar total returns over the period. However, about half of the return on the equity-oriented balanced funds was generated by dividend and interest income, with the remainder coming from capital appreciation. On the other hand, more than 70% of the total return on the income-oriented balanced funds was generated by income, with capital appreciation accounting for the remainder. The income-oriented funds achieved a slightly lower return than the equity-oriented funds, but with considerably less market risk. (Both balanced fund groups incurred less risk—as measured by the contribution of income to their total returns—than the total stock market.) The table reinforces the need to give considerable weight not only to total return but to its capital and income components as well.

TABLE 7-3
Average Annual Rates of Return (15 Years Ended December 31, 1992)

Balanced fund category	Income return	Capital return	Total return	Income as a percent of total return
Equity-oriented	+6.5%	+6.9%	+13.4%	49%
Income-oriented	+8.9	+3.6	+12.5	71
S&P 500 Index	+4.8%	+10.7%	+15.5%	31%

The history of asset allocation funds is too limited for meaningful comparison.

Let me emphasize that the remaining standards of stock fund performance evaluation reviewed in Chapter 4 are equally applicable to balanced funds. You should continue to focus primarily on ten-year rates of return, limit comparisons to the results of funds with similar investment policies and objectives, and recognize that, even if past fund performance could be evaluated precisely, it would be of limited value in predicting the future.

The futility of using past returns to predict future returns can be evaluated in special detail with respect to balanced funds. Since the number of

---

CAVEAT EMPTOR: *The Survival of the Fittest*

There were 28 equity-oriented balanced funds in operation at the end of 1972. However, only the 16 funds included in our performance ranking (Table 7-4) survived the ensuing two decades. The 12 that disappeared—a "fatality rate" of more than 40%—included 7 that were merged into other funds and 5 that changed their investment policies (4 became bond funds and 1 became an equity fund). Among the remaining 16 funds, 6 management companies were merged into others, and there were 2 name changes. Only eight funds survived the period with their investment objectives, managements, and names intact. If you are investing for a lifetime and seeking a consistent investment approach, this record of evanescence is a sober warning against taking the continuity of any fund's existence for granted. It is also a reminder of Charles Darwin's theory that only the fittest—the most vigorous and healthy—survive. Funds that do not survive make life difficult for the long-term investor.

TABLE 7-4
Balanced Fund Relative Rankings by Decade

1982–92			1982–92		
*Annual return**	*Rank*	*1972–82 rank*	*Annual return**	*Rank*	*1972–82 rank*
+15.5%	1	15	+13.4%	9	3
+14.6	2	12	+13.1	10	1
+14.4	3	9	+12.7	11	4
+14.3	4	6	+12.6	12	8
+14.2	5	16	+12.3	13	7
+14.2	6	13	+12.2	14	14
+13.9	7	10	+12.2	15	2
+13.5	8	11	+11.8	16	5

*Excludes impact of sales charge.

balanced funds with an extended performance history is quite limited, I have considered the returns of each of the 16 equity-oriented balanced funds that have been in operation over the past 20 years. (There were only three income-oriented balanced funds in existence 20 years ago.) My objective is to examine the relationship of total returns during the first decade to total returns during the subsequent decade. Since the group consists of only 16 funds, it is easy to look at each individual fund. Table 7-4 shows the returns achieved during the ten-year period ended December 31, 1992, and how each fund's rank compared with its rank in the previous decade. Here are the major conclusions:

- The returns of balanced funds during the first decade were a poor forecaster of superior relative returns during the subsequent decade. For example, the best performer in the decade ended December 31, 1992, was the second worst performer of the previous decade. The second worst performer in the decade ended December 31, 1992, was the second best performer in the previous decade.

- There were remarkably small variations in the returns of individual balanced funds around the overall average of +13.4% annually for the past decade. Of the 16 funds, 14 provided returns in the range of +12.2% to +14.6%; one fund provided a return of +15.5% and another of +11.8%, scarcely major departures from the range.

- Costs mattered. The four best performers during the past decade

---

CAVEAT EMPTOR: *Do Not Forget the Sales Load*

The returns shown in Table 7–4 were calculated without taking sales loads into account. However, note that, after adjusting each fund's return for the impact of any sales loads, the four no-load funds in the comparison ranked 1, 2, 3, and 11 during the decade. The average annual return of the no-load funds was +14.1% versus +12.2% for the load funds. The final value of $10,000 invested at the start of the decade would have been no-load funds $37,400 and load funds $31,620. Given the remarkable consistency of balanced fund returns, the sales charge is an especially important factor in selecting a balanced fund.

---

incurred annual expenses (including the impact of sales charges) of 0.95%; the four worst performers incurred expenses of 1.96%.

Again, I want to underscore the importance of professional management in attending to a balanced fund's fundamental investment objectives and policies, administering its investments, and diversifying its portfolio. Nonetheless, with equity-oriented balanced funds, past performance rankings are, if not meaningless, at least imponderable forecasters of future relative returns. The "predictability premium" is extremely small when you take into account the odds against picking the winners based on past returns and the modest increase in return you would achieve even if you could defy the odds. So it is left to you to study the structural elements of balanced funds, to consider carefully the nature, composition, and relative stability of their past returns, to take all costs into account, and finally to make your selections on the basis of reasoned judgment.

SUMMARY

As I said in the summary to Chapter 4, even the most careful approach to evaluating groups of mutual funds provides no assurance of success. In the case of the traditional balanced funds, however, the smaller universe of funds from which to choose makes the investor's task somewhat more manageable. But it is a fallible exercise nonetheless. Here are just a few ideas to consider:

CAVEAT EMPTOR: *Balanced Funds Top Stock Funds*

For the ten-year period ended December 31, 1992, the +13.6% annual return for the average traditional balanced fund actually exceeded the +13.2% average return achieved by mainstream common stock funds. This anomaly resulted largely from the fact that interest rates fell sharply during the decade, driving bond prices higher and providing a singularly favorable environment for bonds. Does this relationship violate our assumption that lower returns should accompany lower risk? Yes—but only for the 1982–92 decade. In most past decades, balanced funds provided lower relative returns, and in the coming decade return relationships are inevitably imponderable. You would be ill-advised to assume that balanced funds will continue to earn marginally superior returns even as they assume significantly lower risk. The long-term merits of balanced investing are quite sufficient in and of themselves, and their suitability should not rest on unrealistic expectations of future returns.

- Invest principally in mainstream balanced mutual funds, giving important weight to your current income requirements.
- Differentiate carefully among the traditional balanced funds, the income-oriented balanced funds, and the asset allocation balanced funds. They present three distinct investment strategies.
- Determine which type of balanced fund is most suitable to meet your objectives. Then compare its investment characteristics and performance with those of other funds within the same category. Comparing like with like is critical.
- Focus primarily on fund returns for the previous ten years or, for a newer fund, its lifetime. Note year-to-year variations in returns relative to competitors.
- Know what makes the fund tick, and carefully consider the technical factors of ExMark, Beta, and gross yield.
- Focus on the quality of a balanced fund's bond portfolio. Award a plus for significant U.S. Treasury and federal agency holdings and a minus if the portfolio appears to be reaching for higher yields by compromising on quality. Doing so is a very risky business.
- Consider the cost of acquiring and owning a balanced fund's

shares. Some funds are no-load and some are not; the difference is important. Some have high operating expenses and some have low operating expenses; that matters too. In a world of relatively narrow return parameters (as exemplified by the traditional balanced funds), minimizing the impact of these costs may provide the only predictable advantage.

Overall, selecting from among traditional equity-oriented balanced funds is more an exercise in good judgment than in forecasting the future. The same is likely to be true for income-oriented balanced funds. The challenge of selecting asset allocation funds is much greater and depends on your willingness to assume risks that may cause your returns to vary from market norms over the short or even the long term.

Most importantly, you should recognize that owning a single carefully chosen mainstream balanced fund is *not* essentially risky. It is the exact counterpart of retaining a private trustee to invest your resources in a diversified list of investment-grade stocks and bonds, the better to obtain the golden mean.

Chapter Eight

Where to Get Mutual Fund Information
Knowledge Is Power

"Knowledge is power." It has been some 400 years since Sir Francis Bacon first set forth this simple aphorism. True as it was as a general principle when he set it down in 1597, it is equally valid today as a maxim for the intelligent investor. This chapter will discuss the different sources of knowledge that will serve you well in understanding particular mutual funds and will help you avoid some of the worst pitfalls of mutual fund investing.

I will review some of the major sources of information for selecting mutual funds, including fund prospectuses and annual reports and major statistical services—especially an extraordinary mutual fund manual called *Morningstar Mutual Funds*. I will then turn to the information provided by the financial press and mutual fund advisory services. At best, the latter two sources provide helpful information; at worst, they offer dangerous misinformation. This chapter will help investors tell the difference.

FUND PROSPECTUSES AND ANNUAL REPORTS

Fund prospectuses are largely tedious documents that tend to obscure some very important information by burying it amid technical matters of limited investment significance. But prospectuses do convey essential information that investors should thoughtfully appraise in assessing a mutual fund's suitability for their particular needs. The main categories of fund information are investment objectives, investment policies, risks, costs, the ten-year per-share data table, and other items of special interest.

Fund investment objectives.   Investors will want to know precisely what a fund seeks to accomplish. For money market funds and most bond funds, the objectives are fairly specific. But for many stock funds—particularly the basic growth funds and value funds—the objectives can get quite muddy (as I noted earlier, even mongrelized). You are entitled to a clear statement of whether a fund seeks capital growth, current income, or whatever. There is nothing wrong with a fund that positions itself as some of each, but it should state that fact clearly.

Fund investment policies.   At best, investment policies describe the principal types of stocks and bonds the fund will hold: for example, stocks with above-average yields and below-average price-earnings ratios; or, long-term bonds rated BBB or above. Again, specificity is better than generalization to minimize prospective investors' confusion.

Risks.   Most prospectuses handle risk in general rather than specific terms. Typically, the risk statement relates to variations in total return, but capital risk and income risk should also be described. Further, the investor should be informed whether the risk in a particular stock fund, for example, is expected to be significantly more than, less than, or about the same as the risk in a fully diversified portfolio of stocks (using, say, the Standard & Poor's 500 Stock Index as a benchmark). It is probably going too far to require mutual funds to disclose their Betas and ExMarks, given the imprecision of these statistics. On the other hand, they are far more stable than a fund's past performance; their disclosure would do more good than harm and would relieve the investor of the burden of searching out this information in a statistical manual.

Costs.   Thanks to a vigorous effort by the SEC in 1988, prospectuses now do a generally good job of setting forth the costs of fund ownership. Table 8–1 is typical. Every investor should examine this cost table with care. The key item is the total expenses incurred by the investor, shown in the bottom line. The expenses are projected based on an initial investment of $1,000 and applying the fund's current expense ratio. They assume that shares are held for one, three, five, and ten years. To illustrate that expenses rise with fund asset values, the table assumes an annual rate of return of +5% for the fund.

The greatest cost variable is the sales load. The prospectus will state whether the fund is a no-load fund or sales commissions are paid on

TABLE 8–1
Fund Expenses

Shareholder Transaction Expenses

Sales charge on purchases	5.00%
Sales charge on reinvested dividends	None
Redemption fees	None
Exchange fees	None

Annual Fund Operating Expenses

Management fees	0.89%
12b–1 distribution fees	None
Other operating expenses	0.31%
Total operating expenses	1.20%

The following example illustrates the expenses that you would incur on a $1,000 investment over various periods, assuming (1) a 5% annual return and (2) redemption at the end of each period.

1 Year	3 Years	5 Years	10 Years
$62	$87	$115	$197

---

purchases of shares. While a load in almost any amount will represent the major portion of expenses if the fund shares are held for one year, its impact on annual return is reduced when spread over ten years. A 5% load would represent a cost of $50 on the $1,000 investment in the first year but would represent a cost of roughly $5 per year over ten years. For a fund with a 5% initial load and a 1.2% annual expense ratio, the cost of ownership would be $62 for one year and $197 over ten years.

Ten-year per-share data table. Always placed near the front of the prospectus, the ten-year per-share data table has several important pieces of information: net asset values, investment income, expenses, dividends, and capital gains distributions, all shown on a per-share basis. These data are helpful in assessing the stability of income and the extent to which taxable gains are realized annually (as distinct from being unrealized and remaining in the fund's net asset value). In addition, the fund's total return for each fiscal year is presented. Finally, the table also shows the fund's total assets, expense ratios over ten years (which reflects past fee increases or reductions) and the dividend yield net of operating ex-

---

CAVEAT EMPTOR: *The Multiplier Effect*

The cost table has two major weaknesses. The first is that using the $1,000 initial investment as the basis for comparison trivializes the costs of acquisition and ownership. Investors should be careful to multiply the cost figures shown in the table by the amount of their expected investment. Costs on a $50,000 investment will be 50 times as large as the prospectus indicates; in the example in Table 8–1 the $197 ten-year cost would rise to $9,850. The second is that funds whose sponsors are waiving fees temporarily sometimes extend the no-fee or low-fee projections out in time, although it is dubious at best that the fee will be waived for a full decade.

---

penses over the preceding ten years. The portfolio turnover rate is also provided, giving a clue to the fund's investment tactics.

Special items.   An investor should know if a fund departs from industry norms in any particular manner. Some examples might be selling stocks short, using derivative instruments, owning bonds that may enhance income at the expense of principal (such as certain collateralized mortgage obligations), speculating in foreign currencies, and the like.

Summary.   The best prospectuses (1) provide straightforward information on the fund's suitability for particular investors and the role it is designed to play in an investor's portfolio, (2) highlight the most important information, and (3) are written with some sense of the standards and grace of the English language. Many prospectuses fail the first two tests; with their emphasis on legalese, nearly all fail the last.

Fund annual reports provide a wonderful opportunity for management to tell its story to fund shareholders. However, most of the mandated information is quantitative rather than qualitative. As a result, many annual reports have become providers of information generally interesting only to accountants and regulators. Each report includes a listing of the fund's portfolio holdings at market value; a statement of income and expenses, and capital appreciation (or depreciation) for the year; the total unrealized appreciation (or depreciation) of the portfolio at year-end; a statement of changes in net assets, focusing on investor purchases and liquidations over

TABLE 8-2
Financial Highlights

	1992	1991	1990	1989	1988
Net asset value per share, beginning of period	$19.18	$13.27	$14.44	$11.14	$10.31
Income from investment operations					
Net investment income	−0.02	−0.01	0.01	0.15	0.15
Net gains or losses on securities (both realized and unrealized)	−0.52	7.40	−0.23	3.35	0.83
Total from investment operations	−0.54	7.39	−0.22	3.50	0.98
Less distributions					
Dividends (from net investment income)	0.00	0.00	0.00	−0.15	−0.15
Distributions (from capital gains)	−0.74	−1.48	−0.95	−0.05	0.00
Returns of capital	0.00	0.00	0.00	0.00	0.00
Total distributions	−0.74	−1.48	−0.95	−0.20	−0.15
Net asset value per share, end of period	$17.90	$19.18	$13.27	$14.44	$11.14
Total return	−2.8%	+54.3%	+0.8%	+31.4%	+9.5%
Ratios/supplemental data					
Net assets, end of period (in millions)	$661.3	$546.6	$301.4	$298.1	$244.6
Ratio of expenses to average net assets	2.07%	2.28%	2.18%	2.21%	2.20%
Ratio of net income to average net assets	−0.82%	−0.11%	0.54%	1.46%	0.81%
Portfolio turnover rate	96%	147%	96%	112%	126%

Table must be shown for lesser of ten years or life of fund.

the prior two years; and a repeat (or update) of the per-share information in the prospectus. Everything is footnoted to a fault.

To shareholders, however, the main information that can be gleaned from these mandatory accounting disclosures comes from a review of the fund's largest holdings. The nature of the companies owned will hint at the fund's objectives, quality standards, and portfolio concentration (the percentage of assets invested in, for example, the ten largest holdings). A highly concentrated fund might have 50% or more of net assets in this group of ten; for a small cap fund, the figure might be as low as 15%.

The statement of changes in net assets may be worth a glance, showing as it does the cash flow into and out of the fund. A successful fund might be expected to have large cash inflows (purchases of fund shares) and small outflows (redemptions of shares) relative to its asset base; for a poor performer, the reverse pattern might be typical. To a fund accepting (or catering to) market timers, both purchases and liquidations may be high. Unfortunately, publication of the *ratios* of these flows to assets, a useful indicator, is not legally required. These ratios therefore are almost universally ignored in fund reports.

Beyond the mandated information, all uniformity in fund annual reports goes up in smoke. The review of the year's results ranges from the cursory in some funds to the complete in others. The annual report is a tipoff to the amount of information the management company's chief executive officer—writing in his capacity as the fund's chairman—wishes to communicate to the fund's shareholders. This listing presents my view of the minimum information that should be presented in an annual report.

- Total return for the year divided, at least in the case of income-oriented funds, into its capital and income components.
- Total return for the year of appropriate benchmarks, including unmanaged market indexes and funds with similar objectives (for example, the average growth fund), or even peer groups of competitors that have similar investment characteristics.
- An evaluation of the fund's performance during the year, including an explanation of the major factors that contributed to the relative superiority or inferiority of the fund's return.
- To provide perspective, benchmark comparisons should also be presented for longer periods.

From a review of the annual report, investors will learn, in the best case, what made the fund tick. In the worst case, they will learn (by omission) what information the company managing the fund believes is none of their business.

STATISTICAL MANUALS

There are two major mutual fund statistical manuals, and the difference between them tells a great deal about how much the mutual fund industry has changed and how modern computer programming technology has changed the name of the game. The format of the annual *Wiesenberger*

Investment Companies Service manual has remained essentially unchanged since 1941. Originally focused on closed-end investment companies, the manual began to include open-end mutual funds in 1944, when it provided profiles for 45 large funds with combined assets of about $570 million. *Morningstar Mutual Funds,* first published in 1986, is presented in a large looseleaf binder, with the data for the various types of stock, bond, and balanced funds updated sequentially every two weeks. Both manuals are available in many public libraries.

The 1993 Wiesenberger manual (now published by a division of Computer Directions Advisers Investment Technologies, Inc.) provides statistical information—including expense ratios, sales charges, and inception dates—for some 3,000 mutual funds (including money market funds). It also provides for each fund an illustration of a $10,000 investment over periods ranging from 5 years to 25 years.

The most valuable part of the manual is the individual fund analysis, presenting detailed information about roughly 800 funds in individual sections. Included are an overview of the fund's objectives, a description of its investment adviser, and a statistical history over the previous 12 years (or for a newer fund, its lifetime). The Wiesenberger manual is a solid source of basic information.

Without a doubt, however, the most comprehensive source of information about individual mutual funds is *Morningstar Mutual Funds*. Since its initial publication, its format has been continually enhanced. Early in 1993, it provided information on more than 1,300 mutual funds. Money market funds and some new or small funds are not covered. The comprehensive Morningstar list covers almost every regular mutual fund deserving consideration by the intelligent investor.

If you have ever seen the *Value Line Investment Survey* of individual common stocks, Morningstar will look very familiar. Each fund is covered on a single page, with a line chart showing its cumulative return over 13 years, both on an *absolute* basis and *relative* to a major market index (for stock and balanced funds, the S&P 500 Index; for bond funds, the Lehman Government/Corporate Bond Index). Each fund is classified by its broad investment objective. The equity group includes growth, growth and income (which in this book we call value), equity income, small company, international, and concentrated specialty funds. The hybrid group includes balanced, asset allocation, and high-yield bond funds. The bond group includes government, municipal, and corporate funds.

The amount of data Morningstar presents on that single page is remarkable. Here is some of the information included for each fund:

1. Annual rates of return for 13 years and quarterly rates of return for the most recent six years. (It is unfortunate that performance during the disastrous fourth quarter of 1987 for stock funds and the second quarter for bond funds will not be shown for much longer, but their lessons should not be forgotten.) Also shown are income dividends and capital gains distributions each quarter for three calendar years.

2. The principal costs involved in investing, including sales loads, expense ratios, management fees, and (as a rough measure of transaction costs) portfolio turnover.

3. Performance and risk statistics showing each fund's ExMark (using the traditional designation of R-squared), Beta, and other performance measurement data.

4. A simple nine-block matrix indicating, for a stock fund, one of three styles (growth, value, blend) and one of three size categories (large, medium, and small companies). For a bond fund, the matrix shows one of three portfolio quality standards (high, medium, low) and one of three maturity categories (short, intermediate, long).

5. The characteristics of the fund's portfolio. For stock funds, the data include the average price-earnings ratio and weightings by industry sector; for bond funds, average effective maturity, interest coupon structure, and credit quality; and for both categories, a listing of the fund's 30 largest holdings.

6. A brief narrative commentary on the fund's record, updated roughly twice each year.

7. A rating of shareholder annual reports, evaluating the nature and extent of the information each fund provides to its shareholders.

Figures 8-1 and 8-2 show a sample page for a bond fund and a stock fund. The key below highlights some principal features of the analysis.

Morningstar provides nearly everything you need to know about specific mutual funds. Information that is not presented on a fund's page in Morningstar is probably not worth knowing. Exceptions include a statement of the unrealized portfolio appreciation included in the fund's net asset value, as well as any gains realized but not yet distributed during the current year; an examination of the sources of yield in bond funds, including the extent to which derivative securities (which I discussed in Chapter 5) are adding to income yield at the expense of capital return.

I am concerned about the way in which Morningstar's fund ratings combine reward and risk. The system for evaluating the reward half of the formula is simple enough. The total returns (less any sales charges) of each stock and bond fund for various periods are compared with the average returns, respectively, of all stock and bond funds tracked by Morningstar. Using a base of 1.00 for the average, each fund then receives its reward rating. If a specific fund's return was +11%, and the average fund's return was +10%, that fund's reward rating would be 1.10 (a rise 10% greater than the norm).

The risk half of the formula is less straightforward. It is based essentially on the accumulation of all monthly shortfalls for the fund relative to the monthly returns on U.S. Treasury bills, divided by the months in the period. This result is compared with the average stock or bond fund, as appropriate. Again, a base of 1.00 for the average is used. If a fund's cumulative monthly shortfall relative to Treasury bills was −2.2%, and the decline for the average fund was −2.0%, the relative risk rating would be 1.10 (a decline 10% above the norm). This concept is elusive, and small differences in risk can make large differences in the "risk-adjusted return." Morningstar derives this risk-adjusted return by combining the fund's risk ratio and its reward ratio, giving each figure equal weight.

For example, if a stock fund's annual return has been, say, 20% above that of the average equity fund, its return measure would be 1.00 + .20, or 1.20. If its average monthly shortfall to Treasury bills has been 30% less than that of the average equity fund, its risk measure would be 1.00 − .30, or 0.70%. Its risk-adjusted return would be 1.20 + (1.00 − 0.70), or 1.50. That the calculation is so simple does not make it wrong. But there are many kinds of risks in investing that are ignored when past price volatility is the sole measurement standard. Based solely on its short-term price volatility and ignoring the speculative nature of its portfolio, a junk bond fund, for example, could look less risky than a long-term Treasury bond fund.

The equal weight accorded to risk and return in the Morningstar concept seems arbitrary. Table 8–3 illustrates how the system would work in practice. Have the two stock funds shown really performed equally? It is not any easy question to answer. Both have ratings of 1.15 or +15% above the average stock fund. But the average annual return of Fund A was +13.2% for the full period, far above the +9.2% return of Fund B. This

FIGURE 8-1
Morningstar Analysis—Bond Fund

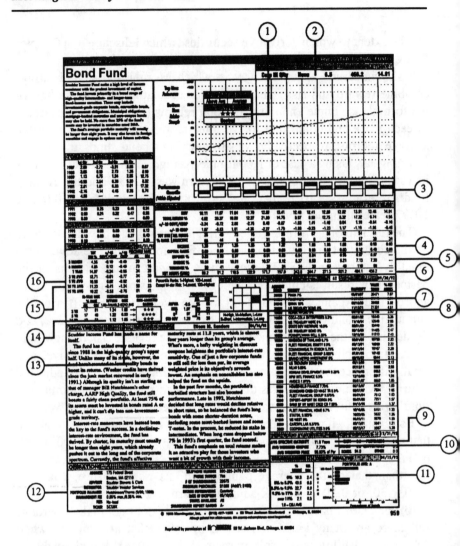

Some Key Points:

1. Rating – Three stars (average)
2. No load, especially important in a bond fund.
3. Solid annual rankings relative to corporate bond funds. Most recent third quartile appearance in 1982.
4. Little capital gains realization in past.
5. Gross income yield of 8.3% less expense ratio of 1.0% brings net income yield to 7.3%.
6. Net assets of $450 million.
7. Style matrix: medium quality, long-term maturity.
8. Beta (1.07) and ExMark (0.97) close to those of long-term government/corporate bond index.
9. Effective maturity of 11.8 years.
10. Low coupon consistent with holding some discount bonds.
11. Mix of top quality and below investment-grade bonds gives portfolio average rating of A.
12. Same portfolio manager since 1986.
13. Morningstar risk. About the same, over time, as average bond fund.
14. Morningstar return. Nicely above average bond fund.
15. Ten-year average return - 1.2% below unmanaged government/corporate index.
16. Five-year average return about equal to government/corporate index.

FIGURE 8–2
Morningstar Analysis—Stock Fund

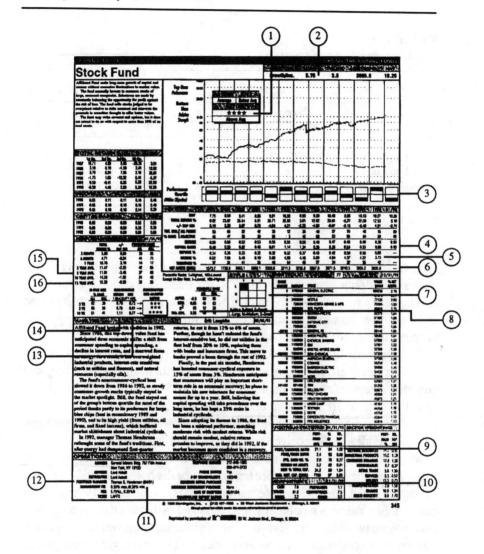

1. Rating – Four stars (above average).
2. Sales load of 5.75% on purchases.
3. Steady quartile rank among growth and income funds through 1990, then in last quartile in 1991 and first quartile in 1992.
4. Consistent and substantial capital gains distributions.
5. Low expenses of 0.60% in 1992 reduce gross income yield of 4.33% to a net income yield of 3.73%.
6. Net assets of $3.8 billion.
7. Style matrix: large company value-oriented fund.
8. Relatively low risk (Beta .85); high ExMark of 93%.
9. Portfolio price-earnings ratio of 21.1 times, 2% above S&P Index.

10. Fairly fully invested in equities (82% stocks, 8% convertibles); cash 8%.
11. 12b-1 distribution fee of 0.25%.
12. Portfolio manager relatively new (1991).
13. Morningstar risk about 20% below average equity mutual fund.
14. Morningstar return in past five years about 20% below average equity mutual fund.
15. Five-year average return: Fund +11.8%; S&P 500 Index +15.3%.
16. Fifteen-year average return: Fund +15.4%; S&P 500 Index +15.9%.

TABLE 8–3
The Morningstar Rating System

	Absolute Results		Relative Results (Base 1.00)		
	Three-year rate of return	Average shortfall	Reward	Risk	Score*
Stock Fund A	+13.2%	−1.7%	1.15	1.00	1.15
Stock Fund B	+ 9.2	−1.1	0.80	0.65	1.15
Average stock fund	+11.5%	−1.7%	1.00	1.00	1.00

*Reward + (1 − risk).

substantial advantage is eliminated, however, by a seemingly small relative increase in down market risk: −1.7% for Fund A and −1.1% for Fund B. The heavy weight given to small differences in negative returns incurred in just a few months seems excessive. Simplistically combining these ratings also leaves a great deal to be desired.

The combined rating, however, is at the heart of the Morningstar system. The funds are ranked in accordance with their combined rating and awarded a certain number of stars. The top 10% receive five stars (highest), the bottom 10% receive one star (lowest); the next 22.5% receive, respectively, four stars (above average) and two stars (below average); and the middle 35% receive three stars (average or neutral).

My primary concern with this system is that it is based solely on what happened in the past. It therefore tends to favor the hot stock funds recently in vogue (in the late 1980s, international funds; in the early 1990s, health care funds). There is a point at which fads and fashions change, however, and in these two cases, the five-star funds either have moved or are quickly moving to two-star or even one-star status. The same syndrome placed junk bond funds, which had high returns and low apparent risk, in the five-star status during the late 1980s. Morningstar changed its system for rating junk bonds in 1991, so comparable present ratings are not available. If such ratings did exist, they too would now cluster in one-star or two-star territory.

In my view, the system also has limitations in its comparative groupings. For instance, an investor who determines to purchase a gold fund will discover that all gold funds receive a one-star rating. This result is hardly surprising in light of the fact that the precious metals sector of the market was by far the worst-performing investment over the decade ended December 31, 1992. Nevertheless, some managers of gold funds have been more successful than others, and a rating system that somehow compared risk and return within the precious metals investment objective would be a more useful evaluation tool. The same principle—comparing like with like—would also hold true for international funds, small capitalization stock funds, high-yield bond funds, and so on.

This comparison of apples with oranges is evidenced in the bond rating procedures as well. Long-, medium-, and short-term bond funds are all lumped together in the same category. Given the heavy weighting accorded to risk in the combined ratings, not one of the 25 taxable bond funds awarded five-star status by Morningstar early in 1993 was a long-term fund. The idea that there are no top long-term bond funds seems ironic, especially for the investor seeking income durability.

The Morningstar star system, then, appears to have little predictive value. To their credit, its publishers have recognized this fact by abandoning their original five categories of best buy, buy, hold, avoid, and sell. Further, Morningstar now highlights each fund's annual total return relative to the other funds in its objective category, an important step forward. While the star system is a flawed forecaster of returns, Morningstar remains a peerless source of mutual fund financial information. A full understanding of the structure of a mutual fund, of its risks, returns, and costs, is an invaluable asset to the intelligent investor.

THE FINANCIAL PRESS

Magazines and newspapers provide an abundance of timely and helpful statistical information. The end of the year brings extensive tables of bond and stock fund performance from *Money, Financial World, Business Week, U.S. News and World Report, Barron's*, and others. *Forbes* also publishes its excellent mutual funds issue, usually in September. Any one or two (but not all) are worth the investor's review, simply to keep up with industry trends.

One of the problems with all of this information is that the publishers, in this age when only simple answers are allowed even to complex questions, feel required to publish a single rating purporting to evaluate a fund's performance. Usually, grades of *A* through *E* are selected to identify the "best" and "worst" funds.

It would be a happy event if the complex world of investing permitted these simple gradations. But the fact is, to fairly evaluate a fund's past performance, you must compare it to funds with similar investment characteristics. Too often, however, different types of stock funds are compared either with an average of all stock funds or with the S&P 500 Index. In this kind of comparison, any small company fund would likely be given the dreaded and undeserved *E* if the evaluation period favored large blue-chip stocks, but the gratifying and equally undeserved *A* if the period favored the smaller company stocks.

The problem is worse in the bond fund group since each fund is compared to an average of all bond funds, irrespective of credit quality or length of maturity. It follows as night follows day that a short-term bond fund will garner an *A* in an environment in which interest rates rise and bond prices decline, while long-term bond funds will garner an *E*. When rates decline, the grades will be exchanged. What these ratings have to do with the competence of a bond fund's management is not clear.

These performance evaluations are (for the worse, I think) presented daily in *The Wall Street Journal*. On Tuesday, each fund's grade for the past year is published; on Wednesday, the grade for the past three years; on Thursday, for the past four years; and finally, on Friday, for the past five years. It is possible for a fund to receive an *A* on Tuesday, a *B* on Wednesday, a *D* on Thursday, and an *E* on Friday. Even when the case is not this extreme, it is not clear what action an investor who respects the system should take. Should a fund that slides from *B* to *E* be liquidated? Incidentally, each Monday, the *Journal* publishes valuable information on expense ratios and sales charges instead of cumulative returns. Perversely, these costs, which are persistent and stable compared with performance returns, are not graded and the rating column lies blank.

Moving beyond the abundant statistics provided, I would give much of the press failing grades on its breathless quarter-by-quarter designations of the "best" portfolio managers. (And by ignoring the "worst" managers is not some sort of discrimination being practiced?) Each top manager is lionized with a photo or drawing and a paragraph or so discussing the reasons for his or her success—usually measured over the past quarter, year, or five years. No note is made of luck, nor of earlier failure, nor of the contribution of the fund's objective to its performance superiority. When biotechnology stocks boom, even an incompetent manager of a

CAVEAT EMPTOR: *Figures Can Lie*

The performance data reported to the press by the statistical services is, to be generous, incomplete. It ignores sales loads, mutual funds that have failed to survive, and the actual results achieved by investors.

- With the sole exception of *Consumer Reports*, the press ignores the impact of sales loads on investment returns. As a result, the returns of funds that carry loads are overstated. This practice, difficult to justify, is indefensible when the data are mischaracterized. One of the largest statistical services, for example, refers in its performance tables to "return on initial $10,000 investment." However, because of the sales charge (8.5% in this example), an initial investment of $10,930 would have been required to realize the final total value after five years, shown as $16,910.

- Survivorship bias means ignoring in the presentation of mutual fund returns those funds that failed to survive over a given period. Since it is almost always the poorer performers that drop out of the race, aggregate returns are overstated. For example, over the 15-year period ended on December 31, 1992, the annual return of all general equity funds in operation for the full period was +15.6%, but the annual return of all general equity funds, including those that fell by the wayside, was +14.8%. Over 15 years, the cumulative returns were +781% and +689%, respectively. It is the former figure that is published, a material misstatement of the facts.

- Time-weighted rates of return are universally used, meaning that the returns in each year are equally weighted irrespective of the amount of assets in a fund. The reality of the fund business, however, is that many investors place their money in the fund *after* the best returns have been achieved. Dollar-weighted rates of return, reflecting actual investor experience, are consistently lower. For example, the annual time-weighted rate of return on global short-term bond funds was +8.3% from the time that the funds began in 1989 through the close of 1992. However, the dollar-weighted rate of return—the return actually achieved by investors—was +3.1%, less than half of that amount.

The intelligent investor, then, should realize that figures can lie and should critically examine reported fund performance. It comes with a consistently upward bias over the returns that investors have actually achieved.

biotech fund should be among the top performers when compared with managers of common stock funds of all types.

MUTUAL FUND NEWSLETTERS

As the industry booms and the number and diversity of funds proliferate, a remarkable number of mutual fund newsletters have come into being. Most recommend individual funds selected from the total fund universe; several limit their recommendations to funds in a single fund family. The quality of their advice is uneven at best. Some are valuable and helpful, but most are worthless or even counterproductive.

Despite the warning that you can't judge a book by its cover, my initial judgment of these advisory services has been shaped largely by the quality of their promotional efforts. Most use glossy brochures with headlines that either promise easy wealth or predict impending disaster. These examples, all direct quotations, illustrate the hyperbole:

- A millionaire-maker (the highest I.Q. on Wall Street?) outsmarts the market, again . . . makes 28 straight correct calls [on the direction of the stock market] against odds of 268,435,456 to 1. . . . Get aboard one of these 10 hot undiscovered growth funds.

- Don't let a mediocre mutual fund SHRINK your biggest dreams! Using nothing but the most conservative, safest, most consistent mutual funds, we have reaped an average gain of +14.1% per year for the past 18 years. [Note: the offered advisory service had been in operation for just five years.]

- *Absolute winners* for next year, plus the "double-digit-returns-forever investment strategy."

- 100 days to inevitable wealth . . . seven best mutual funds now.

- America's #1 mutual fund expert . . . one of the world's highest paid investment advisors at $1,800 an hour . . . reveals the hottest no-load mutual funds . . . produced an average annual return in excess of 50% per year . . . send your profits into hyperspace.

- COMING MUTUAL FUND DISASTERS [picture of volcano erupting] . . . 8 out of 10 fund investors will be in the WRONG FUNDS in 1992. But here's how you can come out 30% richer and sleep better at night, too.

Alas for the newsletters, these claims of past success can be evaluated.

CAVEAT EMPTOR: *The Coin-Flipping Contest*

It is interesting, if not entirely fair, to compare the mutual fund performance derby that attracts so much press attention to a coin-flipping contest. In the contest, 100 persons begin flipping coins; at the end of ten flips, the most likely outcome is that 25 persons will have flipped five heads and five tails. The chances are virtually nil that anyone will flip either all heads or all tails. The upper chart illustrates the pattern of the expected outcome of the coin-flipping contest. The lower chart illustrates the actual outcome of the contest among equity fund managers for performance over the ten years ended December 31, 1992. The 100 largest growth and value fund managers had average annual gross returns of +15.6%. The table shows that 28 provided returns between +15% and +16%, 17 provided returns between +16% and +17%, and 21 provided returns between +14% and +15%, and so on. Three of the 100 managers defied the averages, as it were, two by earning returns of more than +20%, and one by earning a return of less than +11%. As you can see, the patterns are remarkably similar. A winning coin flipper commands no press interest; a winning fund manager is acclaimed a near genius.

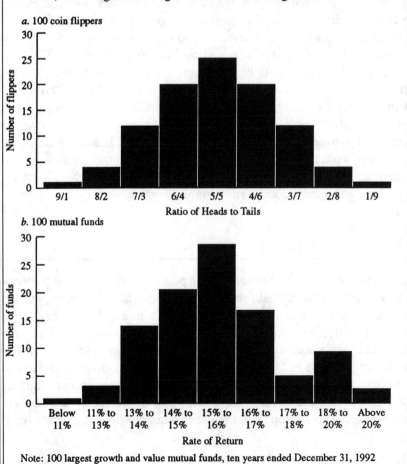

Note: 100 largest growth and value mutual funds, ten years ended December 31, 1992

The Hulbert Financial Digest does exactly that. It measures the returns achieved by a hypothetical investor, in effect, by following each adviser's recommendations over time. During the ten years ended December 31, 1992, for example, the cumulative total return of the average adviser in operation for the full period was +139.9% for the period, a rate of +9.1% annually. For the Wilshire 5000 Index of the total stock market, its cumulative return was +318.6%, a rate of +15.4% annually. That these results seem to defy the law of averages and the rule of regression to the mean is hardly a compliment.

During that decade, only three of the 36 advisers in operation during the full period outpaced the unmanaged index of the total stock market. Things took a turn for the better during the five-year period then ended, however, and 20 out of 87 advisers outpaced the unmanaged buy-and-hold index. These figures suggest that an investor who follows the advice of a newsletter has at best just a little better than one chance in five of adding value and at worst about one chance in twelve. These are not very good odds. They surely do not suggest that advisers as a group add to the returns achieved by investors who stay the course.

Yet the dream of easy riches, however seldom fulfilled, lives on. The number of advisory newsletters has grown from just 24 in 1980 to 135 at the end of 1992. It must be a very profitable business. But even at a typical subscription cost of $150 per year, a newsletter consumes 0.60% of the return on a $25,000 mutual fund holding. Thus, the newsletter would cost more than the $125 all-in annual cost of owning a mutual fund with a 0.50% expense ratio. All newsletters cost the investor good money; most offer dubious value.

SUMMARY

So, knowledge is power, but only up to a point. The abundance of information available about mutual funds is so extensive as to be overpowering. Investors must be extremely selective as to where and how they spend their time collecting information. Reading the important parts of a fund's prospectus and annual report is essential. Almost everything else worthwhile can be found in Morningstar. Accept the press tabulations as valid indicators of a fund's past success, but realize that past success is largely irrelevant to the future. Beware when portfolio managers are lionized when a fund achieves top performance in a quarter or a year, since funds that rank #1 are generally those carrying extra risk. And only if you have money to spare should you subscribe to a fund advisory service that makes irresponsible claims. The purpose of all of this information is for greater understanding, not for forecasting.

PART

III

NEW PERSPECTIVES
ON THREE KEY ISSUES

Part III covers in some detail three subjects that are too often insufficiently understood, and sometimes even ignored, by investors: (1) the elegantly simple case for index funds, (2) the overbearingly large impact of costs on mutual fund returns, and (3) the impact of taxes on fund returns and some ways to minimize this impact.

In each case, I have endeavored to present new perspectives designed to raise your interest, awareness, and understanding of these three subjects to the level of importance each deserves.

Chapter Nine

Index Funds
And There Is!

Chapter 4 focused on the challenges involved in selecting from among the incredible variety of some 1,400 stock funds. At this point you may be asking: "Isn't there a better answer to the question of predicting, at least implicitly, the future relative performance of the fund chosen? Isn't there an alternative to moving from one fund to another as hope about a fund's strategy or its implementation by the fund's investment adviser turns to disappointment, and then again from disappointment to hope as the shares of the first fund are redeemed and the second purchased?" Speaking of this phenomenon among corporate pension funds, James Vertin, a pioneer in capital market theory, put it this way:

> After twenty years of watching investment practitioners dance around the fire shaking their feathered sticks, I observe that far too many of their patients die and that the turnover of medicine men is rather high. There must be a better way.

He concluded, "And there is!"

What there is, of course, is the index fund. Simply put, an index mutual fund is a fund that owns a full participation in some particular segment of the financial market. By far the most common variety of index fund—and the one with the longest history behind it—is a fund that replicates the Standard & Poor's 500 Composite Stock Price Index. This index is heavily weighted by the stocks with the largest market capitalizations (for example, Exxon, General Electric, Philip Morris, AT&T, Coca-Cola, and Merck) and historically has represented about 70% of the value of all U.S. common stocks.

Such funds have now been operating for a fairly long time. The indexing concept was formally introduced to the giant institutional pension plan market in 1971 and to the mutual fund industry in 1976. Aggregate equity indexed assets now approach $400 billion, about one-tenth the market value of all U.S. stocks. The records of these funds have been a tribute to the fact that the efficient market theory—developed during the early 1960s by a group of brilliant academicians, five of whom subsequently earned Nobel Prizes in economics—actually works, not just in theory but in practice.

THE EFFICIENT MARKET PRINCIPLE IN THEORY . . . AND IN PRACTICE

The original efficient market theory of the academics was quite complex and difficult for industry practitioners to follow, let alone agree with. Even Nobel laureate Paul Samuelson, one of the brilliant proponents of this great body of theory, admitted "I must confess to having oscillated . . . between regarding it as trivially obvious (and almost trivially vacuous) and regarding it as remarkably sweeping." It is both of these things.

The complex formulation of what has become known as modern portfolio theory can be reduced to two obvious facts:

1. Since all investors collectively own the entire stock market, if passive investors—holding all stocks, forever—can match the gross return of the stock market, then active investors, as a group, can do no better. They too must match the gross return of the stock market.

2. Since the management fees and transaction costs incurred by passive investors are substantially lower than those incurred by active investors, and both provide equal *gross* returns, then passive investors must earn the higher *net* returns.

As the logicians would say, QED. So it is demonstrated.

If there were ever two elementary, self-evident certainties in a financial world permeated by uncertainties, surely they must be these. But while you should applaud the extensive equations and elegant proofs developed by the academic community, you should also recognize that you need not drive to the furthest reaches of the "efficient frontier" to find simple solutions that, like the proverbial "Acres of Diamonds," often lie undiscovered in your own backyard.

The hypothesis that passive equity management should outpace active management turns out to work, with considerable accuracy, in practice.

An overwhelming body of data confirms that, on a long-term basis, the average investment adviser has been unable to outperform the stock market as a whole.

Passive management quickly came to be known as indexing, a designation adopted in 1971 when the concept became reality through its application to the management of actual investment portfolios. Then, the broad-based Standard & Poor's 500 Stock Index, heavily dominated by large blue-chip companies, was chosen as the index standard. At that time, it represented the soundest indicator of stock market returns, comprised a dominant proportion of the stock market's total capitalization, and was relatively easy to replicate. Further, no valid measure of the capitalization of the entire stock market was then available.

There now exists an all-market measure: the Wilshire 5000 Index, which includes the 500 stocks in the S&P Index, plus some 4,500 remaining stocks that are actively traded in U.S. markets. While the year-by-year returns on the S&P 500 Index have been imperfectly matched to the returns of the Wilshire 5000, over extended periods of time the cumulative returns of the two indexes have been virtually identical. During the period from December 31, 1970 (the inception of the Wilshire 5000) to December 31, 1992, the S&P 500 annual return was +11.8%, incredibly close to the +12.0% rate of return for the Wilshire.

This remarkable similarity in performance suggests a technical distinction without a substantive difference between the two indexes. Nonetheless, the all-encompassing index is theoretically the sounder standard. In this chapter, therefore, I use the Wilshire 5000 rather than the S&P 500 Index as my measurement standard, unless otherwise specified. I refer to the Wilshire Index by name or by the phrase "total stock market."

Now I turn to the annual returns actually achieved by the two largest groups of equity investors—mutual funds and pension funds—relative to the total stock market during the 1970–92 period. In summary:

- *Equity mutual fund return +10.8%. Total stock market return +12.0%.* The return of the typical average equity fund fell −1.2% short of the total stock market. This actual shortfall in relative return was somewhat better than the theoretical annual shortfall of roughly −2.2%. That is, given an average annual expense ratio for fund advisory fees and operating expenses of 1.3% during the full period, and an estimated 0.9% representing the cost of fund portfolio turnover, we would have expected a

FIGURE 9-1

Total Stock Market versus Average General Equity Mutual Fund and
Average Equity Pension Fund—Cumulative Returns (1971-92)

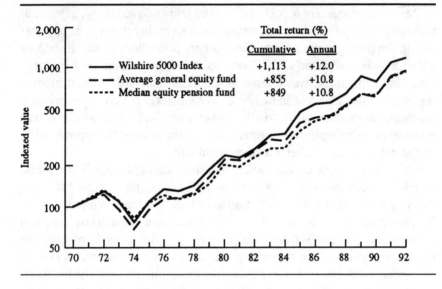

−2.2% shortfall to a cost-free portfolio comprising all of the
stocks in the market.

- *Pension equity fund return +10.8%. Total stock market return
  +12.0%.* The average annual return of the typical pension equity
  fund also fell −1.2% short of the total stock market. This shortfall, as it happens, is identical to the estimated costs of 1.2%
  borne by the pension funds, with management fees of 0.6% and
  portfolio transaction costs of 0.6%. (Pension account fees and
  portfolio turnover are generally lower than those of mutual
  funds.)

With costs included, the annual returns of both sets of managers fell short
of the market by −1.2%. Leaving all costs aside, however, the actual
mutual fund return was +1.0% better than theory would suggest, and the
actual pension return right in line. It is tempting to conclude that mutual
fund managers simply outmanaged pension fund managers but their higher
costs brought them back into line. Such a conclusion is too facile; the
differences likely lie in our inability to measure aggregate performance
with precision. Figure 9-1 presents the actual results achieved by both
types of managers and the total stock market on a cumulative basis since

TABLE 9-1
Initial Investment of $10,000 (December 31, 1970, to December 31, 1992)

Program	Rate of return	Final value
Total stock market	+12.0%	$121,300
Average equity mutual fund	+10.8	95,500
Average pension equity fund	+10.8	95,500

December 31, 1970. Make no mistake. As the magic of compounding takes effect, seemingly small differences in annual returns make for colossal differences in cumulative returns. For example, the final values of initial $10,000 investments in each equity program are $121,300 in the stock market index compared to $95,500 for the professionally managed accounts.

The manager of an index fund will not quite be able to match the market index, since mutual funds incur administrative and operational costs. If we assume that such costs might amount to 0.2% per year, the annual return on the index fund would have been +11.8% and the final value of a $10,000 initial investment would have been $116,300. Clearly, this remains a healthy margin over the traditional managers.

The returns of the average pension equity fund and the average equity mutual fund reflect a wide range of individual fund returns, and there are inevitably investment managers who outperform the market. Some of these fund managers have done such a good job for such a long time that we can fairly assume they have unusual talents. Warren Buffett, Peter Lynch, and John Neff would surely be among this group. (Nonetheless, when he took early retirement from his job as portfolio manager of what was then America's best-performing stock fund, Peter Lynch said, "Most investors would be better off in an index fund.") These managers' long-term records cover 20 years or more and have been outstanding, although not without a few bumpy years of poor relative returns.

Such extraordinary managers, in any event, not only are few in number but are difficult to identify in advance. A major academic study suggested that only about two of every five equity mutual funds has outperformed the market over time, and only about one of every five has done so when sales charges are taken into account. (Sales charges were ignored in Table 9-1; their inclusion would make the advantages of a no-load index fund

---

CAVEAT EMPTOR: *No Room at the Top*

Indexing precludes the opportunity of owning a top mutual fund with the very best record of performance. Based on the record of past decades, and ignoring the effect of fund sales charges, two out of five equity mutual funds should outperform the total stock market index over time. However, in any given year it has been extraordinary for the index fund to outperform fewer than 40% of equity funds. That the odds of picking the winners are obviously poor need not preclude you from making the bet. But you should carefully decide whether to seek mainstream stock funds, which may provide marginal superiority with relatively comparable risk, or more aggressive funds seeking greater superiority and incurring substantially greater risk in the process. As I noted in Chapter 4, if you want the fund that you own to rank among the top 10% of all stock funds, you should be prepared for it to rank among the bottom 10%.

---

almost overwhelming.) What is more, the consistency of index relative performance is compelling. Since December 31, 1970, the total stock market has outpaced nearly two-thirds of all general equity mutual funds in ten years and failed to outpace at least one-third only once, a difference that is asymmetrical to a fault. During the eleven remaining years, the total stock market returns were in a sort of middle range, outpacing at least 38% but no more than 58% of all general equity funds. Figure 9–2 presents the findings.

The question of consistency is significant, since the above-average managers only erratically repeat their past success and, even when they do, their skills may be insufficient to materially overcome the fees and other costs entailed in acquiring their services. As I noted in Chapter 4, the 20 top-performing equity mutual funds during the decade 1972–82 had an average rank of 142 (among 309 funds) during 1982–92. That they tended to drop from the top of the list to the middle strongly suggests that luck is a major factor in selecting the very best equity advisers, and that regression to the mean—the tendency for the returns of the most successful and least successful advisers in one period to converge toward the average in the next period—is alive and well.

A study published by The Brookings Institution in 1992 confirms that the stock market itself is a tough bogey for professionally managed

FIGURE 9–2
General Equity Funds Outperformed by the Wilshire 5000 (1971–92)

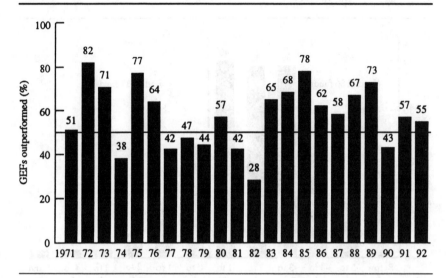

accounts. The Brookings study showed that the average pension equity fund earned an annual total return of +16.0% during the 1983–89 period, compared to +18.6% for the S&P 500. This shortfall of −2.6% per year by the managers, surprising only because of its magnitude, reminded one commentator of this colloquy: "Why are New York bankers so successful? Because they are competing with other New York bankers." If the pension managers had been competing not with each other but with an unmanaged market index, they could hardly have been characterized as successful.

Further, over extended periods, the margin of performance superiority achieved by even the most successful advisers over the total stock market is relatively modest. Figure 9–3 covers the ten years ended December 31, 1992, during which the mutual fund returns that would have been expected in theory (the total stock market return of +15.4% annually, less fund costs of 2.0% during the period, for a net return of +13.4%) exactly coincided with the results generated by the funds in practice (+13.4%). The chart reflects the returns of all 205 mainstream growth funds and value funds in operation throughout the period. It shows that 48 funds underperformed the Wilshire 5000 by more than

FIGURE 9–3
Growth and Value Funds versus Total Stock Market (Ten Years Ended December 31, 1992)

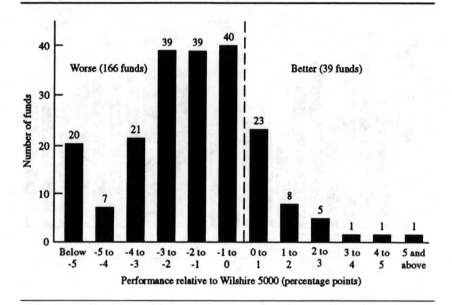

Performance relative to Wilshire 5000 (percentage points)

three percentage points annually, while only three outperformed the index by more than three percentage points. The bias toward underperformance is quite striking.

Even more impressively, Figure 9–3 actually understates the success of an index strategy, because it includes only those funds that remained in operation throughout the entire period. Funds that ceased to exist (in part, we must assume, because of inferior performance) are excluded. In addition, during the 1982–92 decade illustrated, the annual return of the Wilshire total stock market index was somewhat below that of the S&P 500 (+15.4% versus +16.2%, respectively), providing a reduced "hurdle rate" for the funds.

Using the Wilshire 5000 Index rather than the S&P 500 Index puts to rest a major criticism of indexing: that stock prices in the S&P 500 Index were driven up by the very growth of indexing as an investment strategy. This is called the self-fulfilling prophecy theory, but it ignores the fact that most active mutual fund managers also hold their main positions in the stocks in the S&P 500 index. It also ignores the fact that the average annual

---

CAVEAT EMPTOR: *The Role of Fund Expenses*

I have noted the historical tendency of stock market returns to regress to the mean and have demonstrated the practical manifestation of the theory in the case of equity mutual fund returns. I have also noted that poor-performing funds, to some degree at least, have a slight tendency to remain in the lower echelons of performance. What may explain this potential dichotomy—the rich funds becoming average and the poor funds staying poor—is that often poor performers, for obvious reasons, have small asset bases and much higher expense ratios. Perhaps as a consequence, while gross returns tend to regress to the mean, expense ratios do not. Thus, the regression to the mean of the fund's net returns may be somewhat less apparent.

---

total returns of the Wilshire 5000 Index and the S&P 500 Index were close enough that the gap was likely explained by statistical noise rather than by the growth of indexing.

There is one final problem in selecting a winning manager. According to Richard A. Brealey, one of the most respected pioneers of capital market theory, ''. . . you probably need at least 25 years of fund performance to distinguish at the 95% significance level whether a manager has above-average competence.'' Another commentator accepted the 25-year time frame, ''but only if the pension executive is using the *perfect* (italics supplied) benchmark for that manager. Using a less than perfect benchmark may increase the observation time to 80 years.'' Now that is a long time to wait for confirmation. The logic of adopting an equity investment strategy focused at least in part on indexing seems almost overpowering.

There is every reason to assume that in the future index funds will be equally successful in surpassing the long-term results of most professional advisers. In the pension field, the index advantage should result in something like 1.2% of additional return annually, represented by the total costs of investing incurred by the typical pension fund. The institutional index fund, on the other hand, incurs only nominal administrative and custodial fees and, since portfolio turnover is minuscule in an index fund, almost no transaction costs.

In the mutual fund field, even without taking into account sales loads, the index fund advantage should be even larger, a margin of about +2.2%

CAVEAT EMPTOR: *A Fair Comparison*

The stock market index fund, of course, is 100% invested in equities, while most actively managed stock funds maintain equity positions at around 90% of fund net assets. This difference *should* add to the index advantage in rising markets and put it at a disadvantage in declining markets, given its theoretically higher risk exposure. Indeed, in quick and sharp market swings, the fully invested index may be slightly more volatile, given the cash reserves held by most actively managed equity funds. However, statistics suggest that the average equity fund holds somewhat more volatile securities than does the index, which tends to neutralize the impact of cash reserves over extended time periods. On balance, the reward/risk characteristics of equity funds appear quite similar to those of the market index. Thus, the comparison between the two seems fair.

---

of additional return. The average equity fund will probably continue to incur an expense ratio at about the current level of 1.5% and turnover costs of about 0.9%. An index fund can be operated for as little as 0.2% in annual expenses and incurs negligible transaction costs. Given this expected net margin of +2.2%, index funds (in an industry in which uncertainty is the order of the day) seem virtually certain in the years ahead to exceed, yet again, the results of most actively managed no-load funds, and to exceed by even larger margins the results of actively managed load funds. And with their low portfolio turnover, index funds are substantially less likely to realize and distribute capital gains. Thus, the index advantage should be further enhanced for taxable investors.

What can go wrong with this thesis? Nothing, unless you want to argue that the passive managers will somehow lose track of their target index or their computers will take on a sudden virus. Despite all of the uncertainties of investing, it is *certain* that passive equity investment strategies have, will, and must, outperform active equity investment strategies in the aggregate. If nothing can go wrong, I hasten to add, at least three things can *appear* to go wrong:

1. When subsets of the equity market provide different results from the market as a whole. The most notable case is the use of the S&P 500 as the market standard, when it in fact comprises large capitalization stocks and presently includes only about 70% of

---

CAVEAT EMPTOR: *Not an Either-Or Proposition*

Many market pundits are either for or (more likely) against indexing seemingly as a matter of principle. However, no sweeping principle is involved. It is simply a matter of cost. A managed equity fund with a very low expense ratio has a much better chance of beating the market index than a managed equity fund with a very high expense ratio. By the same token, an index fund with a low expense ratio will come closer to matching the index itself than an index fund with a high expense ratio. If expense ratios and turnover costs are ignored, the average returns of managed funds and index funds should be about equal (although the returns of the individual managed funds, unlike those of the index funds, will diverge sharply from one another.) Obviously, the average equity fund, with estimated annual costs of 2.4%, is carrying extra baggage in a race against an index fund with annual costs of 0.2%. However, some index funds incur annual costs of 0.50% to 1.25%, and thus will fall short of the market by that amount. The lower the index fund's cost, then, the closer it is able to match its benchmark. Therefore, you should invest only in those index funds with the lowest expense ratios, and you should never pay a sales load when you invest in an index fund.

---

the stock market's total value, leaving 30% unaccounted for. While the long-term return on the S&P 500 Index has been virtually identical to that of the total stock market, it will likely outperform the total stock market in some periods (as it did in 1986–90) and will underperform it in others (as it did in 1975–81). I believe the all-encompassing Wilshire 5000 Index should be the preferred indexing standard.

2. When one subset of active managers provides better equity results than another subset. It is quite possible that, given their differences in portfolio structure, actively managed mutual funds will, on average, outpace the market in particular periods. However, under this circumstance, one or more of the other subsets—say, bank trust accounts, pension funds, or individual investors—must underperform by a commensurate amount. In any event, there is no evidence whatsoever that these disparities occur over extended periods.

3. When exact measures of the returns of active managers are not available. There is really no way to measure precisely the re-

turns of individual investors. Pension fund data are also notoriously crude. And what we refer to as the "average general equity fund" is unweighted by fund size. (An asset-weighted return would be a far more exact standard.)

I hope you will grant the validity of my passive/active thesis. It is accepted, implicitly at least, by scores of large pension funds, which have committed something like $370 billion to the indexing concept. Yet in the mutual fund field, indexed equity assets total but $18 billion, equal to only 4% of the assets of all equity mutual funds. Why, after 17 years of existence, do index funds remain only a marginal factor in the mutual fund field? I believe there are three reasons:

- First, indexing is decidedly counterintuitive, as in "You mean *no* management is better than professional management?" Few mutual fund investors would have the patience and discipline to labor through the proof I presented earlier in this chapter.

- Second, indexing is far less profitable to investment advisers than their actively managed accounts. It flies in the face of reality to expect that an active manager with an advisory fee of 50 to 100 basis points (0.5% to 1.0%) would offer a client—at least with much enthusiasm—an index fund with an advisory fee of 1 to 5 basis points (0.01% to 0.05%).

- Third, hope springs eternal. Some investors, although inevitably a minority, will choose funds carefully and outpace the market; some will make lucky choices and do the same. Those investors—usually two out of five or one out of five—will point to their success with pride. The other active investors will be envious, but little will be heard of their results.

NEW WAYS OF INDEXING

Until recently, the appeal of indexing depended upon two propositions: first, that the S&P 500 Index would match the returns of the total U.S. stock market (even as it comprised only about 70% of its total value) and that other market segments were not suitable for investing; and second, that owning the S&P 500 Index would provide the appropriate risk and reward characteristics for nearly all investors—implicitly assuming that most of them had roughly comparable investment objectives.

That the first proposition has been completely reliable for as long as we have been able to measure the returns of the *total* stock market—since December 31, 1970—does not guarantee similar reliability in the future. Nonetheless, it is difficult to conceive of a strong overall stock market in the face of general weakness among the large corporations that comprise 70% of its value. Whatever the case, the practice of indexing has now been expanded to include investment portfolios representing an index that comprises the entire U.S. stock market. The standard for such funds is almost invariably the Wilshire 5000 Index. So if you have a concern about the future relative returns achieved by the S&P 500 Index, you now have the option of selecting an index fund that is virtually certain to match the market in totality (before expenses).

The idea of owning the total stock market—rather than a fund modeled strictly on the S&P 500 Index—is a powerful one. With this idea came the first step in the endeavor to tailor index funds to more particular goals. If the "other" stock market—those 4,500 stocks not included in the S&P 500 Index—has an independent existence, why not structure an index to match it? And so the "mid-cap" index fund, heavily weighted by stocks with medium-size market capitalizations, came into existence in 1987. (At the end of 1992, the average market capitalization of the stocks in the S&P 500 was $12.6 billion; the average capitalization of the smaller stocks in the Wilshire 4500 Index was $1.0 billion.)

There is some historical evidence that stocks with very small market capitalizations have distinctively different performance characteristics from those of large and medium-size issues, at least over particular time periods. There are generally considered to be several thousand of these small-cap issues, and their performance is usually measured by yet another index, the Russell 2000 Index of small company stocks. The average market capitalization of these stocks was only $260 million at the end of 1992. It was only a matter of time until the Russell Index would be adopted as an indexing standard in the mutual fund field, and the first fund designed to track this index began in 1989. This extension of the principle of indexing—that small capitalization stocks as a group should outpace the results of investment managers actively investing in small-cap stocks—took passive investing another step forward. However, it remains to be seen whether the long-term historical superiority of small stocks over large stocks will continue.

The indexing concept was also being applied to foreign equities. If the U.S. market lent itself to indexing, the argument went, why not the foreign

---

CAVEAT EMPTOR: *Indexing in Inefficient Markets*

A number of market pundits have argued that, even if indexing is an effective strategy for enhancing returns relative to those achieved by investment advisers in the aggregate, the principle holds true only in a highly efficient active market such as that represented by the S&P 500 Index, and not in what appear to be relatively inefficient markets such as smaller capitalization stocks and foreign stocks. The argument is demonstrably wrong. Those who claim active management produces superior returns to passive management under these circumstances imply that active investors as a group will earn better returns than the market because they have knowledge they can exploit to surpass the results of passive investors. But in efficient and inefficient markets alike, all investors own all of the stocks. Thus, no matter what segment of the market is chosen, a low-cost index fund must provide *gross* returns that equal those of active managers in the aggregate in that same market segment. Since the transaction costs associated with investing in less efficient markets are by and large considerably higher than the costs of investing in U.S. stocks with large capitalizations, the inefficient-market index funds, given their low portfolio turnover, may well command an even greater advantage. Nonetheless, it is probably fair to assume that the spread in return between the best- and worst-performing managers in inefficient markets is larger than in efficient markets. Therefore, the extra returns earned by superior managers in inefficient markets should be larger than the extra returns earned by superior managers in efficient markets. These larger returns, however, will be offset, dollar for dollar, by the returns relinquished by inferior managers. Whether in inefficient markets it is easier to identify these two classes of managers in advance remains to be seen.

---

markets? The offshore bourses could, without significant problems, be indexed in their totality. (At the end of 1992, foreign equities represented, in the aggregate, about 57% of the world's total market value, with the remaining 43% accounted for by the U.S. stock market.) And soon they were, with the first international index mutual fund introduced in 1986. With the sharp wave of speculation in Tokyo, it also seemed worthwhile to separate the foreign markets into two distinct segments: the European markets and the Pacific Basin markets. In each case, the new international index funds have been able to track, with a high degree of precision, the markets in which they invest.

The major European and Pacific Basic indexes involve, for the most part, stocks that are traded in markets that are somewhat less efficient and carry significantly higher transaction costs than indexing in the U.S. Thus, indexing abroad should entail even more financial advantages than in the U.S. The actively managed U.S.-based international funds typically have high rates of portfolio turnover and high transaction costs. In combination, these two factors may reduce international fund returns by as much as 2% annually. These actively managed international funds also normally have higher expense ratios—they averaged about 1.8% during 1992—than their counterparts investing in U.S. stocks. Total annual costs, then, may reach 3.8%. If international index funds, with their much lower portfolio turn-over, have transaction costs of, say, 0.5% and expense ratios of 0.3%, their total costs will be 0.8%. Their theoretical annual advantage of 3.0%, then, will exceed the advantage of 2.2% that index funds investing in the U.S. market should theoretically enjoy.

Currency risk is an important consideration for both passive and active international investors. As I noted in Chapter 4, currency fluctuations will either enhance or reduce the returns to U.S. investors in international markets in any given period but should be about neutral over the long term. International index funds, so far, do not engage in currency hedging, while actively managed funds have at least a limited charter to do so. That they can hedge their currency risk successfully enough to recoup their inherent shortfall to the index funds seems unlikely.

The second proposition on which the appeal of market indexing de-pended—that most investors would have investment objectives roughly comparable to those of the market as a whole—also came into question. As the understanding of indexing grew, it became increasingly clear that some investors would prefer a particular style of investing. So when Stan-dard & Poor's Corporation and BARRA created, early in 1992, two new indexes that divided the S&P 500 into a value component and a growth component, it was only a matter of months until index funds were created to match these indexes.

These new "style" indexes are constructed by placing each stock in the S&P 500 Index into either the value or the growth category, based primar-ily on its relative price-to-book-value ratio (a corporation's price in the stock market relative to the net book value of its assets). Each of the new indexes comprises 50% of the total value of the 500 Index. This deceptively simple method has two important advantages. One, portfolio turnover—and hence transaction costs—is held to minimal levels, a critical feature

CAVEAT EMPTOR: *Indexing Pays Dividends*

The focus on the yields available in the Growth and Value Indexes drives home yet again the importance of mutual fund operating expenses. The table below compares the actual yields on actively managed growth and value funds with those available from a respective index fund.

Dividend Yields (December 31, 1992)

	Growth Objective		Value Objective	
	Index fund	*Active fund*	*Index fund*	*Active fund*
Gross yield	2.1%	2.4%	3.7%	3.7%
Expense ratio	−0.2	−1.4	−0.2	−1.3
Net yield	1.9%	1.0%	3.5%	2.4%

Note how the growth index fund, despite a lower gross yield than its counterpart active funds, provides, by reason of its low expenses, almost double the net yield. More importantly, note that the income from the value index fund is nearly 50% higher than for the active value funds. An investment of $50,000 would provide annual income of $1,200 for the active value funds, compared to $1,750 for the value index fund. This extra income of $550 per year comes without additional risk. If you are seeking retirement income, it is a compelling advantage.

of passive investing. Two, since each stock belongs to one index or the other, without overlap, the new indexes are pristine. (You may recall my earlier point that many of the largest portfolio holdings of growth mutual funds are also among the largest portfolio holdings of value funds, making it difficult to be certain which type of fund you own.)

I expect that the new style indexes will greatly assist investors in meeting their particular investment objectives. In the accumulation phase of your life, you might be well served by a relatively low dividend yield to minimize your taxes. At retirement and in the distribution phase of your life, you would presumably be better served by a higher yield. At the close of 1992, the 500 Index had a yield of 2.8%, with the Growth Index yielding 2.1% and the Value Index yielding 3.7%. Thus, the Value Index provides

TABLE 9-2
The Index Advantage—Annual Rate of Return (Ten Years Ended December 31, 1992)

	Mutual fund	Index*	Index advantage
Growth objective	+12.8%	+15.5%	+2.7%
Value objective	+13.6	+16.1	+2.5

*Reduced by 0.20% to account for assumed operating expenses incurred by an index fund.

current income that is more than 75% higher than that of the Growth Index. This increase, of course, is not free. The presumption is that the Growth Index will provide over time a commensurate increase in capital appreciation relative to the Value Index.

The record of the past decade—manifested in the Standard & Poor's construction of these two new indexes—reflects the accuracy of the expectation that, in the longer run, the total returns of the indexes may prove to be comparable. In this selected period, the two indexes achieved roughly comparable total returns. In addition, both the Growth Index and the Value Index outpaced by imposing margins the returns of equity mutual funds with corresponding objectives, as shown in Table 9-2.

Again, this period was a singularly favorable one for market indexes relative to professional managers, albeit one that was consistent with theoretical expectations. On the other hand, since the total returns are shown on a pretax basis, it is possible that, given their lower portfolio turnover, the after-tax returns on the two indexes would be further improved over the actively managed mutual funds.

MOVING BEYOND STOCK INVESTING

The principles of stock indexing carry over to bond indexing, and the first bond index mutual fund became available in 1986. This fund uses as its target index the Lehman Brothers Aggregate Bond Index, comprising virtually all investment-grade bonds. Largely because of transaction costs in the less liquid segments of the bond market, bond index funds have struggled to match their target indexes. But they have given a good account of themselves relative to other bond funds, which usually carry even larger

FIGURE 9-4
Bond Funds versus Lehman Bond Index—Cumulative Returns (1983-92)

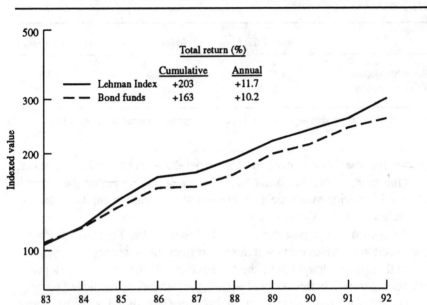

transaction costs and also incur annual operating expenses averaging about 1.0%.

That said, a fund targeting the Lehman Bond Index is suitable only for an investor with an intermediate-term investment horizon. Since the index has a duration of less than five years, such a fund will generally be suitable only if you are seeking greater principal stability compared to a long-term bond fund or greater income stability compared to a short-term bond fund.

In either case, a bond fund seeking to match the Lehman Bond Index has two important advantages. First, since the bond market is dominated by U.S. Treasury and federal agency issues, it has an extremely high-quality portfolio (averaging AAA), meaning minimal credit risk. (The Lehman Index excludes junk bonds and foreign bonds, substantially eliminating both quality risk and currency risk.) Second, it can operate at the same kind of low expense ratio as stock index funds, especially important for the income-oriented investor.

It is possible to make a reasonably fair comparison between the returns of bond funds and the returns of the Lehman Bond Index. Figure 9-4

TABLE 9-3
Initial Investment of $10,000 (December 31, 1982, to December 31, 1992)

Program	Rate of return	Final value
Lehman Bond Index	+11.7%	$30,270
Average bond fund	+10.2	26,300

illustrates the returns of the Lehman Bond Index versus the aggregate returns achieved by all investment-grade corporate bond funds, GNMA funds, and U.S. government bond funds for the ten-year period ended December 31, 1992. Table 9-3 summarizes the results. The Lehman Bond Index provided an average return of +11.7% per year, generating a final value of $30,270 based on an initial investment of $10,000. For the average traditionally managed bond fund of roughly comparable quality and maturity, the total return was +10.2% annually and the final value was $26,300.

The actual positive margin for a bond index of +1.5% per year exactly matches the theoretical margin of +1.5% accounted for by combining the average bond fund expense ratio of 1.0% plus estimated portfolio transaction costs of 0.5%. While this precise explanation of the difference is impressive, such a conclusion, as in the stock index example, is too facile. Given the challenge of developing a fully comparable group of funds in the diverse bond fund arena, this exactness of fit surely represents a series of modest but offsetting measurement errors.

The manager of a bond index fund will not quite be able to match the index of the bond market, given mutual fund administrative, operating, and transaction costs. If we assume that such costs might total 0.3% per year, the annual return on a bond index fund would have been +11.4% and the final value of a $10,000 initial investment would have been $29,430, still a healthy margin over the traditionally managed bond funds.

Since half of all bond funds carry sales loads, I have also calculated the results achieved by the average bond fund when adjusted for an initial sales charge of 5% (0.5% per year over ten years). In this case, the cumulative fund return falls to +9.7% annually, or +152% in total, reducing the final value of the bond mutual fund investment to $25,240. This shortfall of −1.7% to the +11.4% net return of the index fund, then, magnified by the magic of compounding, reaffirms the need to consider all of the

---

CAVEAT EMPTOR: *Bond Indexing and Your Time Horizon*

Paradoxically, a bond index fund is more complex than its stock index cousin. The stock market, in essence, behaves as one market over the long term, but the bond market behaves as many. A particular target bond index may be longer or shorter in maturity, have a higher or lower interest coupon structure, hold bonds of higher or lower quality than the Lehman Brothers Aggregate Bond Index, or place more or less reliance on mortgage-backed obligations. Before using an index fund that is designed to match the entire investment-grade bond market, you should carefully consider its portfolio characteristics in conjunction with your own time horizon and tolerance for volatility risk. The Lehman Bond Index, in substance, is an appropriate choice for investors with an intermediate-term time horizon and seeking top quality. Index funds using longer-term and shorter-term maturities will likely become available in the years ahead.

---

costs of investing. Indexing seems to work at least as well with bonds as stocks, so bond indexing will probably play a growing role in the financial marketplace.

The trend that has prevailed with the spread of indexing—from the S&P 500 Index to the total stock market, then to its mid-cap and small-cap segments, then to the international arena, then to specific portfolio characteristics or styles, such as growth and value, and then to bonds as well—seems no more than logical. The final step (at least for the moment) would be a *balanced* index fund seeking to combine a total stock market portfolio with a total bond market portfolio, and the first such fund was introduced in 1992.

SUMMARY

The critics of equity indexing—and they are strident and numerous—rarely attack its basic principles and self-evident underpinning. Rather, they attack the S&P 500 Index itself and hypothesize that it cannot provide future relative returns comparable to those of the past. They suggest that it is dominated by large capitalization stocks that provided superior returns only as indexing itself raised the demand for those very stocks, a self-fulfilling prophecy. There is no basis in fact for this challenge; even if it were true, it would lack any relevance since indexing is no longer limited to the use of the S&P 500 Index. If you accept this farfetched thesis, you should simply own an index fund that in turn owns the total stock market.

I would suggest that it will be ever more difficult for equity mutual funds, as a group, to significantly outpace an indexing strategy in the years ahead. The largest 300 institutional money managers now direct the investments of some $2 trillion in common stocks, or about half of the $4.3 trillion market value of the total stock market, a level at which performance differentiation is difficult. The result should be even fewer big winners—and, necessarily, fewer big losers—in the future.

No matter what the critics say, index investing is a compelling manifestation of the basic principle of passive investing: in discrete financial markets—stock or bond, large capitalization or small, international or domestic—inexpensive and unmanaged index funds should regularly and consistently outpace the results achieved in the aggregate by the portfolio managers of mutual funds with comparable objectives. Of course, there are many individual managers who will outpace appropriate market indexes. It seems fair to argue that, before taking costs into account, half will and half will not. But two basic questions remain: (1) Can these managers be identified in advance? (2) Will their superiority be sufficient to overwhelm the costs of acquiring their services? The respective answers are: (1) Only with some combination of judgment and luck. (2) Only in the minority of cases.

Despite the powerful conceptual argument for indexing—supported by strong historical performance data—equity index funds presently account for only about 4% of all equity mutual fund assets, compared to 20% of pension equity fund assets. It is easy to forecast with some confidence continued growth and increased market penetration for mutual fund indexing.

Chapter Ten

Mutual Fund Costs
The Price of Everything

According to Oscar Wilde, a cynic is someone "who knows the price of everything, and the value of nothing." True as this sentiment may be about the evaluation of a Renaissance masterpiece, it hardly applies in the ownership of mutual funds. In no other section of the financial services field are cost and value more closely linked. In the case of mutual funds it might be said that knowing the price of everything reveals the value of everything, since each dollar of cost that you pay reduces your return by a precisely equal amount. This principle does *not* lead to the conclusion that you should always own the lowest-cost mutual fund. It simply makes the point that, under good and bad management alike, a fund provides a gross return that is reduced, dollar for dollar, by the cost incurred in its ownership. Other things being equal, lower costs mean higher returns.

In several previous chapters, I referred to the impact of costs on mutual fund investment returns; however, cost is so central to mutual fund investing that it really deserves its own chapter. During the earlier days of this industry, most mutual funds had reasonably low expense ratios (annual operating expenses usually ranged from 0.60% to 1.00% of a fund's average net assets) and all funds were either load (with sales charges of about 8% on purchases of fund shares) or no-load (without sales charges). Then it was a simple matter to calculate the impact of costs. Today, given the number of pricing schemes that have developed in this creative industry, determining costs is a ponderous task.

Cost is but one of the three sides of the eternal triangle of investing; potential reward and potential risk are the other two. But do not underestimate the importance of cost. Consider Table 10-1, which shows the difference that cost can make in yearly returns and over an entire decade. The differences are as dramatic as they are simple.

TABLE 10-1
Mutual Fund Cost Analysis (Initial Investment of $10,000)

| | | | | Total Accumulations | |
Type of fund	Gross return	Expenses	Net return	One year	Ten years
Money market fund					
Low cost	+5.0%	0.3%	+4.7%	$ 470	$ 5,800
High cost	+5.0	1.0	+4.0	400	4,800
Bond fund					
Low cost	+8.0%	0.5%	+7.5%	$ 750	$10,600
High cost	+8.0	2.0	+6.0	600	7,900
Stock fund					
Low cost	+12.0%	0.6%	+11.4%	$1,140	$19,400
High cost	+12.0	2.5	+9.5	950	14,800

- If a money fund earns a gross return of +5.0%, the fund's net return will be +4.7% if it incurs an annual expense ratio of 0.3%. But the fund's net return will be +4.0% if it incurs a 1.0% expense ratio. A yield of 4.7% provides 18% more dollars than a yield of 4.0% in one year and 21% more dollars over ten years.

- If a bond fund earns a gross return of +8.0%, the fund's net return will be +7.5% if it incurs annual expenses of 0.5%. But the fund's net return will be +6.0% if it incurs expenses of 2.0%. A return of +7.5% provides 25% more dollars than a return of +6.0% in one year and 34% more dollars over ten years.

- If a stock fund earns a gross return of +12.0%, the fund's net return will be +11.4% if it incurs annual expenses of 0.6%. But the fund's net return will be +9.5% if it incurs expenses of 2.5%. A return of +11.4% provides 20% more dollars than a return of +9.5% in one year and 31% more dollars over ten years.

The range of annual costs shown in these examples is by no means extreme, since costs may include both expense ratios and sales loads. In each case, there are many funds available at lower costs than those cited and many funds that incur higher costs.

This chapter, then, focuses exclusively on mutual fund costs. First, I discuss sales charges (including the proliferation of 12b-1 distribution fees) and transaction fees; second, operating expense ratios; third, the invisible costs of fund portfolio transactions; and finally, an integrated cost comparison that considers the two visible costs (sales charges and expense ratios). It is becoming increasingly difficult to separate them.

SALES CHARGES

There are no initial sales charges incurred in the purchase of no-load funds. That may be the only definitive statement that can be made about sales commissions in this industry's increasingly complex cost structure. Nonetheless, no-load fund shareholders often pay for marketing and advertising expenses indirectly in the form of a charge known as a "12b-1" distribution fee (so named because it relates to a particular section of the Investment Company Act of 1940). A 12b-1 fee is an extra fee paid to the fund's management company to help finance the costs of marketing the fund's shares. For no-load funds, these costs are included in the fund's total expense ratio. So we will discuss these often burdensome costs at some length later, in the section on expense ratios.

For load funds, the cost picture gets foggier. Load funds are generally sold through stock brokerage firms, banks, or insurance companies, or directly by their sponsors. In each case, the fund's sponsor pays a commission to induce sales representatives to sell the fund's shares. This practice is not inconsistent with normal business operations and certainly is not subject to criticism in and of itself. The rationale for payment of a load, however, presumes both full disclosure and the ability of the sales representative to provide some combination of initiative, education, service, financial planning, account supervision, fund selection, and asset allocation in such dimension as to offset the negative impact of the sales commission. Only if there is value added is a sales charge worth paying.

This overview merely opens the subject of sales charges, but there is much more. Among the variations of sales charges you will want to consider are the regular load, the contingent deferred sales load, and the low-load.

Regular load. A regular load is an initial sales charge deducted before investment of your money in the fund, formerly in the 8% range but today more commonly in the 4% to 6% range. Most reductions in sales loads have been accompanied by the imposition of 12b-1 distribution fees,

---

CAVEAT EMPTOR: *Sales Loads and Fund Performance*

Sales loads have a significant negative impact on the return you earn in a mutual fund. However, sales loads are almost always totally ignored in the tabulations of fund performance that appear in the financial press, which usually show the fund's performance before such loads are deducted. It is difficult to imagine why this situation has persisted for so long. Its proponents claim the tabulations are intended to measure a portfolio manager's ability, not an investor's return. Besides, they argue, the load would have too much of an impact on a fund's results in short periods. These arguments may be respectable as far as they go, but explicit disclosure that sales charges are excluded and references to their precise amount are virtually nonexistent. You must assume the responsibility for assessing the impact of sales loads on a fund's return. The task is not made easier by the fact that some statistical services use the designation "NL" to cover both pure no-load funds and, somewhat disingenuously, funds that have no *initial* sales load but carry substantial 12b-1 fees and contingent deferred sales loads.

---

thereby shifting some of the distribution costs from the investor who purchases the shares to the fund itself. The fee is paid by the fund's existing shareholders to repay the manager for the cost of bringing in new shareholders. To justify paying a front-end sales load, you must expect to hold the fund's shares for a reasonable period of time. The reason is that a 6% sales load reduces a fund's total return by that amount in a day or a year. Over a period of years, however, the percentage impact of the initial load on the fund's annual return declines (e.g., for a holding period of six years, the fund's total return would be reduced by approximately one percentage point per year).

Contingent deferred sales load (CDSL). A CDSL is a regular load in a different guise. An initial load of, say, 6%, is eliminated entirely and replaced by an annual charge (limited to a maximum of 1%, including a service fee of 0.25%) on all the fund's assets. Then, to ensure that the total load paid by each investor in the fund still comes to at least 6% (since the sales representative receives the commission in advance), a deferred sales load (or exit fee) is incurred by each investor, but it is reduced by

TABLE 10–2
Contingent Deferred Sales Load

Year	Annual 12b-1 fee	Cumulative 12b-1 fee	Applicable exit fee	Cumulative sales load
1	1%	1%	5%	6%
2	1	2	4	6
3	1	3	3	6
4	1	4	2	6
5	1	5	1	6
6	1	6	0	6
7	1	7	0	7*
8	1	8	0	8*
9	1	9	0	9*
10	1	10	0	10*

*In some funds, the maximum load is limited to 6%.

1% for each year in which the shares are held. Table 10–2 illustrates how the typical plan works.

It is a conceptually simple scheme, although I have never seen the CDSL rationale explained as clearly in a fund's prospectus. Table 10–2 assumes that the fund sponsor receives the annual 12b-1 fee for as long as the shares are held, so the effective load continues to rise like clockwork with each passing year. If you are a young investor purchasing a fund for your retirement account, your cumulative fee—taking into account total asset-based sales charges and service fees—could exceed 15% or more of the amount initially invested.

This burdensome practice is diminishing under tough new securities regulations that seek to limit total sales charges to a certain percentage of fund sales. (No one knows whether this complex formula will in fact increase or reduce the fee as a percentage of fund assets.) In some cases, however, a separate series of the fund is created without the 12b-1 fee, and an exchange into this series is automatically made after (using the above example) the investor has paid the 6% total. In any event, you will have paid the piper, although to a lesser extent than if the cumulative 12b-1 fee were unlimited. CDSLs are in fact exit loads, and you should be aware that large commissions are payable if shares are redeemed in the early years. The overhang of this cost significantly impairs your investment flexibility.

CAVEAT EMPTOR: *Alphabet Soup*

In recent years, investors' negative perception of the payment of front-end loads has grown. Investors, and sales representatives, seem to perceive a benefit in paying the same sales charge, but in annual increments. Many brokerage firms have responded by offering you a choice. Funds first became available in two series: Class A shares if you desired a front-end load, Class B shares if you desired a continuing load plus a CDSL. Other series are now emerging, including Class C shares, available to brokerage firm employees who are unwilling to pay loads on their employers' funds, and Class D shares, so-called level-load shares, with a 1% load and an ongoing 12b-1 fee of 1%. Investors in these "alphabet soup" funds should be fully aware of the financial consequences of each option to ensure that they have selected the least burdensome plan.

Low load. A low-load fund has a below-normal initial sales charge, usually in the range of 1% to 3.5%. While a low load is a lesser charge, it can have a significant impact on the return achieved by a short-term investor in a stock fund and even by a longer-term investor in a bond fund. (A 3.5% low load on a bond fund held for five years would alone reduce the yield by 0.7% per year—say, from 7.0% to 6.3%.) The fact is that *any* load should be considered consequential. Low-load funds should be clearly distinguished from no-load funds.

Loads on Reinvested Dividends

There is yet another form of sales charge, a subtle one that competition and common sense have almost, but not quite, driven out of practice. Some funds continue to charge sales loads when a shareholder's dividends are reinvested in the fund. Somewhat euphemistically, this practice is called "dividend reinvestment at offering price." Presumably there is no sales effort required to sell the reinvestment of these dividends each month or quarter. A sales charge of 6% on the reinvestment of dividends would reduce the advertised yield on a bond fund from, say, 8.0% to 7.5%. Of course, the sponsor publicizes only the higher yield. It is difficult to imagine why investors would own shares in a fund with such hidden

---

CAVEAT EMPTOR: *When Never to Pay a Sales Load*

The oppressive impact of the sales load increases as (1) the price stability of a fund increases and (2) the ability of a portfolio manager to differentiate the fund's returns from those achieved by other advisers decreases. At one extreme, no money market fund carries a front-end load. (However, many assess 12b-1 fees.) At the other extreme, nearly 60% of all common stock funds are load funds, which presumably have the opportunity to differentiate themselves by providing premium performance to justify the load. But there is absolutely no evidence that the returns on stock funds that charge a load are sufficient to overcome the drag of their sales charges. It seems unlikely that it could happen, unless the existence of a sales force somehow endows a portfolio manager with superior stock-picking ability, a farfetched notion. In any event, it is a mystery why an otherwise intelligent investor would pay a load on funds that meet these two criteria. Certainly, most short-term bond funds (especially those investing in U.S. government and agency issues) meet both criteria. The second criterion would be met by funds investing principally in intermediate- or long-term U.S. Treasury obligations, insured long-term municipal bonds and, to some extent, GNMA mortgage-backed securities. Sales charges on funds whose portfolios are locked in to specific, definable classes of securities should be viewed with skepticism.

---

charges. But if you do own such a fund you should, almost without exception, take your dividends in cash and reinvest them in a comparable no-load fund in which such charges will not be assessed.

Transaction fees. Sales loads are by far the predominant form of transaction charge applicable to fund shares (that is, charges paid *directly* by the investor making the transaction, as distinct from the fund itself). These loads are usually shared by a fund's sponsor, distributor, and sales representative. In that sense, they contrast with two other transaction charges: the redemption charge (often 1% of assets), paid when shares are liquidated or exchanged into shares of another fund, and the transaction charge, paid when fund shares are purchased. Both charges are normally paid not to a sales representative but to the fund itself. (You should find out which is the case.) Here, the costs of selling portfolio securities (in the first case) and purchasing portfolio securities (in the second) are borne by the investor making the transaction, rather than by the fund itself (i.e., all of the shareholders who remain in the fund). These charges—provided they are *paid to* *the fund itself*—should not be considered as sales loads in any sense. They have the effect of indicating to existing shareholders that the costs incurred in investing additional cash flows (or in liquidating securities when there are cash outflows) will tend not to dilute their interests. So it is hard to see that transaction fees are anything but equitable both to new and existing shareholders.

EXPENSE RATIOS

The expense ratio usually represents the most significant cost you will incur in owning a mutual fund. Essentially, the expense ratio represents the total cost of ownership (as distinct from acquisition) of a fund's shares. As I noted earlier, each increase in a fund's unit operating expenses reduces total return by an identical amount. If a fund earns +10% before a 1% expense ratio, it will provide net earnings of +9% for the shareholder after expenses. There are four major expense categories that comprise a fund's total expenses, three of which involve services that are generally necessary in a fund's operations.

Investment advisory fees.   The first major expense category is the investment advisory fee (often called the management fee) paid to the fund's adviser for portfolio supervision and for general management of the fund's affairs. This fee exists to compensate the adviser for the expenses it incurs for providing its services, plus a profit that often amounts to half of the fee or more. Advisory fees range from 0.50% to 1.00% of average fund assets. Sometimes the fee entails an incentive/penalty provision, resulting in an increased fee if the fund outperforms the returns of a particular market index or other appropriate benchmark and a commensurately reduced fee if the fund underperforms these same standards. While it is doubtful that an incentive/penalty fee enhances a fund's performance, it is difficult to argue with its fairness in aligning the interests of the management company with those of the fund shareholders.

Administrative costs.   The second expense category is the cost of administration, incurred largely to provide recordkeeping and transaction services to fund shareholders. Sometimes these costs represent additional fees paid to the fund's adviser itself, on which it may make an additional profit. Other times, the fees are paid to banks and fund service

---

CAVEAT EMPTOR: *The Price of Poker*

Recordkeeping costs of mutual funds are shared equally by all investors in the fund, irrespective of the size of their accounts. Assuming the average account balance in a fund is $10,000 and the cost of account maintenance is $30 per account, each investor in the fund pays an annual cost of 0.30% of assets. However, the actual cost incurred equals 1.00% for a small shareholder with $3,000 invested in the fund and only 0.06% for a large shareholder with $50,000 invested. Given these differences, some fund sponsors are establishing new funds for larger investors, to attract these valuable accounts. Such funds can provide an additional cost saving of perhaps 0.24% per year (0.30% minus 0.06%). Given the economies applicable to large accounts, this price segmentation will doubtless proliferate. The price of poker is going down.

---

organizations, which provide such services independently. These costs usually range from 0.20% to 0.40% of average fund assets.

Other operating expenses. The third expense category, "other operating expenses," includes charges incurred directly by the fund itself for such items as custodial fees, state and local taxes, legal and audit expenses, and directors' fees. These costs normally range from 0.10% to 0.30% of average fund assets. Combining these three expense categories would suggest that the typical fund's operating expense ratio ranges from 0.80% to 1.70% annually, before adding in any 12b-1 distribution fees.

12b-1 distribution fee. The fourth category of fund expenses is worthy of special comment. Unlike the first three, it is not essential to a fund's operations. It is a special charge known as a 12b-1 distribution fee, and normally ranges from about 0.25% to 1.00% of a fund's assets. Some 2,600 mutual funds—more than 60% of all funds in existence—assess 12b-1 fees, which are spent on advertising, marketing, and distribution services or, as noted, on commissions to sales representatives. The primary reason the fund's adviser imposes these fees is to increase fund assets in order to earn higher management fees—the better, presumably, to hire a larger and more competent staff and/or to increase the profits earned on the business of managing the fund.

CAVEAT EMPTOR: *A Rule of Reason*

While our focus is on expenses relative to fund assets, you should also consider the actual dollar amount of expenses that a fund incurs to see if it meets some "rule of reason." In the case of certain very large funds, the aggregate dollars do not seem to meet this test. For example, in 1992 a large equity fund paid a fee of $136,278,000 to its investment adviser for picking stocks, plus a performance fee of $24,965,000 for having picked them well. A large GNMA fund paid its adviser $58,948,000 for picking mortgage-backed securities whose interest and principal payments are guaranteed by the U.S. Treasury. A large "government income plus" fund owned only a handful of U.S. Treasury and agency obligations, yet paid an annual advisory fee of $18,512,000 (after graciously rebating $616,000 to the fund), plus 12b-1 fees of another $26,633,000. It is difficult to imagine how fees of these dimensions could be required to compensate, in the first case, a single portfolio manager and the attendant security analysis and research support; or in the second and third cases, one or more portfolio managers who clearly need undertake no credit research, given that none is necessary to evaluate the credit of the U.S. Treasury. Such fees cannot be justified by the costs incurred. They can be justified only by the principle that the fund's sponsor is entitled to amass most of the compelling economies of scale that exist in fund management to its own benefit, rather than sharing them with the fund shareholders.

Nonetheless, this argument is rarely presented to fund shareholders. Rather, these other arguments are typically set forth. (1) The fund needs to grow to an asset size at which it becomes economically viable. (2) Without distribution facilities, the fund would have to incur the costs of gradually liquidating portfolio securities. (3) The fund's shareholders will receive certain economies of scale if fund assets rise and management fee *rates* decline.

There are any number of problems with these arguments, but I shall mention just three of the most obvious. First, the larger fund groups (with $500 million of assets or more) are already quite economically viable. Second, the costs of liquidating portfolio securities would normally be trivial relative to the amount of the 12b-1 fee. In any event, they would certainly be of no greater magnitude than the costs of *purchasing* portfolio securities if the 12b-1 fee succeeds in bringing additional assets into the

---

CAVEAT EMPTOR: *Hidden Distribution Fees*

The fact that a mutual fund subsidizes the distribution of its shares with a 12b-1 fee should not be taken to indicate that a fund without a 12b-1 fee does not subsidize distribution. Sometimes the distribution costs are simply paid out of the adviser's management fee, or, as the adviser would have it, out of its profits. Either way, fund shareholders pay the bill. Whatever the case may be, you would be unwise to favor a fund with a 1.25% advisory fee (much of which may be used to finance marketing activities) over a fund with a 0.75% advisory fee plus a 0.50% distribution fee. It is the 1.25% total that counts.

CAVEAT EMPTOR: *A Right to Life*

Taken to its logical conclusion, the argument for 12b-1 fees suggests that a fund must grow and that no fund should be allowed to die. If distribution of shares is faltering and capital outflow is rising, so the rationale goes, then simply spend more money on distribution and never mind that poor performance or poor markets may be the culprit. This argument presumes that funds with 12b-1 fees enjoy an increase in sales of their fund's shares, but there is no evidence whatsoever that this is the case. It also presumes that, unlike any other type of corporation in America, a mutual fund has some sort of right to life, no matter what.

---

fund. Third, the reduction of management fee rates as fund assets rise is usually disproportionately small relative to the amount of the 12b-1 fee. For example, a 10-basis-point (0.10%) reduction of the fee on *additional* assets attracted to the fund, compared to a 12b-1 fee of 0.25% on *all* of the fund's assets, will never reduce the fund's expense ratio. Bigger funds are not, as such, better, except insofar as they generate economies of scale to the shareholders. While management resources are indeed larger for the larger fund complexes, it is clearly more difficult to manage a large portfolio than a small one. The evidence suggests that size is only one of many differentiating factors—sometimes favorable, sometimes not—in the comparative returns that funds achieve.

Taking into account *all* operating expenses incurred by the fund—but excluding the impact of sales loads—Figure 10-1 shows the profile of expense ratios in stock, bond, and money market funds. As you can see, there is an ample selection of funds with low expense ratios in each category. The availability of funds with high expenses is rife, especially in the equity fund arena. The need to maximize current yield (as distinct from total return) has helped to constrain fees among bond and money market funds, so it is in these segments that holding costs to rock-bottom levels is most important.

Given the clear financial impact of expenses on mutual fund performance, along with the exponential growth of industry assets, we might expect that fund expense ratios would have declined over the years. However, the reverse has proved true: expense ratios have risen. Figure 10-2 shows the annual expense ratios of common stock mutual funds since 1961.

As the figure shows, the expense ratio of the average stock fund rose from 0.70% of assets in 1961 to 1.50% in 1992, a more than twofold increase. Equity fund assets rose from $23 billion to $463 billion during the period, a 20-fold increase. Crudely applying the higher expense ratio to a much higher asset base, the expenses paid by fund shareholders may have risen by as much as 50-fold.

To a small extent, this increase in aggregate expenses may reflect a higher cost (per dollar of fund assets) of mutual fund administrative and recordkeeping services. But to a far greater extent it reflects (1) a plethora of fee rate increases implemented by fund management companies and (2) the formation of new funds with higher management fee structures. The economies of scale in managing money are enormous. For example, holding the expense ratio constant at 1.0%, if an equity fund grows from $50 million to $1 billion the fees paid to the investment adviser would rise from $500,000 to $10 million. It is almost inconceivable that the costs paid by the fund's shareholders to the investment adviser could increase nearly that much. What we are witnessing is not only the failure of managers to share economies of scale with fund shareholders but also their penchant to increase costs to fund investors at an even faster rate than fund asset growth.

THE INVISIBLE COST

Perhaps surprisingly, there is yet another category of expenses borne by funds. So far I have been describing the visible costs incurred by mutual

FIGURE 10–1
Distribution of Expense Ratios (1992)

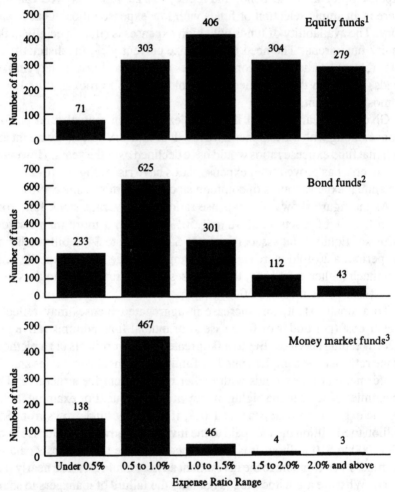

1. Includes asset allocation and equity-oriented balanced funds.
2. Includes income-oriented balanced funds.
3. Excludes institutional money market funds.

funds. There is one large *invisible* cost, often ignored because of its invisibility. It is the cost the fund incurs in executing its portfolio transactions. Buying and selling stocks and bonds can be an expensive business. This cost includes not only commissions but also dealer bid-asked spreads and

FIGURE 10–2
Equity Fund Expense Ratios (1961–92)

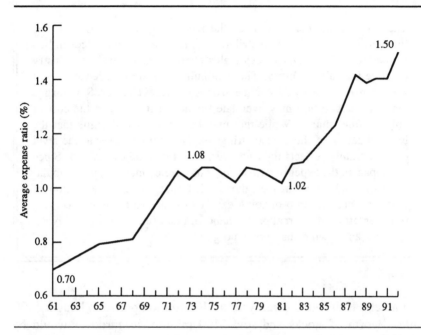

what is called "market impact," meaning that the buyer of a stock tends to push its price up and the seller to push its price down.

Transaction costs are difficult if not impossible to calculate with precision. They vary widely depending on the liquidity and marketability of a fund's portfolio securities. A variety of studies suggest that they approximate 0.5% to 2% of fund assets per year, with higher costs for smaller funds with high rates of portfolio turnover and lower costs for larger funds with lower turnover rates. That this cost, however invisible, is automatically reflected in the fund's stated performance results is no reason to ignore it in considering the drag on return that might occur in a mutual fund's future performance. The important thing is that you should be aware when you compare fund expense ratios that the expense figures do not include transaction charges the fund will necessarily incur.

Portfolio turnover in common stock mutual funds is a good bit higher than—perhaps double—the turnover rates of other large institutional accounts such as pension funds. Turnover is basically defined as the lesser of purchases *or* sales of portfolio investments as a percentage of average

---

CAVEAT EMPTOR: *It's an Ill Wind*

There is yet another reason for the rise in expense ratios. It is the imposition of asset-based distribution (12b-1) and service fees in lieu of the transaction-related fees (sales charges) that were the industry practice for half a century. The continuing rise in expense ratios is to some degree offset by the decline in one-time sales charges. Some argue that this substitution may overstate the actual increase in the cost of holding fund shares. While that may be true, I would argue that the internalization of these costs brings expense ratios closer to the level that accurately reflects the true overall cost of fund ownership. Since the impact of the expense ratio is understandable, and since most tabulations of fund performance ignore sales charges, any translation of front-end charges into ongoing expenses makes for a more accurate representation of the real performance mutual funds deliver to investors. It's an ill wind that blows no good.

---

fund assets. If during a given year a $100 million portfolio bought $100 million worth of stocks and sold $100 million, its turnover would be calculated as 100%. However, the fund in fact executed $200 million of purchases and sales in the aggregate. If transactions costs (commissions plus market impact) were 0.6% of the combined figure, there would be a drag equal to 1.2% of fund assets.

Here's a good rule of thumb for determining the potential drag on performance from transaction costs. (1) Double the fund's reported turnover, (2) multiply that figure by estimated transaction costs of 0.6%, and (3) calculate the resultant number as a percentage of the fund's average assets. Because of the way turnover is calculated, this rule of thumb will *understate* the transaction costs incurred by funds with very large capital inflows (generating additional purchase transactions) or very large outflows (generating additional sale transactions). To fairly approximate the impact of this cost, you should know the fund's turnover in each of the previous three years.

Considering the impact of portfolio transaction costs is not to suggest that the portfolio manager may not be engaged in an ongoing process of selling less attractive securities and recycling the proceeds into more attractive issues. Sometimes portfolio managers are successful at doing

CAVEAT EMPTOR: *Another Kind of Expense Ratio*

There are in fact two methods of calculating mutual fund expense ratios. One, almost universally accepted and the method I use in this chapter, is the ratio of fund expenses to average fund *assets*. The other, almost universally ignored, is the ratio of fund expenses to fund gross *income*. The latter ratio simply shows the percentage of your income that goes to fund management fees and operating expenses. These examples of the ratio of fund expenses to gross income are based on 1992 data:

Fund category	Percent of Assets			Percent of gross income consumed by expenses
	Gross income	Expenses	Net income	
Stock funds	2.79%	1.50%	1.29%	54%
Balanced funds	5.35	1.27	4.08	24
Bond funds	8.75	1.07	7.68	12
Money market funds	3.48	0.62	2.86	18

Note that, even for the most income-oriented funds, expenses consume a substantial amount of your investment income. In this context, choosing between funds with high and low expense ratios makes an important difference in the amount of income you receive. This table shows the fund expense ratio analysis using the gross income yields shown above:

Fund type	Gross income	Low Expenses				Higher Expenses			Increase in income in low-expense fund
		Expense ratio	Net income	Percent of income consumed		Expense ratio	Net income	Percent of income consumed	
Stock	2.79%	0.70%	2.09%	25%		2.00%	0.79%	72%	+165%
Balanced	5.35	0.60	4.75	11		1.50	3.85	28	+23
Bond	8.75	0.50	8.25	6		1.40	7.35	16	+12
Money market	3.48	0.40	3.08	11		1.00	2.48	29	+24

Particularly if you depend on investment income to help meet your retirement expenses, the table poses the question: "Why should you relinquish 30% of your income when perfectly good alternatives exist at a cost that consumes barely more than 10% of your income?" It is a rational question that demands a rational answer.

CAVEAT EMPTOR: *Searching for Precision*

It is no mean task to calculate the costs of the portfolio transactions in which a given fund engages. Commission costs vary with the size of each transaction and may range from as little as 0.1% on larger transactions to 0.5% or even more on smaller ones. Market impact costs—pushing prices upward when buying and downward when selling—are probably significantly larger, particularly among impatient portfolio managers demanding hair-trigger executions. A 1993 study in the *Financial Analysts Journal* suggested that the measurable cost of an average transaction was equivalent to about 0.6%, depending on the factors outlined above. Assuming that each purchase transaction is accompanied by a sale transaction, the total transaction cost would represent about 1.2% of the combined purchase and sale. These rough numbers are probably as close to reality as is possible, given the wide variety of stock prices, timing, order sizes, markets, and types of trades. Many other studies suggest substantially higher transaction costs, ranging from 1.0% to 2.0%. However, I rely on the conservative cost figure, 0.6% of the dollar amount of the transaction. So for an average fund with 75% turnover, transaction costs would represent an annual drag on performance, other factors held equal, of about 0.9%. While many individual funds endeavor to calculate transaction costs, few publicly reveal the data. In any event, precision is not possible. But neither is it necessary.

---

so, and sometimes they are not. The point is, for funds with high or even average turnover, transaction costs can have a major impact on the cost of doing business. Given the imprecision of this measure, however, I have reluctantly excluded turnover-related costs from the calculation of aggregate mutual fund costs in Figure 10–3.

TOTAL COSTS PAID BY SHAREHOLDERS

In the final analysis, you must determine the total costs involved in the ownership of fund shares before making your investment decisions. I shall now deal solely with the *visible* costs. Since operating expenses are paid annually but sales charges are paid only when shares are purchased or redeemed, the only way to integrate the two costs is to assume a certain

FIGURE 10-3
Annual Costs of Mutual Fund Ownership (Three-Year Holding Period Excludes Money Market Funds)

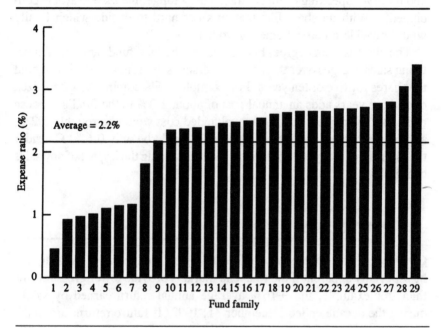

holding period for the investment and then "amortize" the sales charge over this period. A 5% sales charge would represent an annual cost of about 1% per year if you held your shares for five years.

The SEC has made this exercise fairly simple. As I noted in Chapter 8, the SEC requires each mutual fund to set out in a table at the front of its prospectus the fund's annual operating costs in each major expense category as well as the sum total and the impact of the initial sales charge on investors who own the fund for holding periods of one, three, five, and ten years. In mid-1992, *Money* magazine evaluated the prospectuses of each of the stock funds and bond funds in the 29 largest complexes and calculated the average costs of ownership, assuming the fund shares are held for three years. The *Money* analysis is shown in Figure 10-3.

The chart reflects five principal facts: (1) The average cost of owning a mutual fund is about 2.2% per year. (2) In the highest-cost fund family, investors incurred annual costs of almost 3.5%. (3) In 21 of the 29 largest mutual fund families, investors incurred annual costs ranging from about

2.0% to 3.0%. (4) In only six fund families were the annual costs as low as about 1.0%. (5) For the lowest-cost fund family, the annual cost was about 0.4%. Speaking of that extraordinary range, the *Money* article concluded, "With numbers like that, it's not hard to decide which family would provide a better home for your money."

The chart is, to a degree, biased against the load fund families. Amortizing sales charges over three years overstates the annual costs if you hold the shares for five or ten years. For example, a 6% commission amortized over three years adds an annual cost of about 2.0% to the fund's expense ratio. But over five years the annual added cost would be roughly 1.2%, and over ten years the annual added cost would be only 0.6%. Consider the likely length of your holding period in assessing the impact of any sales charge.

SUMMARY

Clearly high costs impose a significant drag on fund returns. The drag will be especially apparent if the financial markets provide lower gross returns than, for example, the +16% average annual return earned by stocks during the decade ended December 31, 1992. If future returns are in the area of +10%, a 2.2% annual cost will consume fully 22% of the market's return; a cost of 0.4% will consume but 4% of the return. So costs matter. You should be fully aware of them and be concerned about their potential impact on your investment returns.

If the old saw that you get exactly what you pay for were true in the mutual fund arena, costs might not matter. But the fact is that the reverse is true: the more you pay, the less you earn. After all is said and done, higher costs always entail relatively lower returns in money market funds and generally do so in bond funds. For stock funds, there is simply no credible evidence that paying higher costs results in receiving higher returns. Oscar Wilde's cynic was on the right track: to realize maximum value, the mutual fund investor must know the cost of everything.

Chapter Eleven

Taxes and Mutual Funds
The Power to Destroy

"The power to tax involves the power to destroy." So wrote John Marshall, Chief Justice of the United States. While there was no federal income tax when he penned those words back in 1819, such a tax was instituted in 1913, and Mr. Chief Justice Marshall's warning was extended to include individual taxpayers. It would be wonderful to return to a world without income taxes, but that would be an unrealistic expectation. So this chapter will examine (1) the impact of taxes on the rates of return earned by investors, (2) some special tax considerations involved in owning mutual fund shares, and (3) some ways to defer or even to eliminate income taxes using investment programs readily available through mutual funds.

TAXES ON INVESTMENT RETURNS

I shall begin this chapter with Table 11-1, which shows the powerful impact of taxes on the returns generated in the modern era by our three basic classes of financial assets. Over the long term, taxes have consumed as much as 25% of the nominal returns on financial assets. However, investors live today, and not "on average" over past years. The highest marginal federal tax rate was 25% in 1926. The rate reached 94% by 1940, was reduced to 70% in 1965, to 50% in 1982, to 28% in 1988, and then was raised to 31% in 1991. In 1993, the maximum marginal rate is expected to rise to 39.6% for investors with the highest incomes. We may not see rates as low as those in force from 1988 to 1992 soon again.

Of course, the tax impact is made far more serious by the fact that you must pay taxes on *nominal* returns (before inflation), but taxes are deducted, in effect, from *real* returns (after inflation). Table 11-2 shows the impact of federal taxes on financial investments, assuming a +7%

CAVEAT EMPTOR: *A Fool for a Client*

In this chapter, I intend to sketch the structure of various tax-deferred and tax-exempt investment programs available through mutual funds, as well as certain tax disadvantages of mutual funds that you should consider. They say that "a lawyer who acts as his own counsel has a fool for a client." In this same spirit, you should know that I am not a lawyer, and only a foolish investor would want to be my client. Given the great complexity of federal and state tax codes, it goes without saying that you should seek tax advice only from qualified professionals.

TABLE 11-1
Real After-Tax Returns (1926–92)

	Nominal return	Tax impact	After-tax nominal return	Inflation impact	After-tax real return
Common stocks	+10.3%	−1.1%	+9.2%	−3.1%	+6.1%
Long-term bonds	+ 4.8	−1.2	+3.6	−3.1	+0.5
Cash reserves	+ 3.7	−0.9	+2.8	−3.1	−0.3

income return for bonds and a +10% total return for stocks (+3% income and +7% capital growth). The table also assumes that capital appreciation is realized at different junctures. I call your attention to the different returns earned on stocks through the various investment strategies.

- The first reflects a high turnover strategy. It assumes you realize and are taxed on all of your capital gains each year like clockwork.

- The second reflects a more restrained turnover strategy. It assumes you pay income taxes on annual dividends earned but realize no capital gains until the end of year ten, at which point all of the accumulated gains are realized and taxed.

- The third reflects a zero portfolio turnover strategy. It assumes you pay income taxes each year on dividends earned but die holding your original portfolio. Then, at least under present tax law, your heirs get a stepped-up cost basis, and thus a portfolio

TABLE 11-2
Impact of Federal Taxes on Stock and Bond Returns

| | | Stocks* Realization of Capital Gains | | |
	Bonds	*Annually (high)†*	*Tenth year (low)†*	*At death (zero)†*
Pretax nominal return	+7.0%	+10.0%	+10.0%	+10.0%
Taxes on income	−2.3	−1.0	−1.0	−1.0
Taxes on capital gains	0.0	−2.0	−1.6	0.0
After-tax nominal return	+4.7%	+7.0%	+7.4%	+9.0%
Inflation rate	−3.0	−3.0	−3.0	−3.0
After-tax real return	+1.7%	+4.0%	+4.4%	+6.0%
Pretax real return	+4.0%	+7.0%	+7.0%	+7.0%
Taxes as percent of real return	58%	43%	36%	14%

*Dividend yield of 3%; capital growth of +7%. Table assumes a 33% marginal tax rate for income and 28% for capital gains.
†Rate of portfolio turnover.

with no unrealized appreciation. This tax nuance gives new, if ironic, meaning to the phrase, "going to one's reward."

Table 11-2 shows that the combination of taxes and inflation has a truly staggering impact on the average annual returns achieved from bonds, composed entirely of taxable income. In this example, taxes consume 58% of the pretax real return on bonds each year. At the other extreme, for the buy-and-hold equity investor, taxes consume less than 15% of the pretax real return. For the two groups of equity investors realizing gains during a decade, taxes consume 43% of the return for the high-turnover investor and 36% of the return for the low-turnover investor.

While it is almost certain that the assumptions in Table 11-2 will be wrong, we have no way of knowing whether returns and tax rates will be higher or lower than those shown. Nonetheless, Table 11-3 illustrates the ten-year accumulations based on the assumed after-tax real returns, applied to an initial investment of $10,000.

In a sense, even this gloomy picture is too kind, because many financial instruments (among them certificates of deposit, U.S. Treasury bills, money market funds, and short-term bond funds) may have such low nominal returns that their real after-tax returns are negative. For example,

TABLE 11-3
Final Value of Initial Investment of $10,000 (Ten-year period)

| | | Stocks* Realization of Capital Gains | | |
	Bonds	Annually (high)†	Tenth year (low)†	At death (zero)†
Pretax nominal value	$19,670	$25,940	$25,940	$25,940
After-tax real value	11,840	14,800	15,380	17,910

*Same assumptions as Table 11-2.
†Rate of portfolio turnover.

a 33% tax rate would reduce a yield of 4.0% on a Treasury bill to 2.7%. If this 2.7% yield were earned during a time when the inflation rate was 3.0%, the real after-tax return would be a loss of -0.3% annually. And economists wonder why America's savings rate is so low.

TAXES PAID BY MUTUAL FUND SHAREHOLDERS

The impact of taxes on mutual fund shareholders varies widely. Of the industry's total assets of $1.582 trillion on December 31, 1992, $352 billion were held in qualified retirement and pension plans, all of which are not subject to current income taxes. In addition, $291 billion comprised municipal bond and money market funds, which provide tax-exempt income. (Municipal bond fund capital gains are fully taxable.)

Even if you own fund investments in these two categories (representing combined assets of $643 billion, or 41% of the industry), you will need to understand the basic elements of mutual fund taxation. Mutual funds pass along to shareholders each year all interest and dividends from net investment income and any net realized capital gains. Since the funds themselves are, as a rule, not subject to federal taxes, when you receive these payments from a fund you must pay taxes as if you held the portfolio securities directly, with the fund simply acting as an intermediary.

If you are a bond fund shareholder, the tax situation is substantially the same as if you held the bonds directly. The interest income is fully taxed in both cases, although in the case of the fund, it is the net interest income after fund expenses that is taxable. A significant difference, however, is that if you buy bonds at par and hold them to maturity, you eliminate the possibility of realizing capital gains or losses. A bond fund, on the other hand, buys and sells bonds as cash flows into and out of the fund and as its manager alters the structure and composition of the fund's portfolio. So, in periods following sharp declines in interest rates (resulting in higher bond prices), bond funds may well realize and distribute capital gains, in some cases without any deliberate intention of doing so. While such gains may be modest in a given year and may not recur, if you are a bond fund shareholder you should not ignore them.

If you are an equity fund shareholder, the tax situation with respect to income dividends is no different from the treatment of bond interest. Taxes are payable on net dividend income, after fund expenses. However, the remainder of an equity fund's return consists of capital appreciation, typically taxed (when gains are actually realized) at lower rates than dividend income. As shown in Table 11-2, your total return as an equity fund investor is taxed at a lower effective rate than your total return as a bond fund investor.

At this point, the subject gets even more complicated. Mutual funds are, in essence, managed as if they are tax-exempt investment pools. Most portfolio managers ignore the tax impact of their investment decisions for three principal reasons. First, the managers are evaluated in terms of the total return that they achieve for the fund. For better or for worse, total return is what investors perceive as the ultimate measure of a manager's ability. This return is consistently presented without consideration of potential tax liabilities. Second, calculating the impact of taxes is problematic, since fund shareholders may be in high tax brackets or low, or may earn returns that are tax deferred or tax exempt. Third, there is no evidence that investors consider potential capital gains taxes as a negative factor in selecting funds, so the realization of capital gains has had surprisingly little impact in the fund marketplace.

SPECIAL TAX CONSIDERATIONS FOR MUTUAL FUND INVESTORS

Given these circumstances, there is a potential, if little recognized, disadvantage that is part and parcel of mutual fund ownership. It is that mutual funds tend to realize capital gains over time and then distribute them, while

CAVEAT EMPTOR: *Built-in Capital Gains*

You should not purchase the shares of a mutual fund without being aware of two highly significant figures: (1) the capital gains that have been realized but not yet distributed by the fund and (2) the unrealized capital appreciation or depreciation in the fund's portfolio. Both figures should be available on request from the fund's sponsor.

1. **Realized capital gains.** If you are a taxable investor, you should *never* purchase the shares of a fund immediately before it distributes a substantial capital gain (or, for that matter, a substantial income dividend). While the total value of your investment would be the same after the "ex-dividend" date as before, that value would be effectively reduced by the taxes incurred on the distribution. Assume that a fund with a net asset value of $10.00 per share distributes a $1.00 per share capital gain. Other factors remaining equal, the fund's net asset value automatically drops to $9.00 per share; however, including the capital gains distribution of $1.00, there is no change in the adjusted net asset value of each share. But a federal tax of $0.28 per share must then be paid, leaving an adjusted net asset value of $9.72. There is no reason to accept this penalty; simply wait until after the ex-dividend date to invest your assets. Waiting a few days to invest is only common sense; waiting a few months may or may not be profitable depending on the increase or decrease in the fund's net asset value. Whatever the case, you should carefully assess the amount of a fund's realized gain when you are considering the purchase of the fund's shares.

2. **Unrealized capital gains.** You should also be aware of the amount of unrealized gains in the fund's portfolio, which may later be translated into taxable realized gains, or unrealized losses which may be used to offset future realized capital gains. If you purchase shares in a fund with a $10.00 net asset value and a cost basis of $8.00 per share, ultimately the $2.00 gain is likely to be realized and distributed, and you will be subject to taxes when it is. Alternatively, if the net asset value is $10.00 and the cost basis is $12.00, the fund can (during the subsequent five years) realize $2.00 of gains, none of which need be distributed or taxed. In an extreme example, assuming each fund realized an additional $2.00 of gains, the first fund might distribute $4.00 of gains and the latter nothing. Although most comparisons are unlikely to be that extreme, you should consider the potential tax liability or the potential tax benefit of a fund, by ascertaining the cost basis of the fund's shares.

TABLE 11-4
Impact of Taxes on Capital Returns (Ten Years Ended December 31, 1992)

	Fund A	Fund B	Fund C
Percent of gains realized	96%	41%	13%
A. Before taxes			
Initial investment	$10,000	$10,000	$10,000
Capital gains distributions	18,211	7,830	2,450
Unrealized capital gains	850	11,070	16,460
Increase in value	$19,061	$18,900	$18,900
Final before-tax value	$29,061	$28,900	$28,900
B. After taxes			
Initial investment	$10,000	$10,000	$10,000
Capital gains distributions	$15,834	$7,288	$2,411
Tax on distributions (28%)	−4,434	−2,041	−675
Unrealized capital gains	660	10,488	16,132
Increase in value	$12,060	$15,735	$17,868
Final after-tax value	$22,060	$25,735	$27,868
Rate of capital return			
Before taxes	+11.3%	+11.2%	+11.2%
After taxes	+ 8.2	+ 9.9	+10.8

investors in individual securities can, by holding on to them, defer the realization of gains indefinitely, and at death eliminate all unrealized gains by conveying the assets to their heirs at a stepped-up cost basis.

The impact of any acceleration in the realization of capital gains should be taken, generally speaking, as a negative factor. As is the case with dividend income, when capital gains are realized, taxes are incurred. The 1982–92 decade provides a good illustration of the arithmetic of capital gains realization. Table 11–4 shows the results of an initial investment of $10,000 in the shares of three mutual funds with virtually identical capital returns, selected to illustrate actual divergences in the extent to which their capital gains were realized. Part A of the table reflects the funds' results assuming that no taxes are paid on their annual capital gains distributions. Part B of the table assumes that the tax liability is paid each year from the proceeds of the capital gains distributions, with the remainder reinvested in additional shares of the fund.

TABLE 11–5
Impact of Taxes on Capital Returns (Ten Years Ended December 31, 1992)

	Fund A	Fund B	Fund C
Percent of gains realized	96%	41%	13%
Final after-tax value (before sale)	$22,060	$25,735	$27,868
Unrealized capital gains	660	10,488	16,132
Tax liability (28%)	−185	−2,936	−4,516
Final after-tax value (after sale)	$21,875	$22,799	$23,352
Rate of capital return	+8.1%	+8.6%	+8.9%

As you can see in Table 11–4, in each case the full capital return is not available if you are a taxable investor. Unsurprisingly, the after-tax return rises as the extent of capital gains realization declines; the after-tax annual return of +10.8% for Fund C (low gains) exceeds the +8.2% after-tax return on Fund A (high gains) by 32%. The +9.9% after-tax return on Fund B, with roughly half of its gains realized and half unrealized (the more typical case), falls between the other two fund returns.

If we consider the *potential* tax liability that exists on the three funds the return gap would narrow. As shown in Table 11–5, the return of Fund C would fall to +8.9% if the shares were liquidated at the end of the ten-year period and all gains were realized by the shareholder. That return is nearly one percentage point higher than that of Fund A. Even that difference understates the added return for Fund C since (1) the gains need not be realized for an extended period and (2) no taxable gains would be realized if the shares were held until death.

While Tables 11–4 and 11–5 reflect the taxability of funds in three distinct circumstances, industrywide data for the decade ended December 31, 1992, show that 69% of the annual capital return of +10.3% for the average equity fund was accounted for by the reinvestment of taxable capital gains distributions and only 31% by the unrealized appreciation of the fund's net asset values. This period was one in which stock prices were in an ever-ascending bull market. During the decade 1967–77, when capital returns for stock funds were negative, only 6 of the 121 funds in existence realized less than 100% of their total capital appreciation. On average, a $10,000 fund investment at the start of the period had a value of $9,120 at the end, yet distributed $2,330 of taxable capital gains. This means that shareholders were taxed on more gains than the amount of

---

CAVEAT EMPTOR: *The Challenge of Cost Basis*

One of the tax recordkeeping problems associated with mutual fund investing is the need to keep a careful record of the *cost basis* of your shares. Typically, an investor has made multiple purchases (often through reinvestment of dividends and capital gains distributions), so each "lot" of shares acquired has a different cost basis. When shares are redeemed, you must calculate the average cost of those shares or identify the cost basis of the specific shares being sold. In either event, maintain complete records of your fund transactions. Help is on the way. Most major fund complexes can now or soon will be able to provide the average cost basis of the shares in your account. Nonetheless, keeping careful records of each transaction will enable you to select your highest-cost lots for redemption and defer the redemption of lower-cost lots, thus deferring the realization of capital gains.

---

capital appreciation they actually enjoyed. Given the extreme high and low market returns generated during the two periods, it may be reasonable to assume that, over a typical decade, 100% of an equity mutual fund's capital return will be subject to taxation.

There are two ways to minimize the negative impact of taxes on capital gains. One is to consider the *unrealized* appreciation of a fund's shares before making a purchase. Say you have a choice between two funds; each has a net asset value of $10, but one has a portfolio cost basis of $8 per share and the other of $12 per share. Other factors held equal, the latter fund is infinitely more likely to give you the higher after-tax return. Being cautious about "buying" unrealized capital appreciation and the accompanying potential tax liability is just common sense. Unfortunately, this important information is almost never promulgated, although the astute investor can calculate it from data in a fund's annual and semiannual reports. The easiest and most timely way to approximate the capital gain for which you may ultimately bear the tax burden is to request information on a fund's cost basis per share and then subtract the number from the current net asset value of the shares.

The second way to minimize the negative impact of taxes on capital gains is to invest in funds with very low rates of portfolio turnover. For the typical equity fund, the rate of portfolio turnover has averaged about

TABLE 11-6
Annual Portfolio Turnover of Common Stock Funds (1992)*

Annual rate of portfolio turnover	Number of funds
Under 25%	114
25% to 50%	112
51% to 75%	85
76% to 100%	62
101% to 150%	61
More than 150%	61
Total funds	495

*Includes common stock funds with assets greater than $100 million.

80% annually, with considerable consistency over the years. This rate means that a mutual fund with $1 billion of assets would sell $800 million of securities during the year and buy $800 million of securities to replace them. (Capital flow into or out of the fund would increase one or the other figures over the indicated $1.6 billion of total transactions.) This is a large volume of transactions, and it generates not only large transaction costs but, at least during extended bull markets, large capital gains tax liabilities for the shareholders of the fund.

A fund with no portfolio turnover generates no extra tax liability for as long as you hold its shares. However, given that funds experience unbalanced cash inflows and outflows from investors, the no-turnover scenario is hardly likely. But 226 of the 495 equity funds with assets greater than $100 million generate annual turnover of less than 50%, including 114 with turnover below 25%. The likelihood that funds in this latter group will realize substantial gains early in the holding period is greatly reduced. Table 11-6 shows 1992 annual turnover rates for this group of common stock funds.

There is no hard and fast correlation between the level of a mutual fund's portfolio turnover and the extent of its realization of capital gains. But there is fragmentary evidence that investing in mutual funds with very low turnover rates effectively reduces the realization of capital gains. This general conclusion is logical. Nonetheless, so many factors affect the realization of capital gains—stock market appreciation or depreciation and the relative performance of the fund, the cost basis of the securities that are sold, the timing of capital flows into and out of the fund, the growth

TABLE 11-7
Mutual Fund Portfolio Turnover (Ten Years Ended December 31, 1992)

Level of turnover	Annual portfolio turnover rate	Percent of Capital Return	
		Unrealized	Realized
Low (under 25%)	16%	67%	33%
Below average (25%–50%)	36	53	47
Average (51%–100%)	66	22	78
Above average (more than 100%)	150	18	82

in the fund's asset base, to name just a few—that any conclusion must be tentative.

That said, I did study the relationship of portfolio turnover to unrealized capital gains in a selected sample of 24 funds. I selected six funds with minimal turnover (under 25%), six with below-average turnover (25% to 50%), six with average turnover (51% to 100%), and six with above-average turnover (more than 100%). I then examined the extent to which each fund's gains were realized over the ten-year period ended December 31, 1992. Table 11-7 shows the results.

The mutual funds used in this analysis were selected to make the point, not that there is a causal relationship between lower portfolio turnover and lower realized gains, but merely that low turnover *may* help to defer capital gains. I believe the table is correct in showing that the percentage of a fund's unrealized gains tends to dwindle as the turnover rate rises. However, once turnover exceeds a 50% rate, most of the tax advantage of gain deferral is eliminated. This conclusion is consistent with that reached by other, more complete studies.

In total, the impact of taxes on both realized capital gains and investment income significantly reduces the rates of mutual fund return reported by the press, the statistical services, and the funds themselves. To make this point, Table 11-8 illustrates the pretax and after-tax returns of two stock funds—one with a high level of gains realization, the other with a low level of gains realization—over the ten-year period ended December 31, 1992. The funds were selected as typical examples of each type of policy, and the choice of two funds with nearly identical pretax rates of total return was deliberate.

TABLE 11–8
Impact of Taxes on Total Returns (10 Years Ended December 31, 1992)

	Pretax total return	After-tax total return	After-tax value of $10,000 initial investment
Fund A	+12.2%	+11.1%	$28,580
Fund B	+12.3	+9.6	25,080

You can see that the after-tax return of a shareholder in Fund A (a low realizer of gains) was +11.1%, compared with +9.6% for Fund B (a high gains realizer). As indicated earlier, however, if the investor in Fund A redeemed all shares at the end of the period, the tax liability would increase. Of course, the investor could avoid incurring any tax liability simply by maintaining the investment in the fund.

It is important to recognize three simple facts regarding mutual funds and taxes. (1) Mutual funds are generally managed without regard to tax considerations. (2) As a result, both income taxes and capital gains taxes reduce, to a greater or lesser degree, the total pretax returns earned by most fund investors. (3) Mutual funds with low (or no) unrealized appreciation in their portfolios and funds with low portfolio turnover are likely to generate capital gains distributions either lesser in amount or later in the holding period (or both) than other funds. I now turn to tax-deferred mutual fund accounts and tax-exempt municipal bond funds, two options that are remarkably effective in mitigating this tax burden.

HOW TO DEFER TAXES

Fortunately, there are legitimate ways to defer taxes on both investment income and capital gains. Taking advantage of tax-deferred investment programs will give you a truly remarkable increase in the total returns you enjoy. I will illustrate the dramatic financial advantage of such plans in a moment, but I want to emphasize that you should commit every dollar you can reasonably afford to investment programs that may be funded with pretax dollars and that enjoy tax-deferral of income and capital gains under explicit Internal Revenue Service regulations or federal tax laws. In the accumulation phase of your life cycle, such programs should have top priority over all other courses of financial action.

The four principal tax-deferred investment programs are (1) individual retirement accounts (IRAs); (2) qualified pension and profit-sharing plans (Keogh plans) for the self-employed; (3) 401(k) plans, frequently made available by corporations to their employees; and (4) 403(b) savings plans made available to the employees of most educational and charitable institutions. Mutual funds, with their diversification, professional management, convenience, and recordkeeping services, constitute an ideal medium for funding these tax-deferred plans.

Table 11–9 shows the difference between a taxable and a tax-deferred savings program, each earning a +10% rate of return on annual investments of $5,000. For the taxable account, we assume that taxes are deducted from the investments before they are put to work (i.e., after-tax dollars), and that taxes are paid on the full amount of total return earned each year. Since most tax-deferred programs allow the use of pretax dollars, neither type of tax liability need be incurred.

Table 11–9 also takes into account the taxes that would become payable on a tax-deferred account once the total investment accumulations are withdrawn. Suffice it to say, however, that nearly all investors will benefit by withdrawing only the income they require to meet their living expenses so that the remaining capital and income will continue to accumulate on a tax-deferred basis. This practice allows taxes to be deferred indefinitely and paid on income only as it is distributed. (A minimum yearly distribution, based on the joint life expectancies of the holder and the beneficiary, must begin at age 70½.)

As you can see in Table 11–9, the miracle of compounding, combined with the financial advantages of investing pretax dollars and earning tax deferred income, has a dramatic impact on an investment program. The $5,000 annual investments grow on a tax-deferred basis to more than $900,000 after 30 years. On a taxable basis, however, the annual investments grow to just $320,000. Even after taking into account the tax liability if the tax-deferred account is liquidated at the conclusion of the 30-year period, the tax-deferred account provides nearly twice the final accumulation, at $606,160. If 30 years seems too long a period to anticipate, bear in mind that a working career may well cover 40 years.

There are significant limitations on the availability of tax-deductible IRAs and the amounts you can contribute to any of the tax-deferred pro-

TABLE 11-9
Taxable versus Tax-Deferred Investment Programs (Annual Investments of $5,000)

Value at end of year	Total Accumulations*		
	Taxable account	*Tax-deferred accounts†*	*Tax-deferred accounts‡*
10	$ 48,690	$ 58,800	$ 87,760
15	87,770	117,080	174,750
20	141,820	211,060	315,010
25	216,580	362,410	540,910
30	319,960	606,160	904,720

*Assumes +10% annual rate of return and a 33% tax rate applied to the annual investments in the taxable account and to its entire annual return.
†Net of taxes payable on withdrawal from tax-deferred account at the end of each period.
‡Assumes no withdrawal from tax-deferred account at the end of each period.

grams mentioned earlier. While we will not attempt to define the complex factors involved, the present limits include:

- Maximum annual contribution is $2,000 for an IRA account ($4,000 if working spouse is included), with all earnings tax deferred. All or part of your maximum individual contribution may be tax deductible if your annual income is below $35,000 ($50,000 if your spouse is employed). Further, if you are not eligible for a corporate savings plan, your entire contribution is tax deductible whatever your income level. Even if the contribution must be made from after-tax income, the tax deferral of earnings is a valuable feature you should not overlook.

- Maximum pretax contributions for qualified pension and profit-sharing plans (including Keogh accounts) may equal the lesser of $30,000 or 20% of net earnings for self-employed individuals.

- Maximum pretax employee contribution in 1993 is $8,994 for participants in 401(k) plans. (This maximum is increased each year to keep pace with increases in the cost-of-living index.) Typically, your employer will allow you to set aside 2% to 4% of your salary in the 401(k) plan and then may make a matching contribution of 50% to 100% of the amount you have set aside. You may also have the opportunity to make additional voluntary, but unmatched, contributions. In 401(k) plans in which your employer matches all or part of your contributions, you gain valuable financial leverage.

- Maximum pretax employee contributions to 403(b) savings plans are generally limited to $9,500 per year. Some such programs allow you to contribute up to 16% of your gross salary.

Millions of investors have the opportunity to invest pretax dollars in a savings program and enjoy tax deferral on their total returns. If you qualify for any such programs, they should usually command the first dollars that you can afford to commit. The only possible drawbacks are that any withdrawals made before age 59½ may be subject to penalty, and that minimum withdrawals must be made beginning at age 70½.

VARIABLE ANNUITIES

Given the limitations on the qualified federal programs, many investors seek further opportunities for tax deferral through other sources. The most common alternative is the variable annuity. This tax-deferred investment program is accessible through mutual funds designed especially for the annuity plan. It may be a stock fund or a bond fund of one type or another or even a money market fund; the funds may be exchanged for others within the same variable annuity fund family without incurring any tax liability. Taxes on dividends and any realized or unrealized capital gains are deferred until the assets are withdrawn, and then paid only on assets that are withdrawn (for example, amounts needed for living expenses). So far, so good; the variable annuity shares the features of the other tax-deferred plans.

But there the similarity ends. On the one hand, an almost unlimited number of standard, garden variety mutual funds may be used in tax-deferred plans operated under the aegis of special provisions of the IRA, Keogh, 401(k), and 403(b) regulations. On the other hand, there is a limited selection of the specially created variable annuity funds (often with higher expense ratios), on which a premium—akin to a life insurance mortality charge—must be paid on an annual basis. It is this "insurance" feature, such as it may be, that permits the tax deferral to exist under federal law. The net result is that the rates of return earned on variable annuities are certain to be significantly lower than the pretax returns earned through direct ownership of the underlying mutual funds.

I begin with a hypothetical comparison of $50,000 invested in a fully taxable mutual fund account versus a variable annuity account, both held in identical mutual funds earning gross returns of +10% annually. It

---

CAVEAT EMPTOR: *Lump Sums versus Regular Investments*

Variable annuities are ordinarily more appropriate for the accumulation investor who has a lump sum of dollars to commit. If you are saving smaller amounts on a regular basis, variable annuities should rarely be used until all other tax-deferred plans have been fully utilized. The reason is simple: contributions to IRAs, qualified pension plans, and 401(k)s are effectively made with *pretax* dollars, while contributions to variable annuities are made with *after-tax* dollars. For an investor in a 33% tax bracket, $10,000 invested over time in an IRA would compare, for example, with $6,700 available to invest in an annuity.

TABLE 11-10
Variable Annuity Fund versus Taxable Mutual Fund* ($50,000 Initial Investment)

Value at end of year	Taxable mutual fund	Tax-deferred variable annuity†	Tax-deferred variable annuity‡
10	$ 89,800	$105,470	$ 87,170
15	120,340	153,190	119,140
20	161,270	222,490	165,570
25	216,120	323,150	233,010
30	289,620	469,340	330,960

*Assumes +10% average annual gross return, 33% tax rate, and annual expenses of 1% for the taxable fund and 2.25% for the variable annuity fund.
†Assumes no withdrawal from annuity at the end of each period.
‡Net of taxes payable on withdrawal from annuity at the end of each period.

assumes that fund expenses are 1% per year, resulting in a net return of +9%, and that the variable annuity insurance premium adds 1.25% per year to the cost of the underlying fund, bringing its total costs to 2.25% per year and the net return to +7.75%.

While the higher costs of the annuity program substantially reduce its gross return, the deferral of taxes creates a more-than-countervailing advantage, particularly as the holding period lengthens. For example, as shown in Table 11-10, the total 15-year accumulation of a $50,000

TABLE 11–11
*Variable Annuity Cost Comparison ($50,000 Initial Investment)**

Value at end of year	Average-cost variable annuity	Low-cost variable annuity
10	$105,470	$115,680
15	153,190	175,960
20	222,490	267,640
25	323,150	407,100
30	469,340	619,220

*Based on +10% annual return, reduced by costs of 2.25% and 1.25%, respectively. Assumes no withdrawals from either account.

investment in a taxable mutual fund would be $120,340, compared with $153,190 in a tax-deferred variable annuity. After 30 years, the respective accumulations would be $289,620 and $469,340, a dramatically favorable margin.

Should you withdraw from the annuity program and pay taxes on your total accumulations, the annuity advantage plummets. Taxes on a withdrawal after 30 years, for example, would reduce the total accumulation from $469,340 to $330,960, as shown in Table 11–10. Indeed, as suggested by the table, it would take nearly 20 years for the value of the annuity after taxes were paid on the withdrawal to exceed the results of the taxable mutual fund investment (respectively, $165,570 and $161,270).

The examples in Table 11–10 assume a complete withdrawal of the variable annuity investment at the end of each period. However, in order to mitigate the tax burden, the investor faced with a need for cash should consider withdrawing only a small percentage (say, 5% to 10%) of the annuity's value each year. Any withdrawals before the investor reaches age 59½ are subject to a 10% penalty, one more reason that you should probably not even consider a variable annuity for assets that you may need to liquidate in the foreseeable future.

Since the range of variable annuity costs is wide, you need to understand the powerful impact of costs on the returns actually realized. Table 11–11 compares the results of the variable annuity program illustrated in Table 11–10 (annual costs of 2.25%, roughly the industry norm) with a lower-expense variable annuity program with annual costs of 1.25%. You can easily see the dramatic role that cost can play in the returns you might earn

---

CAVEAT EMPTOR: *Losers and Winners*

The variable annuity, with its inside build-up of income and capital appreciation on a tax-deferred basis, produces reduced tax revenues to the federal government for an extended period. This tax advantage has come under periodic challenge by the Internal Revenue Service, since the U.S. Treasury is a loser to the extent of this tax deferral. The sponsors of the plan receive higher revenues on variable annuity mutual funds than on regular mutual funds, so the insurance company administrator and the marketing agents receive higher profits and are winners. Investors are, in many instances, neither winners nor losers. Since the higher costs of annuities offset their tax benefits for a decade or more, you may end up being ''return neutral'' in choosing between an annuity and a directly taxable fund investment. Since investing in a variable annuity program is less flexible than simply owning a mutual fund outright and may involve significant tax and other financial penalties on withdrawal, carefully balance out these factors before locking up your money for an extended period.

---

by investing in a variable annuity fund. For example, after 15 years, the average-cost variable annuity fund would provide a total capital accumulation of $153,190, while the lower-cost annuity fund would provide an accumulation of $175,960. After 30 years, the respective accumulations would be $469,340 and $619,220. The sole reason for these remarkable advantages is the cost differential. Tax deferral is a marvelous financial advantage, but only if it is provided at a reasonable price.

In light of the differences illustrated in Tables 11–10 and 11–11, you should consider the cost of a variable annuity program, the length of time you expect to own it, and any financial penalties the insurance company may impose upon early redemption. These penalties are often steep and may amount to 5% or more of capital during the first several years. The negative impact of the annuity's higher cost abates as the holding period increases and the tax savings accumulate. But in many cases, unless you can avoid withdrawing your variable annuity investment and thus avoid realizing taxes on the accumulations, a high-cost tax-deferred variable annuity fund will provide *lower* returns than a fully taxable but low-cost mutual fund, even if the variable annuity is held for as long as two decades.

CAVEAT EMPTOR: *A Municipal Bond Fund Is Not a Municipal Bond*

Because of the acceleration of capital gains realization, ownership of equity mutual funds may be less attractive under some circumstances than ownership of individual common stocks. But the reverse is often true in the municipal bond arena. Municipal bond funds are apt to be more attractive than direct municipal bond ownership, because transaction costs in the municipal markets are likely to be substantially higher for individuals than for institutional investors. Even if you intend to buy and hold individual bonds, you will be affected by these costs, as changes in quality ratings and the calling of individual bonds necessitate periodic portfolio transactions.

INCOME EXEMPT FROM FEDERAL TAXES

It will probably not surprise you to learn that municipal bonds—whose interest payments are entirely exempt from federal taxes—have existed as long as the federal income tax has existed (since 1913). However, mutual funds that are able to "pass through" the tax-exemption of municipal bond interest have existed only since 1976, the result of a special provision added to the Internal Revenue Code at that time.

The mathematics of tax exemption are quite simple compared to the complex mathematics of tax deferral. Municipal bonds yield significantly less than taxable bonds, a sort of equalizer that one would expect in America's efficient capital markets. In determining whether tax-exempt income or taxable income provides the higher net return, you need only make a relatively basic calculation: reduce the yield on a taxable bond by your marginal tax rate and compare it with the yield on a comparable tax-exempt bond. The simplified examples in Table 11-12 make the point, using an assumed marginal federal tax rate of 33%. For example, if taxable yields on long-term, high-grade corporate bonds are in the area of 8.0%, an investor taxed at a 33% rate should consider an equivalent municipal bond only if its tax-exempt yield is 5.4% or more. You should always be fully aware of this spread and be prepared to take appropriate action if the relative yields change appreciably.

The value of the tax exemption grows as tax rates rise, as shown in Table 11-13. If you are taxed at a marginal rate of 40% you must earn a taxable yield of 10% to match a 6% tax-exempt yield. But the threshold falls to a

TABLE 11-12
Tax Impact on Various Yields

Taxable yield	4.0%	5.0%	6.0%	7.0%	8.0%	9.0%	10.0%
Less federal taxes*	1.3	1.6	2.0	2.3	2.6	3.0	3.3
Required tax-exempt yield	2.7%	3.4%	4.0%	4.7%	5.4%	6.0%	6.7%

*Assumes 33% marginal tax rate.

TABLE 11-13
Impact of Higher Tax Rates on Tax-Exempt Yields

Marginal federal tax rate	Tax-exempt yield	Equivalent taxable yield
25%	6.0%	8.0%
30	6.0	8.6
35	6.0	9.2
40	6.0	10.0

taxable yield of 8% if you are taxed at a marginal rate of 25%. Each increase in tax rate adds to the relative attractiveness of the municipal bond.

Tax-exempt yields are not set in a vacuum. They are determined in an efficient market that takes taxes into account, so they are consistently below taxable yields. However, the market seems to "clear" at a point well above that needed to make tax exemption attractive to investors in the highest tax brackets. If you are in these tax brackets, tax-exempt income will nearly always provide a higher after-tax yield.

This subject has some complications. In making fair yield comparisons, all other factors must be held equal. That is a difficult task. The principal features to consider when comparing taxable and tax-exempt bonds are quality, maturity, and call provisions.

- *Quality.* Frequently, a relative yield comparison is made between U.S. Treasury bonds and municipal bonds. However, the credit quality of U.S. Treasury bonds is higher than that of even the highest-grade municipal bonds. On the other hand, the credit of many municipal bonds is enhanced by private insurance covering the payment of both principal and interest. If both the issuer and the insurer are top-rated, such insured bonds should provide a slightly lower yield than other high-grade municipal bonds, but with a quality rating nearly equivalent to that of U.S. Treasuries,

---

CAVEAT EMPTOR: *Tax-Exempt Bonds versus Taxable CDs*

In times of particularly low short-term interest rates, long-term tax-exempt rates appear especially attractive. Increasing a certificate of deposit yield of 3.5% *before* taxes to a long-term municipal bond yield of 6.0% *after* taxes seems too good to be true. Alas, it *is* too good to be true. The switch involves a substantial increase in principal volatility in the form of interest rate risk, and at least some increase in credit risk since only the CD is insured by the FDIC. When such comparisons are promulgated by fund sponsors without prominent and complete disclosure of these differences, they are grossly misleading. That is not to say that the step-up in yield should be ignored. If you are a longer-term investor seeking higher and more durable income, and if you are fully cognizant of the extra principal risk involved, extending maturity and gaining tax-exempt income can combine to make a remarkably attractive alternative to a CD.

---

since insured municipal bonds are almost invariably rated AAA. Under no circumstances should you compromise quality standards on the basis of a yield comparison—between, say, a U.S. Treasury bond and a lower-grade municipal bond—in which there are material differences in credit risk.

- *Maturity.* It goes without saying that the average weighted maturities of the tax-exempt and taxable bond fund portfolios you are comparing should match as closely as possible. It is usually possible to earn higher yields by extending maturities, but with that extension comes a risk of higher price volatility.

- *Call Provisions.* Nearly all municipal bonds are callable (i.e., can be redeemed by the issuer before they mature) after a certain number of years, and so are most corporate bonds. The most common periods for call protection are five or ten years after the bond is issued. Thereafter if interest rates drop significantly below the bond coupon, the bonds will almost always be called, leaving you no recourse but to reinvest the proceeds from the called bonds into bonds with lower yields. However, bonds issued by the U.S. Treasury are rarely callable and thus pay their full interest until they mature.

Given these differences in quality, maturity, and callability, it is problematic to find precise comparative standards for taxable and tax-exempt investments. Nonetheless, you should elicit all available information to approximate a fair evaluation. Generally, the after-tax yield differential between a U.S. Treasury bond and a top-grade insured municipal bond of roughly the same maturity should probably be in the area of 0.5% for the municipal bond to represent an appropriate substitute. For example, if you own a taxable U.S. Treasury bond fund yielding 7.0% and you are in a 33% tax bracket, you will require a top-rated municipal bond fund to yield at least 5.2%. (A 7.0% taxable yield, after assumed income taxes of 33%, would be reduced to 4.7%. Adding back a premium of 0.5% for call protection and quality results in a required tax-exempt yield of 5.2%.)

INCOME EXEMPT FROM STATE TAXES

Especially in recent years, we have witnessed the imposition of income taxes by many state and local governments. As these taxes have become more onerous, a whole new variety of mutual fund has sprung up: the single-state municipal bond fund. These funds provide income that is exempt not only from federal income taxes but from state and local income taxes as well. They accomplish this goal by investing solely in the municipal bonds of a single state, and so usually provide an opportunity for added after-tax yield to residents of that state. The single-state funds typically come in the form of either long-term bond funds or money market funds.

Some of the higher state income tax rates are levied in New York, maximum state income tax of 7.875% (plus an additional 6% for residents of New York City); California, up to 11%; Massachusetts, 5.95%; New Jersey, 7%; and Pennsylvania, 2.8%. State tax-exempt funds frequently (though not always) provide higher after-tax returns than their national tax-exempt cousins. You should make this comparison in much the way as our earlier federal tax comparison. But in a single-state municipal bond fund, you are exposed to a concentration of risk that cannot be disregarded: local events can wreak havoc on a relatively undiversified portfolio. For instance, a sharp decline in the credit of New York, or an earthquake in California, could cause sharp reductions in the value of those respective states' bonds. These types of risks are broad indeed.

In response to these risks it was only a matter of time before the *insured* single-state municipal bond fund was inaugurated. (The insurance feature is not available for short-term municipal bonds.) The major insurers of municipal bonds appear to be well capitalized and capable of meeting their potential obligations and normally raise the rating of the insured bond to

AAA. If the single-state bond fund seems attractive, you should carefully consider the value added by this insurance. The cost of the insurance is modest, entailing a yield sacrifice of as little as 0.10% to 0.25%. And as mentioned in Chapter 5 on bonds, this modest reduction may be more than offset if the particular fund has a significantly lower expense ratio. A low-cost insured fund may provide a higher yield (sometimes significantly higher) than a high-cost fund investing in uninsured and lower-quality bonds. This situation is akin to buying an insurance policy on your home but having the insurance company pay you the premium.

Mutual funds investing in U.S. Treasury bonds and bills also carry exemptions from state and local taxes in all states except Pennsylvania. You ignore this vitally important advantage at your peril. The arithmetic is simple: obligations of the U.S. Treasury yield less than those of high-grade corporate issuers. Interest on both kinds of instruments is taxable at the federal level, but states provide a tax exemption for interest paid by U.S. Treasury issues (whether paid directly or passed through in a mutual fund). Reflecting the premier credit quality of the U.S. Treasury, its bills and bonds often yield something in the range of 0.50% below the highest-grade money market instruments and AAA corporate bonds. However, taking state taxes into consideration, the Treasury obligations may provide you with competitive *net* yields. Table 11-14 illustrates this comparison, assuming a yield of 4.0% for a high-grade money market and a yield of 7.0% for a AAA-rated corporate bond fund.

As you can see, investors owning U.S. Treasury bond and money market funds may earn virtually the same returns, net of state taxes, as investors in corporate bond and money market mutual funds with lesser (albeit high) credit quality. Given the wide range of mutual fund operating expenses, it is not uncommon to find U.S. Treasury funds with extremely low costs available at higher net yields than corporate funds of comparable maturity but with higher costs. This anomaly of higher return coming hand in hand with lower risk is a rare occurrence in the financial markets. You should take advantage of such a powerful combination.

SUMMARY

In a simpler age, the impact of taxes on income and capital gains, tax-deferred returns, and tax-exempt income may have seemed relatively unimportant. Today, however, only the naive, ill-informed investor fails to

TABLE 11-14
Impact of Taxes on Corporate and Treasury Instruments

	Taxable money market fund	Taxable long-term bond fund
Corporate obligation		
Pretax yield	4.0%	7.0%
Federal taxes (33%)	−1.3	−2.3
After-tax yield	2.7%	4.7%
State and local taxes*	−0.2	−0.3
After-tax yield	2.5%	4.4%
U.S. Treasury obligation		
Pretax yield	3.5%	6.5%
Federal taxes (33%)	−1.2	−2.1
After-tax yield	2.3%	4.4%

*Assumes a marginal state tax rate of 6%, net of the federal tax deduction for state and local taxes.

consider the relationship between income return and capital return; the implications of taxes on dividend income and realized capital gains; and the potential taxes on unrealized gains. Only the foolish investor fails to utilize tax-deferred accounts to the maximum possible advantage; to calculate the yield at which municipal bonds break even with their taxable counterparts; and to evaluate the advantage of paying no state taxes on interest earned on U.S. Treasury obligations. No intelligent investor can afford to make these mistakes, lest the power to tax indeed becomes the power, if not to destroy, certainly to confiscate meaningful proportions of the returns you earn on your investments.

IV

PRACTICAL APPLICATION OF INVESTMENT PRINCIPLES

T he first two of the next three chapters will help you apply the principles covered in the previous eleven chapters. I will set forth recommendations regarding the allocation of assets among stock funds and bond
funds, and present eight model portfolios designed to illustrate investment
strategies for various stages of an investor's life cycle.

The final chapter issues a challenge to mutual fund shareholders and
mutual fund directors. It suggests practical courses of action you can take
to help make this good industry an even better one for investors.

Chapter Twelve

The Allocation of Investment Assets
The Intelligent Investor

To invest successfully over a lifetime does not require a stratospheric IQ, unusual business insights, or inside information. What's needed is a sound intellectual framework for making decisions and the ability to keep emotions from corroding that framework. This book precisely and clearly prescribes the proper framework. You must supply the emotional discipline.

So wrote Warren E. Buffett, one of the most successful investors of our time, in his introduction to *The Intelligent Investor* by Benjamin Graham, surely one of the most successful investors of his time. *The Intelligent Investor,* in Mr. Buffett's words, "is by far the best book about investing ever written."

The most fundamental decision of investing is the allocation of your assets: How much should you own in stocks? How much should you own in bonds? How much should you own in cash reserves? According to a recent study, that decision has accounted for an astonishing 94% of the differences in total returns achieved by institutionally managed pension funds. The results of this study have been reaffirmed in countless others. There is no reason to believe that the same relationship does not also hold true for individual investors. The 94% figure suggests that long-term fund investors might profit by concentrating more on the allocation of their investments between stock and bond funds and less on the question of which particular stock and bond funds to hold. (I emphasize that I am speaking of mainstream stock funds and high-grade bond funds.)

Where do we begin? I suggest we start with Benjamin Graham's advice regarding asset allocation in *The Intelligent Investor:*

We have suggested as a fundamental guiding rule that the investor should never have less than 25% or more than 75% of his funds in common stocks, with a consequent inverse range of between 75% and 25% in bonds. There is an implication here that the standard division should be an equal one, or 50-50, between the two major investment mediums. According to tradition the sound reason for increasing the percentage in common stocks would be the appearance of the "bargain price" levels created in a protracted bear market. Conversely, sound procedure would call for reducing the common-stock component below 50% when in the judgment of the investor the market level has become dangerously high.

These copybook maxims have always been easy to enunciate and always difficult to follow—because they go against that very human nature which produces the excesses of bull and bear markets. It is almost a contradiction in terms to suggest as a feasible policy for the *average* stockowner that he lighten his holdings when the market advances beyond a certain point and add to them after a corresponding decline. It is because the average man operates, and apparently must operate, in opposite fashion that we have had the great advances and collapses of the past; and—this writer believes—we are likely to have them in the future.

We are thus led to put forward to most of our readers what may appear to be an oversimplified 50-50 formula. Under this plan the guiding rule is to maintain as nearly as practicable an equal division between bond and stock holdings. When changes in the market level have raised the common-stock component to, say, 55 per cent, the balance would be restored by a sale of one-eleventh of the stock portfolio and the transfer of the proceeds to bonds. Conversely, a fall in the common-stock proportion to 45 per cent would call for the use of one-eleventh of the bond fund to buy additional equities.

. . . we are convinced that our 50-50 version of this approach makes good sense for the defensive investor. It is extremely simple; it aims unquestionably in the right direction; it gives the follower the feeling that he is at least making some moves in response to market developments; most important of all, it will restrain him from being drawn more and more heavily into common stocks as the market rises to more and more dangerous heights.

Furthermore, a truly conservative investor will be satisfied with the gains shown on half his portfolio in a rising market, while in a severe decline he may derive much solace (a la Rochefoucauld[1]) from reflecting how much better off he is than many of his more venturesome friends.

Since this advice was presented nearly three decades ago, the stock market has experienced the madness of the go-go years in 1965–68 (described in

---

1. An apparent reference to the maxim, "We all have strength enough to endure the misfortunes of others."

CAVEAT EMPTOR: *Bonds and Reserves*

Following the lead of Benjamin Graham, I chose not to allocate any part of the portfolio to reserves such as money funds. I adopted this convention because it simplifies the analysis that follows, without materially altering its conclusions. I have three general comments with respect to bonds and cash reserves. (1) Cash reserves, given their low long-term returns, should be held to a modest portion—say 10%—of your total portfolio. Thus, the stock/bond relationships presented in this chapter would be only slightly disturbed. (2) You may wish to use short-term bond funds for a portion of your bond position. Such funds usually enhance yield relative to reserves with only modest principal risk. I have not attempted to deal with the issue of short-term versus intermediate-term versus long-term bonds. Rather, I suggest that the duration of the bond portfolio should bear some relationship to the investor's time horizon—for example, short-term bonds might be emphasized for reserves that might be needed in two or three years, intermediate-term bonds might be emphasized if you are retired, and long-term bonds might be emphasized if you are a younger investor accumulating assets for retirement or an older investor seeking to maximize the amount and the durability of your income. (3) While my reference to a bond portfolio speaks of bonds as a generic category, my underlying assumption is that the portfolio will be dominated by U.S. Treasury bond funds, investment-grade corporate bond funds, or municipal bond funds rated A or above. Maturity should vary with your time horizon, but quality should *not* be sacrificed to meet your income requirements. Both interest rate risk and credit risk must be appropriately limited.

Chapter 4), the subsequent and inevitable collapse in 1969–70, the worst bear market (1973–74) since the Depression, and one of the great bull markets of all time, beginning in 1982 and, despite the great crash of October 1987, continuing into 1993. Nonetheless, the general principles then enunciated remain remarkably intact and the suggested asset allocation percentages still form the basis for a sensible investment program.

Heeding Benjamin Graham's advice that a standard division between bonds and stocks should begin at a 50/50 ratio, I move from this broad generalization to more specific guidelines for mutual funds that take into account your financial circumstances, age, and objectives, as well as the specific phase—either accumulation or distribution—of your investment

FIGURE 12–1
Basic Asset Allocation Model (Stocks/Bonds)

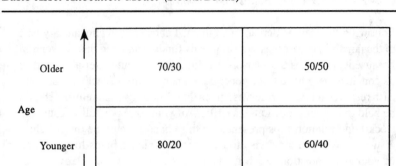

life cycle. During the accumulation phase, you are building assets by making periodic investments of capital and reinvesting all dividend income and capital gains distributions. During the distribution phase, you have ceased adding assets and instead are receiving cash distributions from income as it is earned. Figure 12–1 gives a good indication of how the allocation of assets among stocks and bonds might vary given your age and income requirements.

The two main points of the matrix are merely common sense. (1) Investors seeking to accumulate assets by investing regularly can afford to take somewhat more risk—that is, to be more aggressive—than investors who have a relatively fixed pool of capital and are dependent on income distributions to meet their day-to-day living expenses. (2) Younger investors, with more time to let the magic of compounding work for them, can also afford to be more aggressive, while older investors will want to steer a more conservative course.

Assuming only that the long-term return on stocks exceeds that on bonds (as it nearly always has in the past), your common stock position should be as large as your tolerance for risk permits. For example, my highest recommended target allocation for stocks would be 80% for younger investors accumulating assets over a long time frame. My lowest target stock allocation, 50%, would apply to older investors in the distribution phase. These investors must give greater weight to the short-run consequences of their

---

CAVEAT EMPTOR: *A Simple Rule of Thumb*

If you are seeking a simple rule of thumb for asset allocation, this one may be useful: the bond portion of your total investment portfolio should be roughly equal to your age. The remainder should be invested in equities. If you are 30 years old, you would maintain a 70% stock position and a 30% bond position. At age 50, your portfolio balance would be 50/50; at age 70, it would be 30/70. This concept engenders investment allocations conceptually similar to those shown in the matrix in Figure 12-1. This rule is only a rough guideline; your own circumstances may dictate a substantially different allocation.

---

actions. They must carefully consider that volatility of returns is an imperfect measure of risk. More meaningful is the risk that an investor will unexpectedly have to liquidate assets when they are needed, and perhaps receive less in proceeds than the original cost of the assets.

With that background, and with the basic asset allocations established, I now turn to four additional questions about asset allocation strategy.

1. Which investments should comprise the stock and bond elements of the asset allocation portfolio?

2. Should the asset allocation be rebalanced periodically to the originally desired level, or should it be allowed to reflect the relative returns achieved by its stock and bond sectors?

3. Are there tactical opportunities to alter the allocation of assets to capitalize on changing relative valuation levels in the financial markets?

4. Is there a better way to allocate assets, so as to increase potential returns without increasing portfolio risk? Alternatively, can you hold potential returns constant even while lowering risk?

ELEMENTS OF THE ASSET ALLOCATION PORTFOLIO

This book's entire approach to asset allocation involves the use of mutual funds. The diversity of stock and bond funds available, along with their varied objectives and strategies, allows you to build an investment program tightly linked to your own personal needs and resources. For simplicity, this section will focus solely on the investor with an initial 50%/50% stock/ bond portfolio allocation. The percentages can easily be adjusted to reflect other preferred basic allocations. Here are some examples:

- *A complex managed portfolio* might include for stocks, 20% in two mainstream growth stock funds, 20% in two aggressive growth funds, and 10% in a broadly based specialty equity fund; and for bonds, 30% in two long-term corporate bond funds and 20% in a short-term bond fund.

- *A basic managed portfolio* might include for stocks, 50% in a broadly diversified mainstream value fund; and for bonds, 25% in each of two long-term bond funds (one a U.S. Treasury bond fund and the other a high-grade corporate bond fund).

- *A tax-minimizing portfolio* might include for stocks, 25% in each of two mainstream equity funds (one a variable annuity fund and one a growth fund); and for bonds, 25% in both a long-term and an intermediate-term municipal bond fund.

- *A simple managed portfolio* might include about 85% in a mainstream balanced fund with a policy of maintaining a 60/40 balance and, to bring the stock/bond balance closer to 50/50, a 15% position in an intermediate-term bond fund.

- *A basic indexed portfolio* might include 50% in a total stock market portfolio and 50% in a total bond market portfolio.

- *A ready-made convenience portfolio,* provided the target allocation meets your standards, might include a single balanced index fund, comprising 60% stocks and 40% bonds.

The number of funds in these simplified examples ranges from eight to just one. While many investors own ten funds or more, superior returns in one fund are often offset by inferior returns in another, resulting in an index-like performance but without the requisite feature of minimal cost. A very large number of mutual fund holdings is not likely to add value to the performance of your overall investment portfolio.

The next two principles may seem obvious. First, the number of equity funds you hold can be reduced as their own diversification increases. Two funds with high ExMarks are probably ample, but if ExMarks are low, four funds may be needed. And one stock market index fund (in which 100% of its return is explained by the market's return) would provide complete equity diversification. Second, you should hold the smallest number of bond funds needed to shape the desired duration of your bond portfolio. If your desired duration is six years, one fund with a ten-year

---

CAVEAT EMPTOR: *This Too Shall Pass*

Abraham Lincoln, in a speech in 1859, told this story. "It is said an Eastern monarch once charged his wise men to invent him a sentence to be ever in view, and which should be true and appropriate in all times and situations. They presented him the words: 'And this, too, shall pass away.' How much it expresses! How chastening in the hour of pride! How consoling in the depths of affliction!" This is wise advice on investing in the financial markets: transitory changes in the prices of financial assets must be ignored. Yet many investors simply cannot follow this practice. They feel richer when the stock market rises and poorer when it declines, despite the fact that the aggregate underlying value of the business enterprises that comprise "the market" have changed not a whit. *The Intelligent Investor* cautions against the temptation to "give way to the bull-market atmosphere, become infected with the enthusiasm, the overconfidence, and the greed of the great public, (of which, after all, you are a part) and make larger and dangerous commitments." Benjamin Graham could have easily gone on to caution against the temptation to give way to the bear market atmosphere, become infected with the negativism, the lack of confidence, and the fear of the great public, and slash stock commitments. If you cannot ignore the heat of stock market volatility, you should not commit a very large portion of your assets to the markets. Your success in investing will depend in part on your character and guts, and in part on your ability to realize, at the heights of ebullience and the depths of despair alike, that this, too, shall pass away.

---

duration and one with a two-year duration may be appropriate. It would be pointless to hold two U.S. Treasury bond funds with the same duration when one would serve the same purpose, perhaps at a lower cost.

This brief review of the elements of portfolio asset allocation is intended only to set general parameters. More specific ideas on asset allocation will be presented in the next chapter.

SHOULD YOUR ASSET ALLOCATION BE REBALANCED PERIODICALLY?

There are, at the extreme, two different approaches to asset allocation. One is to rebalance your portfolio to your initially desired stock/bond mix every year or so. This approach involves liquidating a small portion of the portfolio's position in the asset class that has provided the higher return and reinvesting that sum in the asset class with the lower return, so that at all times the target balance is maintained. (In this section, I assume a 50/50 balance.) For example, if the total return on the stock position was +30% in a given year and the return on the bond position was +5%, the allocation at year-end would shift to about 55% stocks and 45% bonds.

A fixed-ratio strategy would call for the exchange of 5% of your total assets out of the stock portfolio and into the bond portfolio, restoring the 50/50 target balance. The advantage of such a policy is to lock in some of your gains and to reduce your equity exposure *after* a sharp stock market increase. Correspondingly, such a policy would increase your equity holdings after a sharp decline had reduced them. These steps are emotionally counterintuitive. It is in the ebullience of a market rise that most investors consider adding to their stock positions. And it is in times of caution or fear, when markets are down, that investors are tempted to reduce their stock positions. Considerable discipline is therefore required to take the appropriate action.

The other major allocation approach is to let the profits run, doing no rebalancing whatsoever. Under this method, changes in the stock/bond ratio may be modest or large, depending on the circumstances of the investor, the returns achieved, and the time horizon involved. For example, Table 12–1 reflects the changes in the stock/bond ratio assuming total returns of +10% on stocks (+3% income, +7% capital) and +7% on bonds (entirely income). The choice of these returns is arbitrary on my part, reflecting a combination of market valuations at the close of 1992 and historical norms. The fact is, since 1872 the total returns on stocks have averaged about four percentage points above those on bonds (a 4% risk premium, rather than the 3% premium used in the example).

As you can see in Table 12–1, for the accumulation investor seeking to build capital, these assumed total returns would carry the initial 50/50 balance to 57/43 in favor of stocks at the end of 10 years and 67/33 at the end of 25 years. By way of contrast, for the distribution investor spending current income each year, the stock/bond ratios would rise to 66/34 and 84/16, respectively, after 10 and 25 years. These larger increases in the stock holdings of the distribution investor result from the fact that, given the absence of reinvested income, the value of the bond position remains fixed while the value of the stock position grows by 7% each year. A decision to utilize the variable-ratio asset allocation program, of course, also has financial consequences. Even if the variable-ratio program outper-

TABLE 12-1
50/50 Stock/Bond Allocation (25 Years Ended December 31, 1992)*

| | Accumulation Investor | | | | Distribution Investor | | | | |
| | Cumulative Total Value | | | | Cumulative Capital Value | | | | Cumulative Income |
Time span	Stocks (+10%)	Bonds (+7%)	Total portfolio	Stock ratio	Stocks (+7%)	Bonds (0)	Total portfolio	Stock ratio	
Inception	$ 100	$100	$ 200	50%	$100	$100	$200	50%	$ 0
5 years	161	140	301	53	140	100	240	58	53
10 years	259	197	456	57	197	100	297	66	114
15 years	418	276	694	60	276	100	376	73	186
20 years	673	387	1,060	63	387	100	487	79	272
25 years	1,083	543	1,626	67	543	100	643	84	378

*No rebalancing of portfolio. Initial investment of $100 in both stocks and bonds.

forms a fixed-ratio program for a given period, it is never possible to predict what will happen the next day (or year), when a sharp bear market could erode the earlier gains.

By way of example, Table 12–2 shows the results of an assumed investment of $10,000 made 25 years ago for the fixed-ratio investor and the variable-ratio investor, with all income reinvested. I imagine you may be as surprised as I was, not only that the difference in terminal value was razor thin, but that the (less risky) fixed-ratio program actually emerged victorious. At the end of the period, the program in which the portfolio was rebalanced to 50/50 at the end of each year had a value of $100,590, while the program in which the stock/bond ratio was never readjusted had a value of $97,910. (The ratio was 63/37 at the end of the period.)

The annual rate of return on the fixed-ratio portfolio for the period was +9.7%, compared with +9.6% for the variable-ratio portfolio. Most investors would find that outcome contrary to expectations. Nevertheless, during each of the 16 rolling 25-year periods ending between 1977 and 1992, the results achieved by the two programs were quite close, although a small advantage most often accrued to the variable-ratio program. During most of the 25-year periods ending between 1950 and 1976, results favored the variable-ratio program. In total, for all of the 43 quarter-century periods beginning in 1926, the variable-ratio program provided an average rate

TABLE 12–2
50/50 Initial Stock/Bond Allocation (25 Years Ended December 31, 1992)

| | Portfolio Value at End of Each Period | |
| | Fixed-ratio program | Variable-ratio program |
Time span		
Inception	$ 10,000	$10,000
5 years	13,570	13,540
10 years	15,830	15,410
15 years	25,990	24,850
20 years	52,040	49,950
25 years	100,590	97,910

Stock returns are based on the S&P 500 Index; bond returns are based on long-term U.S. government bonds. Initial investment of $10,000 in each program.

of return of +8.6%, nicely ahead of the +7.5% return for the fixed-ratio program.

The major reason for the greater relative success of the fixed-ratio strategy since 1977 is that returns on bonds were closer to those of stocks than in the earlier periods. If you accept my view that the relative returns on bonds and stocks in the coming era seem likely to parallel those of the recent past, you will favor the fixed-ratio program, with its lower risk, over the variable-ratio program. Whatever conclusion you come to, you should not ignore the fact that all past performance results are necessarily "period dependent." So, for that matter, is the future.

TACTICAL ASSET ALLOCATION

Thus far in this chapter, I have been speaking of *strategic* asset allocation, meaning the setting of a durable long-term balance that meets your financial objectives, your risk tolerance, and your return goals. The strategic allocation should be altered infrequently and only as your circumstances change. As noted in the opening quotation from the introduction to *The Intelligent Investor,* you must supply the emotional discipline to maintain the proper framework of a sound investment program. But there is another approach, one that does not assure success but offers the prospect of extra returns at the margin, perhaps with less exposure to market risk. It is called *tactical* asset allocation.

CAVEAT EMPTOR: *The Tax Consequences of Asset Allocation*

As noted in Chapter 11, the tax consequences of any investment decision should be carefully considered. In the case of rebalancing a mutual fund investment program to maintain the desired stock/bond allocation, the consequences are likely to be small, for two reasons: (1) Annual investment income and any additional investments can be used as the first sources of reallocation, minimizing the need to liquidate any mutual fund shares, (2) The mutual funds themselves, as noted earlier, tend to realize capital gains of significant proportions; these gains are taxed when distributed to shareholders, meaning that gains actually realized by the investor when shares in the mutual fund portfolio are liquidated may be relatively modest. Furthermore, for tax-deferred investment programs such as IRAs, 401(k) plans, and variable annuities, the realization of gains is of no significance and reallocation is essentially painless from a tax standpoint.

Tactics are specific actions designed to implement a basic strategy. In the financial markets, tactics consist of varying the strategic asset mix to take advantage of expected differences in the relative valuations of specific types of financial assets. For example, emphasizing small stocks over large, or value stocks over growth, or consumer goods over capital goods are all tactical moves that a fund's portfolio manager might make in the search to improve equity returns relative to the overall market. In Chapter 4, I expressed skepticism that most managers will be able to enhance returns through these tactical moves, or, for that matter, through successfully selecting specific stocks that will provide above-average returns in the future. The record is clear that, for professional investment managers as a group, these kinds of tactics are unproductive.

Another sort of tactical allocation strategy involves changing the stock/bond ratio based on the relative outlooks for the respective financial markets. But since no one can ever be sure of the future path of the financial markets, the tactics I recommend would place severe restrictions on the extent of the allocation changes. Specifically, I would vary the desired strategic balance by no more than 15 percentage points on either side. A portfolio targeted at 50/50 would never have less than 35% in stocks nor more than 65%. Table 12–3 shows the possible impact of these tactics on the basic asset allocations set forth in Figure 12–1.

TABLE 12–3
Stock/Bond Allocation (%)

Basic allocation	Maximum aggressive allocation	Maximum conservative allocation
50/50	65/35	35/65
60/40	75/25	45/55
70/30	85/15	55/45
80/20	95/5	65/35

Are there fundamental guidelines that you can use to make changes to your portfolio allocation? I think there are. But they should be used only if you are prepared to take the risk of being wrong. My favorite guideline is based on projecting future returns by making judgments on the components of stock and bond returns that I discussed in Chapter 1: for stocks, the actual current dividend yield, the expected dividend growth rate, and the expected change in the price the market will pay for $1 of dividends; for bonds, the actual current interest rate.

Using the three components of stock valuation has led to remarkably helpful predictions of long-range returns for some four decades. One of the three components—the current dividend yield—requires no forecasting, since it is a known quantity. A forecast that the other two factors—the dividend growth rate and the change in the price of $1 of dividends—will simply regress to their means established over the previous 25 years proves to be a fairly good assumption.

If the initial stock dividend yield is, say, 3%, and the dividend growth rate has been +6%, the total return in the stock market over the next decade would be projected at +9%. This +9% figure would represent the market's *fundamental* return. But it would prove to be the *actual* return only if the price of $1 of dividends was the same at the end of the decade as at the beginning. If this price were to rise, so would the return, and vice versa. Assuming the price paid for $1 of dividends averaged about $27 over the previous 25 years, a regression to that level from the initial price paid has a measurable impact on return.

Table 12–4 shows that, if $1 of dividends can be purchased for $20 at the start of a decade (a yield of 5.0%) and $27 at its conclusion (a yield of 3.7%), capital will increase by +35%, or +3.0% per year. Adding

---

CAVEAT EMPTOR: *The Cost of Being on the Sidelines*

That you reduce risk by being out of the stock market is well known. What is less well known is that the *opportunity cost* of being out of the market may be substantial. Stock prices tend to achieve their gains and suffer their losses in short periods of time, often when least expected. If you sit on the sidelines, you run a high risk of missing the spasmodic upsurges in the market. You also are unlikely to exit the market, at least with any consistency, just before the downdrafts come. For example, the annual return on stocks over the decade ended December 31, 1992, was +16.2%. However, if you had been out of the market during only the four best market months, you would have earned an average annual return of +11.3%. Therefore, if you had the ill fortune to miss just four months in that 120-month period (if you were out of the market just 3% of the time), you would have enjoyed a gain of +191%, but if you had simply bought and held common stocks for the full period, you would have achieved a gain of +348%. The sidelines is often a costly place to sit.

---

this component to the +9.0% fundamental return, the projected total return on stocks is +12.0%. If the initial price was $35, capital would be reduced by −23%, reducing total return by −2.6% annually, to +6.4%.

Using our single forecasting measure for predicting bond valuations, the current interest rate, has also led to remarkably helpful forecasts of long-term returns on bonds. The use of the current yield as the assumed ten-year rate of return is simply an acknowledgment that it is virtually impossible to forecast interest rates ten years hence, to say nothing of the rates at which ten years of interest payments would be reinvested. Further, it is a recognition that these factors tend to counterbalance one another over time. Higher interest rates, however painful to the short-term investor, raise the returns earned by the long-term investor. When viewed over ten-year periods since 1926, more than 80% of the future total returns on long-term government bonds have been explained by their initial yields.

For both stocks and bonds, this approach to forecasting market returns is strictly *long-term* in nature. (I have used ten-year periods.) To forecast dividend growth over shorter periods is probably not worth the effort; to forecast short-term changes in the price of $1 of dividends (or $1 of interest) is decidedly hazardous. Yet this is what the financial markets are doing every day.

TABLE 12–4
Impact of a Changing Price-Dividend Ratio

Price Paid for $1 of Dividends		Implied Percentage Change in Market Value	
Initial	25-year average	Instantaneous	Spread over 10 years
$40*	$27	−33%	−3.9%
35	27	−23	−2.6
30	27	−10	−1.0
25	27	+8	+0.8
20	27	+35	+3.0
15	27	+80	+6.1
10*	27	+170	+10.4

*These extreme valuations were reached, respectively, only at the 1987 market high and the 1933 market low.

How have ten-year forecasts based upon this simple methodology—relying on just four variables, two of which (the initial yields on stocks and bonds) are known in advance—fared in the past? Remarkably well. Figure 12–2 presents a clear picture of the general similarity of the forecast versus the actual returns of each asset class over ten-year periods beginning in 1948. To place numbers on each bar in the two charts would be overwhelming, so let me highlight just a few examples.

- For the 1970s, the forecast annual return for stocks was +9.0%; the actual return was +5.9%. For bonds, the forecast return was +6.9%; the actual return was +5.5%.

- For the 1980s, the forecast annual return for stocks was +15.0%; the actual return was +17.5%. For bonds, the forecast return was +10.1%; the actual return was +12.6%.

- For the 1990s, based on the relationships existing on December 31, 1989, the forecast return was +7.4% for stocks and +8.2% for bonds. During the subsequent three years ended December 31, 1992, the rates of return have been: stocks +10.8%, bonds +11.0%. "So far, so good" is a reasonable conclusion.

These examples make it clear that, while there were significant differences between forecast and actual returns, both the direction and the

FIGURE 12–2
Forecast Returns versus Actual Returns—Stocks and Bonds

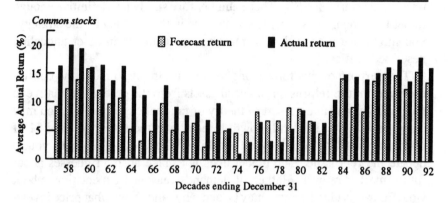

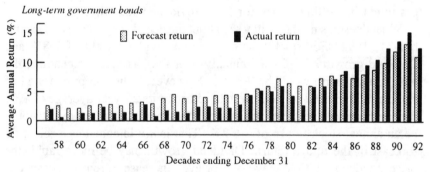

dimension of the change in returns were quite accurately indicated. In statistical terms, the correlation between forecast returns and actual returns was 0.77 for stocks and 0.96 for bonds. (Perfect correlation is 1.00.) In the world of academe, correlations of more than 0.50 indicate a statistically significant relationship. In fairness, I will acknowledge that even the correlation of 0.77 for stocks leaves a great deal of the relationship between the forecast returns and the actual returns unexplained. Overall, the forecasts are telling us something worth knowing—or at least some thing that would have been worth knowing in the past.

From observing the pattern of returns shown in the charts, it is obvious that the actual ten-year average returns moved in fairly close proximity to the forecast ten-year average returns. In fact, the standard deviation between the actual and forecast stock returns averaged about 3% on a mean return of +11%; for bond returns, the standard deviation was 1.5% on a mean return of +5%. These numbers are surely not definitive enough to bet the ranch. However, if you believe in the efficacy of the strategy, you might use it to make the marginal adjustments in asset allocation described earlier.

The purpose of this forecasting method is simply to move the consideration of future returns on financial assets from the purely speculative to the logically sensible—a sort of theory of rational expectations. You may disagree with the dividend growth forecast and the future price of $1 of dividends that I have proffered, but this methodology challenges you to debate the real issue. The model does not make abstract guesses about future market returns. Rather, it demands reasoned expectations about what future dividend growth may be and why, and about what price investors might be willing to pay for $1 of dividends and why.

What does this methodology say about the decade beginning on December 31, 1992? For stocks, with an initial dividend yield of 2.8% and dividend growth of +6.0% annually over the past quarter century, the base annual return would be +8.8%. However, if the $35 price for $1 of dividends at the end of 1992 were to return to its 25-year average of $27, that return would be penalized by −2.6% annually. The net result would be an annual stock return of +6.2%. That is *not* intended as a scientific forecast of the future return. Dividend growth may be more rapid; the price-dividend multiple may hold (or even increase, a remote prospect). The forecast long-term bond return, using my methodology, would be +7.3%, based on the yield of the 20-year U.S. Treasury bond on December 31, 1992.

Even more simplistically, but offered without apology, the stock market can be viewed as a game of chance; the odds change along with changes in the yields prevailing at the time of your investment. During the 1926–92 period, the stock market provided a total return averaging about +10% annually. The chance of reaching or exceeding this average during any ten-year period has been shaped importantly by the initial dividend yield at the start of each period, as shown in Table 12–5.

Of course, in our asset allocation portfolio, the stock market's potential return must be contrasted with the potential return in the bond market. Since future bond returns have been shaped in large part by their initial yields, we can establish chances based on that factor as well. Table

---

CAVEAT EMPTOR: *Limits on the Power of Forecasting*

By way of full disclosure, I should acknowledge that the forecasting power of my stock return model was not in evidence during the years surrounding the Great Depression of the early 1930s. The volatility of dividends during this turbulent time, and the prices paid for them, simply overwhelmed the forecasts. (The bond model, however, worked fairly well.) The conclusion would seem to be that the model for forecasting stock returns can be used effectively if "normal" business and market conditions prevail, but not if we experience conditions wholly beyond historical experience.

TABLE 12–5
Stock Returns (Decades Ending 1935–92)

Initial yield	Chances of return greater than $+10\%$ over subsequent decade
Less than 3.5%	1 in 16
3.5% to 4.5%	7 in 15
4.6% to 6.0%	13 in 17
More than 6.0%	6 in 10
Total	27 in 58*

*Out of 58 ten-year periods, 27 had average returns greater than $+10\%$.

12–6 shows the chances, based on past experience, that the return on long-term bonds will fall within a given number of percentage points of the initial yield. As you can see, the odds are compelling that future bond returns will cluster around the initial interest rate. In over 80% of the periods (47 out of 58), annual returns have remained within a margin of two percentage points or less.

Taken together, Tables 12–5 and 12–6 provide interesting odds as we look past the end of the century to the year 2002. At the close of 1992, with the yield on stocks well below 3.5%, historical experience suggests that there is no more than one chance in 16 that stocks will achieve a return of more than $+10\%$ annually during the next decade. On the other hand, history suggests that there are roughly three chances out of five that annual

TABLE 12-6
Long-Term U.S. Government Bond Returns (Decades Ending 1935-92)

Future returns versus initial yield	Chances of occurrence
Within 1.5%	34 in 58
1.5% to 2.0%	13 in 58
2.1% to 2.5%	8 in 58
Greater than 2.5%	3 in 58

returns on U.S. Treasury bonds will fall within 1.5% of the 7.3% yield at the close of 1992 (i.e., within a range of 5.8% to 8.8%).

It is up to you to decide whether these odds are significant enough to call for tactical changes in your basic strategic asset allocations. They are based only on history, and we know the financial markets do not subject themselves to actuarial tables. But at the very least, these forecasts suggest that the returns on financial assets during the 1990s will almost surely fall well short of those earned during the 1980s. The forecasts also suggest that the premium returns earned by common stocks over bonds could fall significantly below long-term historical norms. Since unpredictable risks always exist—"anything can happen" is a good rule of thumb for the financial markets—canny investors may wish to lower their allocation to stocks by an appropriate amount.

CAN YOU INCREASE RETURN WITHOUT INCREASING RISK?

We have all heard that there is no such thing as a free lunch. It is generally true. And I believe it is universally true in the financial markets. Reward and risk do indeed go hand in hand, and you cannot enhance potential return without exposure to greater risk. So, the answer to the question—can you increase return without increasing risk?—ought to be a resounding "no."

As the question applies to the mutual fund field, however, the answer is in fact a resounding "yes." These seemingly contradictory answers can be reconciled because large variations in *costs* can make a substantial—indeed, a definitive—difference in returns. When the relative costs of mutual funds are taken into account, there may well be a free lunch for

TABLE 12-7
The Relationship between Cost and Quality

	U.S. Treasury bond fund	BBB quality bond fund
Assumed gross yield	7.0%	8.2%
Assumed annual cost	0.3	2.3
Yield to investor	6.7%	5.9%

investors. The universal truth, then, applies only to the financial markets in the abstract, since their returns are measured on paper without real-world frictions—transaction costs, advisory and custody fees, administrative expenses, and the like—that inevitably diminish the theoretical returns achieved in the ideal world. In the mutual fund field, therefore, costs assume a tremendous importance for the long-term investor. Other things held equal, lower costs mean higher returns.

This principle has important implications regarding how you allocate your assets. For it follows that you can own a fund with a lower expected *gross* return and a lower risk, and earn the same or higher *net* return as on a riskier fund—provided that the costs of investing in the lower-risk alternative are materially less than those in the higher-risk alternative. As an example, Table 12-7 shows that a long-term U.S. Treasury bond fund can easily earn more than a BBB-quality bond fund (lowest investment-grade rating) when the cost differential is large.

The extreme range of bond fund costs illustrated in the table is by no means unusual in the mutual fund field. On the low side, it is simply a matter of fact. On the high side (and many bond funds incur even higher annual costs than 2.3%), it is based on a 1.3% expense ratio (the average is 1.0%) and a 5% sales charge (about 65% of all bond funds are load funds) spread out over five years at the rate of 1% per year. The U.S. Treasury bond fund provides 14% more income on a portfolio essentially without credit risk.

With the example in the caveat emptor that follows as background, I turn to the implications of applying the concepts of risk premium and cost penalty to asset allocation. If you assume, a bit more optimistically than was suggested by my earlier projection, that the average annual return for stocks during the decade beginning December 31, 1992, might be +10% and that the return for bonds might be +7%, you can compare the returns

---

CAVEAT EMPTOR: *Risk Premium versus Cost Penalty*

It is basic economics that riskier types of assets demand higher returns than more secure types, as compensation for the higher risks assumed. "Risk premium" is the scholarly term for this anticipated difference in return. For example, the expected risk premium required on an investment-grade bond portfolio might be a yield one percentage point above the yield available on a U.S. Treasury bond. Or the expected risk premium required on a stock portfolio might be based on a prospective total return of three percentage points more than the yield on a U.S. Treasury bond. Whatever the premium, it is counterbalanced—percentage point for percentage point, dollar for dollar—by a reduction in the costs of acquiring and holding the portfolio. Thus, if an investment-grade bond fund incurred an expense ratio one percentage point higher than that of a U.S. Treasury bond fund, 100% of its risk premium would be confiscated. If a stock fund incurred an expense ratio two percentage points higher than that of a U.S. Treasury bond fund, two-thirds of the three percentage point risk premium to which it should be entitled would be confiscated. Risk premium and cost penalty, ever at war with each other, will soon find their way into the mutual fund evaluation process. It's about time.

---

for three different asset allocation portfolios: One, a portfolio comprising 50% of assets in split between an actively managed stock fund and bond fund, rebalanced to 50/50 annually; two, a similarly balanced portfolio comprising index funds with much lower costs; and three, an index fund portfolio comprising 35% stocks and 65% bonds.

I assume that the actively managed fund portfolio carries a cost of 2.0% annually. (You may recall from Chapter 10 that the average mutual fund carries an annual cost, including operating expenses and amortized sales charges, of 2.2%.) I also assume that the index funds can be operated at about 0.2% annually. Using these assumptions, now consider the remarkable implications for the returns provided:

- *The balanced-risk portfolios.* The first two columns of Table 12–8 compare the returns achieved by two investors, each willing to commit 50% of assets to equities. The investor in the indexed portfolio earns a net return of +8.3%, nearly 30% higher than the +6.5% net return earned on the actively managed fund port-

TABLE 12–8
Sample Asset Allocation Portfolios (Stocks/Bonds)

| | Balanced Risk | | Risk Averse |
	Actively managed funds 50/50	Index funds 50/50	Index funds 35/65
Weighted portfolio return	+8.5%	+8.5%	+8.1%
Assumed cost	−2.0	−0.2	−0.2
Net portfolio return	+6.5%	+8.3%	+7.9%

Return of +10% on stocks and +7% on bonds.

folio. In this case, you can see a compelling increase in reward without any additional risk whatsoever.

- *The risk-averse portfolio.* The third column shows that the investor in the index funds could earn a +7.9% net return with a stock exposure of only 35% of assets, compared with a +6.5% net return for the investor in the actively managed funds with a stock exposure of 50%. Thus, despite a 15 percentage point reduction in risk exposure, reward rises more than 20%.

It could be argued that Table 12–8 stacks the deck by using funds with higher costs than the careful investor truly has to pay and by assuming bond returns that are reasonably competitive with stock returns. So I substitute in Table 12–9 a set of actively managed funds without sales loads and with highly competitive annual costs averaging 1%. I assume that stocks will earn +12% annually during the next decade, rather than the +10% assumption in Table 12–8. Finally, I assume that the risk-averse investor maintains the same 35/65 stock/bond balance.

The risk-averse portfolio again exceeds the return of the actively managed balanced-risk portfolio, despite a 15-percentage-point reduction in equities (35% versus 50%). Holding risk constant at 50/50, the index portfolio return of +9.3% exceeds the actively managed portfolio return of +8.5% by nearly 10%. Thus, while the best-case simulation for actively managed funds narrows the disparity in the risk-return relationship, it does not nearly eliminate it. Given the magic of compounding, each $10,000 initial investment balanced at 50/50 in the actively managed portfolio would grow to $22,610 over ten years, but would grow to $24,330 in the indexed portfolio.

TABLE 12-9
Sample Asset Allocation Portfolios (Stocks/Bonds)

| | Balanced Risk | | Risk Averse |
	Actively managed funds 50/50	Index funds 50/50	Index funds 35/65
Weighted portfolio return	+9.5%	+9.5%	+8.8%
Assumed cost	−1.0	−0.2	−0.2
Net portfolio return	+8.5%	+9.3%	+8.6%

Return of +12% on stocks and +7% on bonds.

So the low-cost principle stands this stern test. It continues to provide a substantially higher return with risk held constant and marginally higher return with a lower risk profile. When you consider the importance of low cost, you have two choices: (1) hold risk constant and add to your expected return or (2) reduce risk and earn a comparable or even higher return than an actively managed fund. Clearly, in the mutual fund field, risk and reward go hand in hand *only if cost is held constant.*

I have three final thoughts with respect to my "risk premium, cost penalty" principle. (1) Money managers may criticize these examples and claim that they can outpace the market indexes by an amount exceeding their costs. Based on past experience over extended time frames, two out of five will be right in the case of no-load funds and one out of five in the case of load funds. It follows that three out of five (or four out of five) will fail to outpace the market by a margin sufficient to recover their costs. (2) For investors in the aggregate, the advantages forecast for the index portfolio (+1.8% in the first case, +0.8% in the second) seem understated relative to past experience. Applying increases of this magnitude to assets held over an extended period multiplies the cost impact remarkably, as the magic of compounding comes into full force and effect. (3) The examples do not necessarily imply that index funds are the sole means of implementation of the program. Carefully selected mainstream common stock funds with low expense ratios may provide a viable alternative.

SUMMARY

As an intelligent investor, you must make five key decisions about your asset allocation program:

- First, and most important, you must make a strategic choice among stocks and bonds. Differently situated investors, with unique needs and circumstances, will obviously make different decisions.

- Second, the decision to maintain a fixed ratio or a ratio that varies with market returns cannot be sidestepped, although the fixed ratio appears to be the more sensible choice.

- Third, a decision must be made on the elements of your asset allocation portfolio, and it comes down to the choice of stock and bond mutual funds. For the stock component, you should select a limited number of equity funds seeking objectives parallel to your own and a very limited number of high-quality bond funds whose maturities match your own time horizon.

- Fourth is the decision as to whether to introduce an element of tactical allocation. It carries its own risks. Changes in the stock/bond ratio *may* add value, but they may not. In an uncertain world, tactical changes should be made sparingly.

- Fifth is the decision as to whether, because of the relationship between risk premium and cost penalty, you have the opportunity to enjoy increased return while assuming reduced risk. If you accept this concept, an index-oriented strategy demands your consideration. But if you are confident of your ability to identify a superior manager in advance and confident that the cost of acquiring and holding the fund does not materially impair that superiority, the traditional active manager strategy is equally appropriate.

All five of these decisions require tough, demanding choices by the intelligent investor. With thoughtfulness, care, and prudence, you can make these choices sensibly and securely.

Chapter Thirteen

Mutual Fund Model Portfolios
Getting Down to Brass Tacks

Turning a rough measurement into a precise one—and, by implication, turning a general principle into a specific course of action—is known as "getting down to brass tacks." This phrase, it is said, came from an old custom whereby merchants measured a yard of fabric from the tips of their noses to the fingers at the end of their outstretched arms. Buyers who were afraid of being cheated could call for an exact measurement, and for this purpose there were rows of brass tacks, 36 inches apart, embedded in the counter.

In this chapter, I shall get down to brass tacks, moving from the principles of asset allocation discussed in Chapter 12 to the selection of the particular types of stock and bond funds that should help you align your long-term reward expectations with the level of risk you are willing to assume. While the broad asset allocation principles presented thus far are uniformly applicable to all investors—from a young person just embarking on an investment journey, to a highly conservative retiree, to a corporate pension plan—I shall now present specific examples of portfolios that reflect an array of lifestyles, ages, objectives, and financial circumstances. I want to be clear that each of the model portfolios presented in this chapter reflects allocations for an *investment* program, as distinct from a *savings* program. All investors should maintain an independent savings program consisting of liquid emergency cash reserves. The rule of thumb for a savings program is that a working person should have available three to six months of living expenses; a retired person might require up to a year's worth of living expenses in reserve.

When you consider that investors number in the millions and mutual funds in the thousands, the possible combinations for investment portfolios seem overwhelming. Obviously, it would be impractical to attempt to deal with every possible circumstance for every investor. It is possible, however, to define specific characteristics that broadly describe large segments of the investment population. I shall present recommendations for investors in five categories:

1. *The accumulation investor,* typically between the ages of 25 and 50, seeks to build capital to achieve some long-term objective. Whether that objective is to accumulate assets for retirement, to meet a child's future college education expenses, or to purchase a home, the guidelines for charting the appropriate investment course are similar. They vary most importantly according to the number of years in which the desired goal is to be reached. (This section applies to both taxable accounts and tax-deferred retirement accounts.)

2. *The transition investor,* roughly age 51 to 65, is gradually moving from an investment program focused on accumulating assets to a program focused on distributing income.

3. *The distribution investor,* once retirement age is reached, seeks to maximize investment income, achieve a modicum of income growth to cope with inflation and, to the extent possible, protect capital. This section includes recommendations for the early and middle years of normal retirement as well as for the later years.

4. *The lump-sum investor* is someone of any age who receives a single pool of capital from an insurance policy or an inheritance. This investor has quite different objectives from the accumulator since the assets have, in essence, already been accumulated and the objective now is to invest to meet the needs of the new beneficiary. My recommendations include programs for both investors who seek further capital accumulation and those who require periodic income distributions.

5. *The institutional investor* has a time horizon that is, if not unlimited, certainly very long. Here I make separate portfolio recommendations for two institutions with very different needs: the corporate pension fund, seeking to accumulate assets to meet future pension liabilities; and the endowment fund, seeking current income, income growth, and preservation of principal.

In presenting each of these programs, I follow the traditional approach to asset allocation: a pie chart showing the percentage of the

CAVEAT EMPTOR: *No Two Snowflakes*

It is said no two snowflakes are alike. Surely the same can be said of human beings. It follows that no two investment programs will be alike; thus, I want to underscore that variations from my recommended model portfolios may be appropriate. You may want to change my suggested allocations depending on your personal circumstances or your outlook for the financial markets. Even if you are a long-term investor accumulating assets in an IRA, if you can't tolerate significant volatility in the market value of your portfolio, you might substitute a short-term bond fund in place of a growth fund, odd though that may sound. If your evaluation is that stocks are overpriced relative to bonds, you might want to reduce your equity exposure, subject to the limitations described in the preceding chapter. An investment program is a personal choice, and the model portfolios are only targets for your consideration.

investor's assets in each of the various major fund categories. The stock fund categories include growth, value, equity income, and broad-based specialty funds (concentrated specialty funds should be held by only the most aggressive investors). The bond funds are assumed to hold only high-grade bonds and are arrayed by maturity: long term, intermediate term, and short term.

This simple formulation enables me to present my recommendations in the most understandable way. However, I want to emphasize that there are other ways to achieve the desired allocations that may involve greater simplicity, lower cost, more favorable tax impact, or some fine-tuning to meet your special requirements. I want you to be aware of these five options before I present my specific recommendations.

- *Balanced funds.* These funds combine the characteristics of mainstream stock funds and high-grade bond funds, and could be the sole holding of the transition investor, the income-oriented lump-sum investor, or the endowment fund. The balanced fund could also comprise a core position in other model portfolios, with the allocation differences reconciled by the marginal use of the other specified funds. An investor who is early in the retirement phase and seeks a 50/50 stock/bond balance could invest

about 85% of assets in a balanced fund with a 60/40 ratio and
the remaining 15% in short- and intermediate-term bond funds.

- *Index funds.* The stock fund position of every investment program I describe could just as easily be supported solely by holding one or more stock market index funds, and the bond fund position could in each case be supported by a core holding in a
bond index fund (providing a combination of long-term,
intermediate-term, and short-term bonds). That such a program
would enhance total return is suggested by historical data, but is
by no means guaranteed; that it would provide markedly higher
income without any increase in risk is beyond debate.

- *Municipal bond funds.* As I noted in Chapter 11, these funds
should be used in place of taxable corporate or U.S. government
bond funds when tax-exempt income provides a significant enhancement on an after-tax basis.

- *Variable annuity funds.* All taxable lump-sum investors with a
long-term time horizon (at least ten years) should consider these
tax-deferred programs, provided they can be obtained at minimal
cost and maximum flexibility.

- *Fine-tuning funds.* You may want to modify my general allocation
recommendations to suit your particular needs. You could own, for
example, a small-cap fund, an international fund, or a utilities income fund to give a particular tilt to your portfolio, even in those
model portfolios that indicate a zero commitment to these types of
funds. (However, such funds should rarely exceed 20% of your
stock portfolio.) Nor is there anything inherently wrong with owning a high-yield bond fund rather than a high-grade bond fund, provided that you are aware of the additional risks and the holding is
limited to no more than 20% of your total portfolio.

With that background, Table 13–1 presents an overview of the various
model portfolios so you can see their interrelationships, similarities, and
differences. Not only do the stock/bond ratios vary from one model portfolio to another, but the composition of the stock and bond segments varies
as well. The model portfolios are dynamic entities and will require tending
to maintain the suggested allocations over time. As I discussed in Chapter
12, there is no easy answer to the question of whether or not to periodically
rebalance your portfolio allocation, but common sense favors some form
of readjustment to maintain your original risk/reward profile. Once you
have selected the model portfolio with which you most closely identify,

TABLE 13-1
Model Portfolio Allocations

| | | | Type of Investor | | | | | |
| | | | Distribution | | Lump Sum | | Institution | |
	Accumulation	Transition	Earlier years	Later years	Growth-oriented	Income-oriented	Pension	Endowment
Stock funds								
Growth	35%	15%	0%	0%	35%	15%	15%	10%
Value	30	30	25	15	20	25	15	25
Equity income	0	15	25	20	0	20	15	25
Specialty	15	5	0	0	15	0	15	0
Total stock funds	80%	65%	50%	35%	70%	60%	60%	60%
Bond funds								
Long term	10%	10%	20%	30%	20%	25%	20%	20%
Intermediate term	10	15	20	25	10	10	10	20
Short term	0	10	10	10	0	5	10	0
Total bond funds	20%	35%	50%	65%	30%	40%	40%	40%
Total portfolio	100%	100%	100%	100%	100%	100%	100%	100%

you may then wish to turn to the later analysis of that particular investment program.

THE ACCUMULATION INVESTOR

For most investors, the process of accumulating investment assets begins sometime between the ages of 25 and 50. I emphasize again how critical it is to invest as much money as you can as early as possible and as often as practicable, despite the obvious financial constraints that nearly all investors face. As we have seen throughout this book, the magic of compounding is inextricably linked to the length of time an investment is held. Therefore, it is common sense that you will be considerably better off if you can invest regularly for 30 years rather than 10.

Perhaps it is less obvious that the longer the time period, the smaller the annual contribution required to reach a given goal. Table 13-2 makes the point emphatically. It shows the monthly contributions needed to accu-

---

CAVEAT EMPTOR: *Less Is More*

How many funds should you own in your portfolio? Far fewer than you probably think. A single mainstream balanced fund, for example, provides extraordinary diversification and is the functional equivalent of having your entire portfolio managed by an investment counsel firm or by a trust officer at your local bank. (The value added by using two banks is dubious.) A single equity index fund can cover the entire stock market and is likely to be the functional equivalent of owning two mainstream growth funds and two mainstream value funds (but at a much lower cost). While it may be desirable to own a high-yield bond fund and a high-quality long-term U.S. Treasury bond fund, holding two funds in the latter category would not make much sense. You may be tempted to add new funds to your portfolio based on extraordinary past performance, and that is all right as far as it goes. But I would limit "extra" funds to the differentiated fund categories including, for example, small capitalization, international, and perhaps concentrated specialty. It is always tempting to own more rather than fewer funds since, assuming the expense ratios are similar, adding funds does not increase your total fund expenses. However, owning a large number of funds means receiving more portfolio statements and shareholder reports. Such a program adds to your recordkeeping and tax reporting chores, but it also provides additional information and a variety of investment perspectives. On balance, the number of funds you own should exemplify the aphorism that less is more; less burdensome detail, more investment focus.

---

mulate $100,000, assuming an average annual return of +10% and that the investments are made over periods ranging from five years to 30 years. You can see that if you allow yourself 30 years of contributions, you can accumulate $100,000 by investing only $44 each month. If you allow yourself only five years, however, the cost is $1,281 each month. The slope of the financial mountain you have to climb gets steeper and steeper as time goes on, from a gradual and manageable slope if you have 30 years to invest to a near-insurmountable precipice if the summit must be reached in just five years.

As the Chinese philosopher Lao-tzu tells us, "A journey of a thousand miles must begin with a single step." If you are a young neophyte investor, the prudent allocation of assets cannot begin until you take the first invest-

TABLE 13–2
Accumulating Investment Assets

Number of years	Monthly investment required to accumulate $100,000
30	$ 44
20	131
10	484
5	1,281

Assumes an annual return of +10%.

ment step. Allocating assets implies that there are assets to allocate. As you begin your investment journey, then, you will likely be best served by investing regularly in a mainstream balanced fund and maintaining that single investment account until your assets have reached, say, at least $5,000. Annual investments of $1,000 growing at a rate of +8% per annum would reach the $5,000 level in just over four years.

Once you have accumulated sufficient assets, the basic investment allocation standard up until the age of 50 should remain fairly constant at 80% equities and 20% bonds as long as you are regularly adding to your program. This ratio may seem somewhat aggressive if all of your assets are currently invested in a money market fund. However, it is based on three factors: (1) the relatively higher long-term historical returns on stocks versus bonds and reserves; (2) the possibility, if not the likelihood, of future inflation; and (3) the smoothing impact of a dollar-cost-averaging program that reduces risk. Figure 13–1 presents the suggested mix.

If you are investing fully taxable dollars, you will most likely benefit by constructing a portfolio that emphasizes minimizing your tax liability. In this case, you might achieve the 80/20 allocation by placing 40% of your assets in a growth index fund, 40% in an actively managed growth fund, and the remaining 20% in a long-term tax-exempt bond fund. Both types of growth funds can serve as effective tax-deferred investments by virtue of the fact that taxable dividend income should be modest. For the index fund, low portfolio turnover reduces the likelihood that large capital gains will be realized and distributed by the fund.

Tax-deferred accumulation investors using IRA, 401(k), 403(b), and qualified self-employed pension plans should follow essentially the same 80/20 model. However, because of tax deferral, income-oriented value funds could be substituted for low-yielding growth funds without tax impact. Tax-deferred programs are extraordinarily productive relative to

FIGURE 13–1
The Accumulation Investor

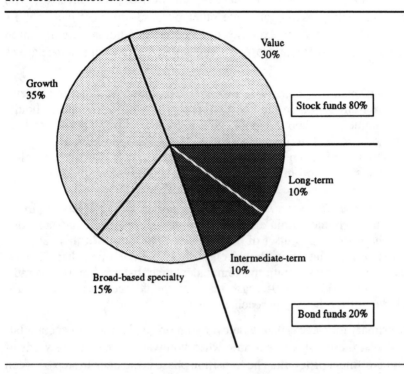

their taxable cousins, and they should be utilized for "first investment dollars" until every eligible tax-deferred dollar has been put to work.

THE TRANSITION INVESTOR

In the latter stages of the accumulation phase you will, with reasonable markets and some good luck, begin to approach the objective that you initially set for yourself. At this point you should begin to prepare for the time when you will want to draw down the income on your accumulated assets. I call this stage of the investment life cycle the transition phase, and the investor in this age bracket the transition investor. In the accumulation phase, an expansive investment horizon allows you to focus more on reward than on risk; as your investment horizon diminishes, risk becomes a more dominant consideration. The transition phase is a time to gradually realign your portfolio allocation to reflect your changing risk/reward profile.

This section focuses on the transition investor who is ultimately seeking an adequate pool of capital to meet retirement needs. For investors who are accumulating assets for some other purpose—to meet their child's future college education expenses or to purchase a home—the transition phase is quite a different prospect. The key issues in each instance are as follows:

- *Accumulating for college expenses.* Assuming that the investment program begins in the child's infancy, the transition phase should commence at about age 14, with a gradual movement of assets from stocks to bonds. By age 18, the stock/bond allocation should shift from 80/20 to 35/65. Investors who initiate the college savings program when the child is older should select a more conservative initial investment allocation.

- *Accumulating for a home.* A person accumulating assets to purchase a home within around five years is arguably in a transition phase from the outset of the investment program. In this case, the initial allocation should only rarely include more than 25% of assets in stocks, with the remainder in short-term bonds. A gradual transition to 100% cash reserves should occur as the purchase date of the home approaches.

The primary message is that, whatever your original reason for accumulating assets, there will come a time when you want to reap the rewards of your investment program. The transition phase is the interim step between accumulation and liquidation.

For the investor accumulating assets for retirement in a lifetime investment program, the transition phase may well begin in the 51–65 age range. In this case, I would recommend a 65/35 stock/bond ratio. Achieving this new allocation will involve gradually shifting assets from your stock portfolio into your bond portfolio so that the 80/20 stock/bond ratio during the accumulation phase becomes a 65/35 ratio during the transition phase.

According to my guidelines, this 15% reduction in the stock position could be achieved by reductions of 20% in the growth component and 10% in the broad-based specialty component, partially offset by a 15% position in an equity income fund. Thus, as the transition takes place the stock exposure not only declines but takes on a more conservative posture. At the same time, the 15% increase in the bond component could be achieved by a 10% investment in a short-term bond fund and a 5% increase in the intermediate-term bond fund position. The final portfolio allocation is shown in Figure 13–2.

FIGURE 13–2
The Transition Investor

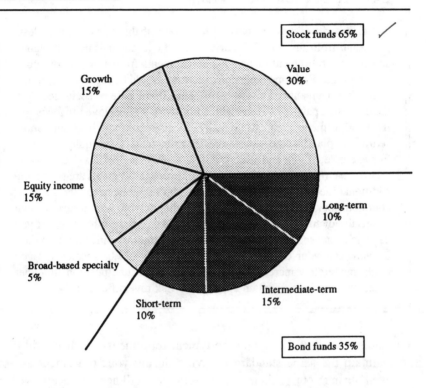

As you contemplate the transition from the accumulation phase to the distribution phase, remember that it need not occur overnight. If, in the search for higher returns, you are willing to accept the greater volatility risk engendered by a larger commitment to equities, you might make the transition at a later age. In the final analysis, you should be guided during the transition phase by your own risk tolerance balanced against your reward expectations.

THE DISTRIBUTION INVESTOR

The *raison d'etre* of a lifetime investment program is to have capital available during your retirement years. For many investors these years will begin in their early 60s, but others will retire earlier and some will

---

CAVEAT EMPTOR: *Social Security*

Social security issues are beyond the scope of this book. Nonetheless, payments from the Social Security Trust Fund count—and importantly so—in your retirement income, as do payments from a private or public pension fund. Retirement plan distributions should be regarded as similar to interest payments on a long-term bond. In the case of social security, these interest payments come with an inflation hedge, given that cost-of-living adjustments are made annually. As a result, if you have substantial retirement plan income, you may wish to increase your equity holdings. For example, if you and your spouse are receiving the maximum social security payment of $27,000 per year and your investments are producing additional income of $10,000 per year, you might want to increase your common stock fund position, possibly adding to your total return without materially disturbing the assurance of income. On the other hand, if you have no social security benefits but receive $25,000 of income from your investments, your effective exposure to risk would be greater and you might moderately increase your long-term bond fund position. In either case, the idea is to maintain appropriate risk diversification.

---

continue to work well beyond the typical retirement age. It is said that, to maintain the same standard of living during your retirement as you enjoyed during your prime earning years, you will need to receive yearly distributions equal to 75% of your average salary. The maximum yearly social security payment for a single wage earner is $13,540; for a working couple it is twice that level, $27,000. So most investors will require at least some additional income to sustain their standard of living during their retirement years. The distribution phase, then, marks the culmination of a lifetime of accumulating assets and the recognition that you may now enjoy the benefits of your disciplined investment program.

In my view, most investors, assuming full awareness of the market volatility involved, should not reduce their normal equity exposure much below the 35% level. While in the later years of retirement their dependence on income will be substantial, they should not lose sight of the risk of inflation. For investors who spend all of the income that is generated from their investment portfolios, it is simple mathematics to conclude that, if inflation persists and there is no countervailing increase over time in the capital value of their investment portfolios, then the real (inflation-

TABLE 13-3
The Impact of Inflation on an Investment Portfolio

Year	Inflation-adjusted value
Inception	$100,000
5	85,870
10	73,740
15	63,330
20	54,380
25	46,700

Assumes 7% income return and 3% rate of inflation. All distributions received in cash.

adjusted) value of their portfolios and the purchasing power of the income generated will gradually be eroded.

For example, an income yield of 7% on a $100,000 portfolio composed entirely of bonds would produce income totaling $7,000 annually. In real terms, however, assuming a relatively modest inflation rate of 3%, your annual distribution would be equivalent to just $4,000. That in itself is a sobering reality. But if you received the full $7,000 distribution in cash each year, the lack of a growth component in your portfolio would result in a gradual erosion in the value of your capital, as Table 13-3 shows. You can see that within 15 years the effective purchasing power of your initial $100,000 portfolio would be reduced by more than one-third. After 25 years the effective value of your investment portfolio, measured in real dollars, would be more than halved.

For the lucky among us (including our spouses), retirement may last for a long time. Figure 13-3 illustrates models for two investors in the distribution phase of their investment programs:

1. The investor from 60 to 75 years of age, with a longer-term time horizon.
2. The investor over age 75, who may wish to enhance income even at the risk of greater principal volatility.

The investment program for the earlier retirement years reflects an overall reduction in the stock fund allocation from 65% during the transition years to 50%. This equal balance between stocks and bonds enhances income and capital conservation. In the later years of retirement, there is a gradual progression toward higher income, reflected in a still lower stock

CAVEAT EMPTOR: *Looking for More Income?*

Despite logic and historical evidence, reasonable persons can disagree that the total returns achieved by a passive stock market index fund will outpace the total returns achieved by most traditional professional advisers. However, there can be no debate about the fact that, when risk is held constant, an index fund will provide a higher current income return, solely by reason of its lower cost. Similarly, a low-cost stock fund and a low-cost bond fund will provide higher income returns than their high-cost counterparts. The magnitude of the income differences may be large, as indicated by the examples in this table.

Impact of Costs on Income—Distribution Investor (Early Retirement Years)

	Portfolio allocation	Assumed gross yield	Net income after annual expenses	
			0.30%	*1.50%*
Value stock fund	25%	4.0%	3.7%	2.5%
Equity income fund	25	5.0	4.7	3.5
Long-term bond fund	20	7.0	6.7	5.5
Intermediate-term bond fund	20	6.0	5.7	4.5
Short-term bond fund	10	5.0	4.7	3.5
Total (weighted)	100%	5.4%	5.1%	3.9%

Given a choice between a yield of 5.1% or 3.9% in two substantially identical portfolios, any intelligent investor would make the sensible selection. For an investor with $100,000 of capital, opting for annual income of $5,100 rather than $3,900—an increase of more than 30%—without any increase whatsoever in risk exposure should not be a difficult decision. So for the distribution investor, the income-oriented lump-sum investor, and the endowment fund, it seems almost beyond argument that a significant portion of assets should be invested in stock funds and bond funds (including index funds) with minimal costs and no sales commissions.

FIGURE 13–3
The Distribution Investor

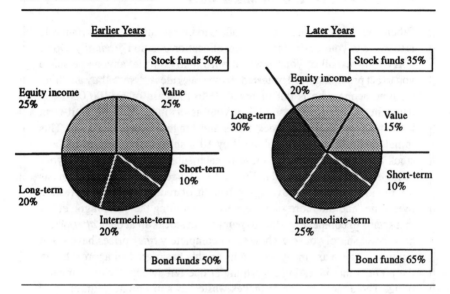

exposure of 35% and a greater emphasis on long-term bonds to reduce the income risk of the portfolio.

THE LUMP-SUM INVESTOR

In the course of a lifetime, many investors will be the recipients of substantial one-time, lump-sum cash payments—from an inheritance, insurance policy proceeds, or even a financial windfall—that they will likely want to add to their investment programs. Since in some cases these assets might fairly be described as found money, there may be a tendency to invest the proceeds in highly aggressive fund offerings or even to eschew mutual funds altogether in the hope of picking that rare hot stock that will double in value overnight. However, based on the evidence we considered in Chapters 4 through 9 and considering the slim odds, not to mention the extraordinary risks, of selecting a home-run stock fund, I urge you to resist this temptation. The same broad principles of investing that I have promulgated throughout this book apply in all circumstances and for all investment dollars. The odds of getting rich quick do not improve simply because your own hard-earned dollars are not at stake.

CAVEAT EMPTOR: *Haste Makes Waste*

When you receive a lump sum of dollars to invest, the most important rule is to move to your desired investment allocation position *gradually.* Don't hurry to invest all of your assets at once, and don't let anyone persuade you to act precipitately. The tested, if cynical, rule is "Never buy anything from someone who is out of breath." In the case of a $100,000 cash payment, you might invest 70% of your assets in reserves or short-term bond funds and 30% in stock funds and longer-term bond funds. This initial allocation might be followed by 10% shifts from reserves to these stock and bond funds at the close of each subsequent quarter until your desired allocation (reflected in Figure 13–4) is reached. This program has the obvious dollar-cost–averaging benefit of reducing risk by investing over time, and the more subtle benefit of avoiding the bandwagon effect that seems to compel investors to plunge into stocks all at once *after* prices have risen sharply or to eschew them completely *after* prices have taken a plunge. There are many variations on this basic gradual approach, but the point is that investing everything at one fell swoop is closer to gambling. The aphorism "haste makes waste" is appropriate counsel.

Unlike the other types of investors I have described, the lump-sum investor is faced with the prospect of making a substantial commitment to stocks and bonds in a relatively short period of time instead of smaller contributions over an extended time frame. The problem is how to balance the clear advantage of a long-term dollar-cost-averaging program against the potential disadvantage of having your assets out of the market and missing a sharp market rally. (I discussed the risk of being out of the market in Chapter 12.)

This important distinction suggests that, whatever your ultimate objective for these lump-sum assets, your portfolio allocation should probably be more conservative than it might be if you were accumulating assets over a lifetime. While an 80/20 stock/bond ratio might have been suitable during the accumulation phase, it seems sensible to reduce your equity exposure when you have not had the luxury of dollar-cost averaging over a working lifetime. On the other hand, it would probably not be wise to maintain too conservative an investment posture, since the investment horizon of a lump-sum investor is often considerably longer than that of a distribution investor. In general, the stock/bond allocation for the

FIGURE 13–4
The Lump-Sum Investor

a. Growth-oriented

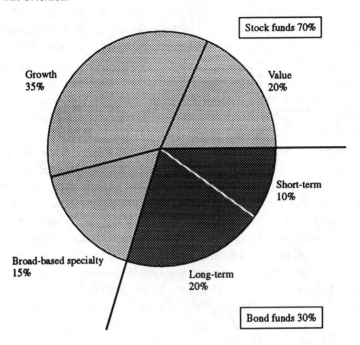

b. Income-oriented

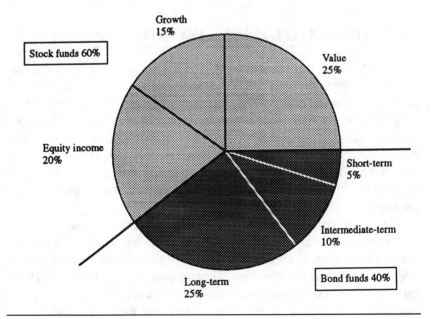

lump-sum investor should fall somewhere between the 80/20 ratio for the accumulation investor and the 35/65 ratio for the distribution investor.

As you consider the best mix of stock and bond funds for your lump-sum assets, you should focus on achieving an allocation that will fit your personal lifestyle. In a broad sense, most investors will want to construct a portfolio that emphasizes either growth in capital or current income. Figure 13–4 shows how two lump-sum investors—one with a growth objective, the other with an income objective—might allocate their investment assets.

Growth-oriented lump-sum investors might gradually invest their assets to achieve a 70% allocation in stock funds, including a small commitment in specialty and value funds but with the lion's share in growth funds. The remaining 30% should be allocated largely to longer-term bond funds. On the other hand, lump-sum investors with a substantial need for current income—such as widows or widowers—might allocate a higher percentage of their assets, perhaps as much as 40%, to bond funds. Since income risk is a major consideration, the income-oriented investor should emphasize longer-term bond funds and keep a small reserve in a short-term bond fund. In the stock portfolio (60% of assets), broad-based specialty funds with lower yields should be replaced by an equity income fund (20%), with the remainder allocated 15% to growth funds and 25% to value funds.

THE INSTITUTIONAL INVESTOR

The major factor that sets the institutional investor apart from the individual investor is the time horizon. Institutions are, in a sense, perpetual in nature. Although many colleges and universities have survived in their original form for more than a century, few U.S. corporations have met that test. This section deals with two major types of institutional investors: the corporate pension plan, whose program bears many similarities to that of the lump-sum growth-oriented individual investor; and the college endowment fund, whose program differs little from that of the lump-sum income-oriented individual investor.

The corporate pension plan has a particular objective: to assure that the corporation will have sufficient assets to meet its pension liabilities to retiring employees. I conclude that a 60/40 stock/bond mix is generally appropriate to meet this objective. The common stock portion should focus on very broad diversification, with assets equally divided among four elements: 15% in each of the three mainstream fund types and 15% in

---

CAVEAT EMPTOR: *Compared to What?*

It is conventional wisdom that an investor should *never* dip into principal. Broadly speaking, that is sound policy. Yet circumstances may arise under which you will need additional spendable resources. In my view, spending principal is often better than increasing the yield on the account. For example, assume that you hold a $100,000 portfolio and need an additional $1,000 cash during the coming year. Withdrawing it would simply reduce the capital value of your account to $99,000. On the other hand, increasing the portfolio yield to earn the additional $1,000, would require a significant change in the very nature of the investment portfolio, as this table shows.

Increasing Yield by Lowering Bond Quality

		Current		Required	
Asset	Amount	Yield	Income	Yield	Income
Bonds	$ 50,000	7.0%	$3,500	9.0%	$4,500
Stocks	50,000	3.0	1,500	3.0	1,500
Total	$100,000	5.0%	$5,000	6.0%	$6,000

For simplicity, I have assumed that the additional income is earned by changing the bond position only, increasing the yield from 7% to 9%. That would mean, essentially, liquidating an all-U.S. Treasury bond fund position and investing the proceeds in a portfolio equally divided between BBB and BB bond funds. Such a reduction in quality, especially for investors who can't afford to incur any credit risk, is beyond the bounds of prudence. So, compared to downgrading the quality of the entire portfolio, occasionally spending moderate amounts of principal makes sense.

---

specialty funds, perhaps including international funds and small capitalization stock funds. The bond portion could include long-, intermediate-, and short-term bond funds but should generally maintain a longer-term bias. Figure 13–5 shows how a sample portfolio might be allocated.

My choice of an equity ratio equal to 60% of assets is unremarkable to a fault, differing little from the 57% average equity ratio for U.S. private pension funds in the aggregate during the 1968–92 period. I would hold this ratio steady, making moderate adjustments, if any, based on the tactical strategy described in Chapter 12.

FIGURE 13–5
The Pension Fund

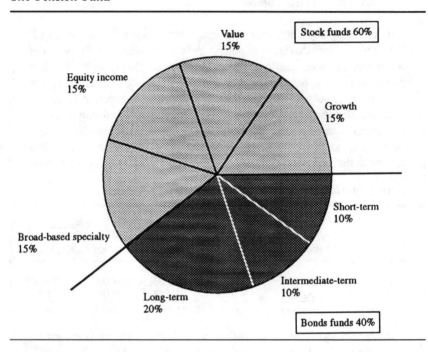

I am mindful that the allocation strategies of private pension plans generally have been poor. Their advisers (or their staffs and trustees) have exhibited a penchant for following the crowd. It has not served them well. For example, the highest equity ratio ever reached by pension plans (71% of assets) was attained at year-end 1972, immediately before the biggest market decline (−43% from top to bottom, as measured by the Standard & Poor's 500 Stock Index) since the Great Depression of the 1930s. The equity ratio was allowed to fall to a low of 51% at the end of 1981, just before the great bull market of 1982–92 began. Despite the market advance, the stock ratio fell to 49% by the end of 1984, again, just before the market's strong advance resumed. This consistently counterproductive shifting of asset allocations provides a powerful argument against guessing at the market's direction, and in favor of staying the course. Apparently coming to precisely this same conclusion (albeit somewhat belatedly), pension funds have maintained a fairly steady 55% to 60% stock commitment since 1984. It totaled 56% at the end of 1992.

FIGURE 13-6
The Endowment Fund

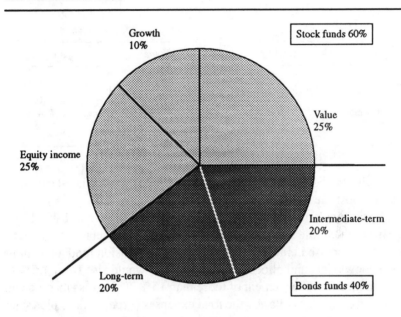

I caution that there is one good reason for altering the equity ratio: to invest the plan's assets in a manner consistent with the plan's liabilities. My model assumes that the work force has a "normal" demographic mix. If the employee population is significantly older, the equity position should be reduced; if younger, the position might be increased.

The endowment fund presents rather different issues from those of the pension fund. They arise principally because beneficiaries of the endowment fund often require that its income be distributed. Thus, the fund must provide reasonable current income, seek income growth to the extent possible and, since it cannot reduce principal risk via the magic of compounding, maintain a conservative bias.

As a result of these considerations, the endowment fund model portfolio, while it maintains the same 60/40 balance as the pension fund, is significantly more income oriented. The common stock position relies less on growth funds and eliminates the position in specialty funds. These reductions are offset by 10% increases in the value and equity income sectors. In the bond position, the 10% commitment to short-term bond

TABLE 13–4
Mutual Fund Gross Yields (December 31, 1992)

Stock Funds		Bond Funds	
Fund type	*Gross yield*	*Fund type*	*Gross yield*
Growth	2.3%	Long term	7.3%
Value	3.7	Intermediate term	6.7
Equity income	5.0	Short term	4.8
Specialty	1.5		

funds is eliminated, with the proceeds shifted into intermediate-term bond funds to boost the overall portfolio yield.

Using the yields available on December 31, 1992, shown in Table 13–4, you can see that these seemingly marginal changes in asset mix engender a substantial increase in income. Moving from the pension fund allocations to the endowment fund allocations, gross yield would rise from 4.5% to 5.2%, an income enhancement of more than 15%. This gross income will be reduced dollar for dollar by the total expenses (expense ratio plus sales commissions) incurred by the investor in the funds. So, low cost should be a priority in all cases.

SUMMARY

After you have carefully evaluated the model portfolios as a group and have decided on one portfolio that best fits your particular circumstances, you may well think, "It's all so obvious." I hope that is the case, for common sense is as important a part of the asset allocation models as careful consideration of the rewards and risks. In the final analysis, each model portfolio is only a rough target, not something to which you should slavishly adhere, but a place to start in developing your individual investment program. It is you, the investor, who must do the work necessary to get down to brass tacks and turn a ready-made portfolio into one that is tailor-made to fit your own objectives.

Chapter Fourteen

A Mandate for Fund Shareholders
The Fault, Dear Brutus

"The fault, dear Brutus, is not in our stars, but in ourselves." So said the protagonist in Shakespeare's play *Julius Caesar.* Most of this book has described how the mutual fund industry works today. But this industry can be greatly improved and can provide far better opportunities for investors. Positive change will take place, however, only if we lay the responsibility for the industry's shortcomings not in our stars but in ourselves as shareholders. If enough investors demand a better mutual fund industry, we will have a better mutual fund industry. All you need to do is stand up for your rights as investors.

It may seem difficult for a shareholder with a relatively small investment to advance change. After all, the average investor owns perhaps a $10,000 holding in a $500 million mutual fund, or a voting interest of something like 2/1000ths of 1%. But if you believe, as I do, that even one person can make a difference, any change that enough mutual fund shareholders demand will surely come to pass. I am not suggesting that mutual fund shareholders must act in concert with each other. That proposition would take organization, tedium, and patience. Rather, I am suggesting that if all shareholders merely act independently in concert with their own financial needs and best interests, the mutual fund industry will soon improve.

In considering exactly what is in your best interests as a mutual fund investor, I suggest that you abide by these four elementary rules: (1) be canny, (2) be thrifty, (3) be active, and (4) be skeptical. In the following pages I will review these rules as if they were mutually exclusive, but intelligent investors will want to incorporate all four into their investment programs.

CAVEAT EMPTOR: *The Industry*

As a term used to describe a group of firms engaged in a common business or financial activity, "industry" is a useful collective identifier. However, the purposes, policies, and practices of all of the firms in a given industry are never identical. These divergences are certainly evident in the mutual fund industry, where there are some 50 major ($5 billion or more of assets) fund complexes. Among them are some that follow what I would regard as the best practices and many that do not. Overall, however, it is my conviction that the mutual fund industry has substantial room for improvement and that even the best firms, without exception, can be much better.

THE CANNY INVESTOR

It seems almost naive to suggest that if investors are canny—wise enough to rely on their own common sense and good judgment—the mutual fund industry will be an even better investment medium. Nonetheless, I believe it to be true. As an industry, it is exceptionally responsive to investors' needs and demands. Through modern, sophisticated direct marketing techniques and energetic, highly motivated sales forces, the industry responds to consumer demands as quickly as any financial services business I have ever observed. The problem is that investors have largely demanded the *wrong* things and have for the most part ignored the right things. So any industry improvement depends first on a change in investors' attitudes—acting wisely and carefully in the selection and ownership of mutual fund shares.

While it seems trivial to suggest that the canny investor begin by reading fund prospectuses, that is where it really *does* begin. Which prospectuses should you read? Surely not those of all of the funds in the industry, nor even the 1,000 or so funds that might be covered in the leading statistical services, nor even the hundreds that might be involved if you decided on, say, a common stock fund. Perhaps a selection of prospectuses from among a dozen stock funds, half as many bond funds, and half that many money market funds, would be appropriate. That gives you just over 20 prospectuses to wade through and review the important points. It is a worthwhile investment of your time.

Where do you begin the process of selecting sample prospectuses? The most logical starting point is to review the prospectuses of some of the funds that comprise the better-known mutual fund complexes. Most fund complexes have been in business for 50 years or more, which suggests that they are doing *something* right. But do not exclude smaller funds or fund families that you may have learned about through mutual fund evaluation services and financial publications. The advice of friends who are experienced investors is often helpful, as are suggestions from your lawyer or accountant. For investors who need more professional advice, reputable financial planners and stockbrokers can provide a useful service at an additional cost.

How should the canny investor read the prospectus? It would be unrealistic to suggest that you read the entire document from cover to cover. For the long-term investor, knowing the fund's objectives, investment policies, returns, risks, and total costs (sales charges, annual expenses, redemption fees, etc.) is probably sufficient. The shorter-term active investor should also know the fund's key transaction policies, such as how to redeem shares, how to exchange shares to another fund, and any transaction limitations such as redemption fees or limits on the frequency of fund exchanges.

Once you have narrowed down the field, turn to the supplemental information provided by the fund's sponsor, including a precise description of the fund, performance statistics, and financial information. After giving appropriate, but not excessive, weight to the fund's past performance—including both capital return and income return—and following the selection criteria I set forth in the earlier chapters, you'll be ready to make your fund selections. The canny investor will look through this information and make sure that all or at least most of it has been provided. If it has not, there are lots of fish in the sea, and there are many similar funds from which to choose.

What is required is that you do your homework and demand useful information, including the fund's compound rate of return over an extended period, the comparative standards used to evaluate this record, a clear statement of risk, and a thorough presentation of cost factors. If enough investors follow this process of selecting funds on the basis of the substance, breadth, and fairness of the information they provide, only those funds that make adequate information available to investors will ultimately remain in business.

THE THRIFTY INVESTOR

If mutual fund investors become more cognizant of the costs they are paying in the form of sales loads, management fees, and other fund expenses, and then act on this awareness, these costs will surely decline. It is as simple as that. If you purchase only the shares of the lower-cost funds (perhaps even by redeeming your investments in the higher-cost funds), mutual fund sponsors will quickly get the message. They'll learn that reducing their costs to investors will help them to increase the level of assets that they manage; failing to do so will lead to an unremitting capital outflow.

This is not a utopian concept. To some degree, this scenario is already unfolding in the mutual fund industry. Consider the money market funds. In a broad sense, the lower the level of a money market fund's expense ratio, the larger the amount of assets it attracts. All of the largest funds have expense ratios that are at or below the industry norm. As far as I am concerned, the jury is now in on the fee waiver issue that I discussed earlier: temporary fee waivers *do* draw in assets. But when the fund sponsor ceases to absorb the expenses of the fund it is promoting and the expense ratio rises to its "normal" level, much of the money that was enticed into the fund by cut-rate costs is enticed out, as it were, by other funds with durable low costs and high yields. That this reversal in cash flow takes place despite the sponsor's failure to notify its shareholders about any fee increases suggests that, at least in the money market arena, investors are not only thrifty but keenly aware of the yields that they earn. In fact, when the first money market funds were formed, several carried sales loads; however, this expense was simply too much baggage for the marketplace to accept, and the practice soon vanished.

In the bond fund arena, the importance of being thrifty appears not to have been fully recognized. It is as if profligacy, not thrift, were the central theme. It is remarkable to me that so many bond mutual funds with assets upward of $1 billion incur annual expenses in excess of 1.25%. At this cost, and assuming a gross yield of 7.0%, expenses consume something like 18% of a fund's income, reducing the fund's dividend distribution to its shareholders by that same 18%. It is astonishing to see that more than half of all bond funds are actually sold with sales charges. The net result is that investors earn their net income (assuming a 5% load) on only 95% of their assets. If you hold a bond fund for five years, the result is an annual sacrifice of 1% each year in yield. At a 1.25% expense ratio, the fund's combined annual costs and sales charges over a five-year period are 2.25%, consuming nearly *one-third* of the fund's 7% gross yield.

As I noted earlier, the ability of any bond fund manager to earn excess returns sufficient to offset these prodigious costs is quite limited. Thus, it is contrary to expectations that nearly 70% of bond fund assets are held by load funds and only about 30% are held by no-load funds. There are hints that these percentages are converging, but a major shift can transpire only when bond fund investors act on their thrifty impulses.

In the stock fund arena, the presales-charge records of load and no-load funds are generally comparable. After adjusting for sales charges, no-load funds carry a distinct advantage. The marketplace seems to see this difference, and nearly 40% of the assets of all stock funds are represented by no-load funds. Most equity funds with very high operating expense ratios (say, over 2.5%) have attracted limited amounts of assets. It is difficult to determine, however, just where the link among high expenses, low performance, and a small asset base begins. Nonetheless, it seems clear to me that two trends will develop in the years ahead: (1) all equity funds—particularly the mainstream funds—will feel the cost pressure as price competition in the marketplace increases and (2) assuming that index funds "work," those that attract the most assets will be the ones that do not charge sales loads and have the lowest operating costs.

THE ACTIVE INVESTOR

Once you own shares of a mutual fund, you gain "certain inalienable rights." Among them are the right to vote proxies, the right to express your opinions to management, and finally the ultimate right, the right to "vote with your feet" and redeem your investment in the fund. This final option frightens fund sponsors greatly. Not only does it suggest that they have somehow failed the investor, but it reduces the fees they receive from managing the fund.

The right to vote proxies is significant, since management fee increases must be approved by mutual fund shareholders. (Curiously enough, so must the almost unheard-of proposals to reduce fees.) It follows that, since investors—after reading the fund's prospectus—tacitly approved the management fee when they purchased their shares, they will want to examine carefully any proposal to change the terms of the contract. Each shareholder *must* vote, and vote intelligently.

To do so, you will need complete and candid information on why a fee increase is being requested. If the proxy does not provide it, a no vote should be automatic. Many proxies, sadly, fall far short of adequate disclosure. Begin with the cover page. It often calls attention to "a vote to amend the fund's investment advisory agreement." Rarely, if ever, does it state "a vote to increase the fees you pay to the fund's investment manager by 25%." So careful examination of the details of the proxy is a must.

Fair reasons for a management to increase its fee rates might be "the need to have the resources to hire additional investment professionals," or "to expand the range of services provided to shareholders." Very few proxies, however, state that these are the reasons. Most suggest that, after long consideration, the fund's directors have approved the fee increase requested by the management company, since the fund's fee rates were below industry norms.

This reason seems more like a rationalization. (Must not half of the funds in the industry always have below-average fees and half always have above-average fees?) The real reason for most fee *rate* increases is to improve the profitability of the management company. Remember that the *dollar* amount of the fee has automatically increased—often enormously— with the increase in fund assets, although in many cases the fee rate is scaled down moderately as fund assets increase. While higher profits for fund managers are not necessarily wrong in the abstract, shareholders are entitled not only to a candid statement of that profit objective but a clear financial tabulation showing the revenues that the adviser receives from the fund both before and after the fee increase, the nature and extent of the fund's expenses, and the margin of profit it realizes on operating the fund.

If an adviser expends $0.50 out of each $1.00 of fee revenue to operate the fund, the pretax profit margin is 50%. If this margin is to go to 75%— an astonishing increase, but hardly unprecedented—let it be so stated. While huge compared to most industries, a 50% profit margin has not been uncommon among the larger mutual fund complexes. In order to merit your favorable vote, the management company should provide these profit margin figures (not only for the fund at issue but for the funds in the complex in the aggregate) and address their reasonableness.

Fund shareholders seem to ignore the issues presented in proxies, even when the fund provides reasonable disclosure. Shareholders of one investment company recently voted to approve a 31% fee increase to a manager who was already making a pretax profit equal to 85% of its gross revenues. Table 14-1 shows the figures, as published in the proxy. The fee paid to the manager rises by some $1.6 million, to more than $7 million. Since the manager's expenses remain at about $800,000, the manager's profit, too, rises by $1.6 million, a 40% increase. As a result, the profit margin

TABLE 14–1
Management Company Profit Margins

	Before *fee increase*	After *fee increase*
Management fees	$5,369,000	$7,055,000
Operating expenses	823,000	823,000
Operating profit	$4,546,000	$6,232,000
Profit margin	85%	88%

on this particular fund rises from 85% to 88%, a level that is surely amazing.

A second issue that demands that shareholders vote is the 12b-1 distribution plan discussed in Chapter 10. Sadly, since more than half of all funds already have such plans, the remaining opportunities to vote to approve or disapprove new plans are likely to be few. And, given the increasingly controversial nature of 12b-1 plans, the likelihood of any funds having the temerity to propose to increase such distribution fees seems remote in the extreme. Suffice it to say that if the fund plans to spend any of the assets that you as a shareholder have entrusted to it simply to bring additional assets into the fund, the justification for the expenditure should be clearly articulated, both in understandable conceptual terms and in detailed financial terms. Otherwise, "just vote no."

Freedom of speech to fund management is another inalienable right of fund shareholders. Few investors are aware that the management of any enlightened mutual fund is interested in the opinions of the fund's shareholders. In my experience, shareholders are rarely heard from except in matters relating to performance and the accurate processing of their accounts. One major area in which shareholders should make their opinions known is the quality of the communications they receive from their fund. Many annual reports are superficial and incomplete. Any annual report worth its salt should meet the standards I suggested in Chapter 8.

Many funds fall short of providing all—or indeed *any*—of this information to their shareholders. In fact, these sins of omission are more the industry norm than the exception. Most funds seem to believe that performance comparisons are odious and, implicitly at least, that "there is no fair standard against which we may be measured." One assumes the fund's

---

CAVEAT EMPTOR: *There Ought to Be a Law*

There is one general instance in which mutual fund fee increases may be implemented without shareholder approval. In recent years, many funds have been offered that have rather hefty fees in their advisers' contracts but these high fees are waived for "a temporary period of time." Most funds that follow this practice, not surprisingly, are money market and bond funds; high fees would impinge on the competitive yields that such funds *must* provide at the outset to gain entry into the marketplace. So the fund begins with a low fee—indeed, often no fee—and it is difficult to offer any objection to that practice. What is objectionable is the practice whereby investors are subsequently saddled with onerous fees, without ever being informed of the change. Whether such funds implement these increases on a one-shot basis or, more likely, a nickel-and-dime progression, the sponsors feel no obligation to inform shareholders that the price of investing has just gone up. Your response might be, there ought to be a law against such a practice. Paradoxically, there *is* a law, a requirement in the Investment Company Act of 1940 that an investment adviser cannot serve a mutual fund "except pursuant to a written contract that *precisely describes* all compensation" to be paid to the fund's adviser. It is difficult to believe that undisclosed and unannounced on-again, off-again fees meet this test of precision. Yet more than 2,100 mutual funds—one of every two funds—are enticing investors by waiving fees. One day, soon I hope, the law will be enforced and this practice put to rest.

---

independent directors themselves receive some comparison and evaluation of the fund's performance. An obvious solution is to make that information available to the actual *owners* of the fund—the shareholders. There is nothing wrong with presenting an imperfect comparison and then describing its limitations. But every fund simply *must* give its investors appropriate and enlightening information in its annual report. The active investor should demand no less.

In April 1993 the SEC, presumably frustrated by the industry's recalcitrance, adopted a requirement that mutual funds provide comparisons of their performance relative to an appropriate index along with a narrative discussion of strategies and factors that materially affected the fund's performance during the year, along with a ten-year comparative chart. While this requirement is a welcome step forward, funds have been given

---

CAVEAT EMPTOR: *A Canard about Cash Flow*

Many proposals for 12b-1 plans argue, speciously, that reducing or avoiding cash outflow will improve investment returns. It is often alleged that cash outflow requires the manager to liquidate attractive securities in the fund's portfolio at low prices. If so, the reverse should be equally true: cash inflow requires the manager to accumulate less attractive securities at high prices. Both arguments are absurd. Mutual funds are *portfolios* of securities, and cash flow requires neither the full elimination of existing positions nor the acquisition of entirely new positions. Rather, each portfolio holding can be proportionally reduced or increased with the ebb and flow of assets, leaving the overall portfolio structure unchanged. What is more, there is no credible evidence that the expenditure of dollars on a 12b-1 plan does increase the fund's cash inflow. The real purpose of the 12b-1 plan is to build up a fund's assets and hence the management fees paid to its adviser.

---

the option of providing the information either in their annual reports or in their prospectuses. Which alternative funds will choose remains to be seen. But it is ironic that many fund sponsors, whose portfolio managers rely on full disclosure from corporations, must be required by a federal agency to provide full disclosure to the shareholders of the funds they manage.

While it is more difficult to articulate, shareholders have the right not only to hold the fund to comparative standards that are consistently applied from year to year but also to a candid evaluation of these returns by the fund's chief executive officer. (In the typical case, the fund's CEO— responsible for *appraising* the results—is also the CEO of the investment adviser—responsible for *generating* the results. As a result, reporting to shareholders with candor is no mean challenge.) The active investor should demand fund reports that begin with something like, "last year, your fund's performance was inferior both absolutely and relative to fair competitive standards," rather than, for example, "the year's most important event was the expansion of IRA eligibility," or "your fund's assets increased by $100 million during the past year."

But the issue does not end with fair presentation of the facts and figures of the mutual fund's performance results and at least some perspective on

---

CAVEAT EMPTOR: *Demand Candor*

You should consider my bare-bones standards for fund annual reports as minimal guidelines. A few moments of thought present a plethora of other opportunities for full disclosure and candor. One excellent example is found in 1987, the year that stocks soared during the first three calendar quarters, only to plummet in the fourth quarter as a result of the great crash in the stock market on October 19. Most stock funds reported total returns for the full year in the range of +5% to −5%, making it look like a so-so, uneventful year. Why did nearly all funds describe this year—which was anything but uneventful—as a totality, rather than separating out performance in the fourth quarter (market down −23%) from performance in the first three quarters (market up +36%)? Was this not a wonderful opportunity to remind shareholders of the inevitable price volatility and risk of stocks? Did the fund's owners not have a *right* to know how their fund performed under conditions of adversity? To ask such obvious questions is, in my view, to answer them. You should demand candor under all circumstances.

---

what they mean. Overall, what is involved is a spirit of candor, in which a fund's failures receive at least as much attention as its successes, and its problems as much emphasis as its opportunities. If even 50 active investors would place this demand for candor before the fund's chairman (copies to the fund's independent directors), I believe many funds would respond affirmatively, for two reasons. First, the fund's management may not have previously considered the issue all that important and may now realize that investors care. Second, the fund's management will ultimately act with an enlightened sense of the fund's (and the adviser's) long-run self-interest.

If the demand for candor is not met even when you let your opinions be known, you can take an even more forceful action. The ultimate nightmare of fund managers is that you vote with your feet, redeem your shares, and walk away from the fund. Of course, many investors redeem their shares under the most normal of circumstances. Reallocating your assets in order to increase or reduce your common stock exposure is one obvious reason. Achieving your original financial goals *demands* redemption (e.g., sooner or later your accumulated education fund will be spent on college tuition bills). Unfortunately, leaving a fund because the fund has let you down may involve otherwise unnecessary penalties. The most obvious are (1) the cost of the sales commission you originally may have paid, especially onerous after a short period of time (i.e., a 5% sales commission reduces a fund's one-year return by −5%, but a five-year return by "only" −1% per year); and (2) the taxes payable on any capital gains you would realize if the net asset value of your shares has increased. Nonetheless, redemption of shares is the ultimate weapon of the active investor.

THE SKEPTICAL INVESTOR

Unlike the active investors, skeptical investors do not yet own a particular fund. They are looking at the information presented to them and deciding whether or not to invest their assets. In this age of aggressive fund marketing and promotional hype, the industry has earned their skepticism. Three areas come quickly to mind: in advertising, the exaggeration of the importance of a fund's past performance; in calculating yields, the inadequate disclosure of low credit quality or substantial use of risky derivative instruments to obtain exaggerated yields; and in promotion, the development of new fund concepts that are based on unproven or untested principles.

All investors want funds that provide good performance. And all funds seek to provide it. But despite overpowering evidence to the contrary, investors seem to believe that past performance is the precursor to future performance. Fund sponsors—good businessmen all—respond to investors' predispositions by exploiting a fund's past performance as if there were some link, however tenuous, between past and future returns.

The most blatant manifestation of this "past performance syndrome" is in mutual fund advertising, especially advertising that proclaims a fund #1, even as the small print reveals that the fund is first only in some limited group, of some limited size, over some limited period. Given the large number of these limited universes, literally hundreds of funds can lay claim to #1 status at any time. And when a particular fund inevitably regresses to the mean, it can be replaced in the advertising by another fund with #1 credentials offered by the same sponsor. If the sponsor operates many highly specialized aggressive funds, this option is always available.

What is important about this issue is something that the sponsors must know but do not say: the chance that a #1 fund in, say, the *past* ten years will repeat as #1 in the *next* ten years is essentially zero. The skepticism of the investor who pays little heed to such claims will be well rewarded.

CAVEAT EMPTOR: *Bought to Be Held*

Mutual funds should be bought to be held. It is hard to imagine why so many investors engage in the frequent shuffling of the mutual funds they own and even harder to imagine that their returns are enhanced by doing so. Nonetheless, there are times when you should adjust your portfolio, even if you are a long-term investor.

- *When a particular type of equity fund consistently underperforms its carefully selected peers.* To each his own as to the amount of time that should be allowed to elapse before taking action, but I suggest that one or two years of unexplained and dramatic underperformance or four or five consecutive years of marginal underperformance are generally appropriate indicators. If your fund's performance does not meet the criteria I discussed in my summary in Chapter 4 for a sustained period, the fund should be liquidated and replaced with one that does.

- *When a fund changes its objectives or policies.* If you have selected, for example, a balanced fund that subsequently becomes a bond fund, it is time for a change. If your fund radically changes its traditional portfolio turnover policy, it may be time for a change. Substantial modifications of any of the criteria that were material factors in your initial selection of the fund are also "grounds for divorce."

- *When a fund's expense ratio rises significantly.* Particularly in bond, balanced, and money market funds, an increase in fees to the manager represents a reduction of income to you and is highly unlikely to be offset by enhanced capital return. Conversely, you should be alert to new low-cost opportunities that may emerge as the industry becomes more price competitive, and should move to a new fund if cost is likely to be a principal factor in determining its performance.

- *When your investment objectives change.* Obviously, as you move through your investment life cycle, changes in asset allocation are required. In this case, while the specific types of funds may change, you may well wish to remain in the same fund family if its funds have earned your respect in the past.

Such circumstances should be regarded as the exceptions rather than the rule. If the funds are soundly selected and then consistently managed by the adviser, a bit of inertia on your part may go a long way toward your enjoyment of productive investment returns.

In fairness, the advertisements state, albeit in the proverbial small print, that past results may not recur in the future. But surely it must be obvious that investors cannot put their money to work today and achieve yesterday's returns. Yesterday is now history. So the skeptical investor should ask the sponsor: "What are the chances this record will be repeated in the years ahead?" If the answer is not candid ("The chances are near zero."), move along to the next fund on your list.

Extreme examples of this type of advertising abound. Take a look at three sample headlines:

- *"The #1 Pacific Fund."* This fund "ranked #1 for the ten-year period ended September 30, 1991, out of *three* (italics added) Pacific Region Funds." The sponsor's sister Pacific Fund—different only in cost structure—"ranked #3." What a rare combination of first and last in a single ad! By actual measurement, the "#1" figure was 19 inches high; the "#3" was one-sixteenth of an inch high.

- *"Now Ranked #1 for Performance*"* The Fund That's Performed Through Booms, Busts and 11 Presidential Elections."* The asterisk referred to a small footnote confessing that this fund was first, not among all mutual funds for the implied 44 years, but first during the third quarter of 1992 among 27 growth and income funds with assets between $250 million and $500 million.

- *"They Must be Smart."* This was the caption on an ad screaming, "#1 of all mutual funds for 30 years." Ignored: a rank of #496 for the previous ten years, #455 for the previous five years, and #1,532 for the previous year.

In their own grotesque way, ads like these have become their own parodies. They count for nothing.

Another, more insidious, form of fund advertising became popular in 1992. In a marketplace where investors are seeking higher yields, ads that promise higher yields prompt high response rates from investors, so bond funds are managed to provide such higher yields. To me, this stands the proper priorities on their head: the objectives and strategies of the fund should come first, the advertising cachet second. This kind of competition may be fair enough, but only if the risks of obtaining higher yields are explicitly and prominently articulated.

The risks are too rarely disclosed and, with the changing structure of the securities markets, can easily be obscured. In the "old days," if you knew only the quality, maturity, and cost structure of bond funds, you could make wise investment selections. Today, however, with derivative instruments (securities broken up into "tranches" with varying claims on principal and income); with many foreign bonds available (incurring, in general, both currency risk and sovereign risk); with varying prepayment provisions (under which mortgage holders may repay their obligations as interest rates fall); and with a variety of accounting options to let the fund maximize its stated yield, making intelligent comparisons among mutual funds is a daunting task. Under these circumstances, "gaming" yields is an easy game indeed for fund sponsors to play.

So when confronted with two short-term bond funds of uniform quality and maturity but a substantial yield differential, the skeptical investor should ask why and how. Many times the higher apparent yield results from a shift of capital return to income return, so consider total return as well as stated dividend yield. The issues posed are complex, requiring careful analysis and guidance. Never lose sight of the fact that, in the financial markets, when costs are held constant there is no extra reward without extra risk. A skeptical approach to investing can pay dividends.

New fund concepts—often glamorized as "new products" or, presumably even better, "hot new products"—are also dangerous. It flies in the face of common sense to think that, after all these years, some new secret can be discovered in the financial markets. Yet the industry continues to offer a variety of fund products that are either unsound, misunderstood, or inappropriately compared with other types of funds. Some examples are the government-plus fund, the prime rate fund, the short-term global fund, and the adjustable rate mortgage (ARM) fund.

The government-plus fund.   It was said a government-plus fund could significantly enhance the yield on long-term U.S. Treasury bonds—despite substantial fund expenses and often sales loads—simply by buying the bonds and selling call options on them (giving the buyer of the option the right to buy the bond from the fund at a specified price). The option premiums received by the fund, often substantial, were added to its yield. However, common sense suggests, and experience quickly proved, that when the price of a bond dropped (higher interest rates) the owner of the option did *not* exercise it. But when the price of a bond rose (lower interest rates), the bond was called away from the fund. In other words, the fund effectively owned long-term bonds when rates rose and short-term bonds when rates fell. Result: the fund lost money when rates rose, but failed to make money when rates fell. It was not a helpful combination. Tens of billions of dollars of this new product were sold to investors. Asset values fell, and few initial purchasers avoided a substantial loss of capital.

The prime rate fund. Prime rate funds were at least tacitly identified as a "modern" type of money market fund. They would own, not marketable short-term obligations of banks, corporations, and the U.S. Treasury, but participations in the loan portfolios of banks, a rather riskier approach. Since such participations were illiquid, the funds did not offer daily liquidity of shares; rather, they agreed (or at least implied) that they would allow shares to be redeemed each quarter. Here was a fund that seemed to provide a higher yield than a money market fund without extra risk. Of course, there *was* extra risk, and at least one prime rate fund has simply not honored its commitment (moral, not legal) to meet the quarterly redemption requests.

The short-term global fund. The short-term global fund presented an opportunity for investors to "obtain higher yields from around the world" without significant currency risk, because that complex risk would be cross-hedged. (I shall spare you a detailed description of how this strategy purports to work, but it comes with an added, if incalculable, cost.) These funds were at least tacitly compared with money market funds, a wholly inappropriate standard. Again, billions of dollars were drawn into them, based on the returns that would have been provided had the strategy been applied in the past. Once again, however, the future stubbornly refused to echo the past, and a widespread failure of cross-hedging in 1992 brought home to roost the currency risks involved. Shareholder redemptions—often at much reduced net asset values—soared.

The ARM fund. Among the newest mutual fund products are funds that invest in ARMs. The selling proposition was that investors could earn higher yields than they would in a money market fund, purportedly with greater yield stability and only modest price volatility. During 1992, however, ARMs were beset with mortgage prepayments when interest rates fell; ARM fund dividends dropped sharply and many of their asset values edged lower. While investors were not materially harmed, as in the earlier three instances, investors who had expected that ARM funds would be a haven from the income risk of money funds were considerably disappointed.

In a sense, there is nothing wrong with new fund concepts. However, in a world in which higher risk and higher reward go hand in hand, the securities and derivative instruments used in these new strategies must, at least in the abstract, be fairly priced to take both risk and reward into account. The problems, it seems to me, are these: (1) in new and untested products, the relationship between risk and reward may be different than the sponsor anticipates, and actual experience may therefore fall short of past indications; (2) despite the risks entailed in these new products, their yields are compared (albeit usually well-hedged with disclaimers) with safer alternatives; and (3) because of their novelty and seemingly miraculous characteristics, initial demand from investors is often large. This last circumstance engenders the obvious, traditional, and justified (at least by economic theory) response from the sponsors: higher prices (i.e., higher expense ratios) for investors.

The cost factor, as I have repeatedly emphasized, fundamentally alters the risk/reward relationship; higher expense ratios always lead to lower rates of return in the aggregate. The skeptical investor will want to be exceedingly cautious about rushing into the latest and hottest new products of this most creative of all industries. The statement "No one ever went broke underestimating the intelligence of the American public" is attributed to H. L. Mencken. My corollary is, "No investor ever went broke failing to invest in a new mutual fund product." You would rarely go wrong by following this simple advice: if it is called a "new product," particularly if it is called a "hot new product," do not invest in it.

THE ROLE OF THE INDEPENDENT DIRECTOR

So far in this chapter, I have placed on mutual fund shareholders the onus of being the agents of change in the industry. That may be asking too much, since each investor is a very small fish in a very large ocean. There is in fact another way to bring about change in the industry, involving not tens of millions of fund investors but several hundred fund independent directors. As a fund shareholder, you elect them. They are your designated representatives, and they owe you a trusteeship duty.

The independent directors of a mutual fund—those not affiliated with the fund's management company—normally comprise a majority of a fund's board of directors. They are therefore in a position to control the activities of the fund and, in particular, to assure that the fund is managed

---

CAVEAT EMPTOR: *The What-If Portfolio*

In considering the division of economies of scale between mutual funds and their management companies, let's contrast the investment returns on the stocks of mutual fund management companies with those of the funds that they manage. It has been much more profitable to own shares in the managers than to own shares in their funds. One outstanding mutual fund manager, describing "one of my favorite what-if portfolios," recently wrote that "in a single year (1989), if you had divided your money equally among eight (management company) stocks, you would have outperformed 99% of the funds that these companies promote." The long-run record appears far more imposing than that. This table compares the results of investing $10,000, equally weighted, in the shares of the two largest publicly traded management companies during the decade ended December 31, 1992, with the returns of their equity funds and the unmanaged Standard & Poor's 500 Stock Index.

Total Return (Ten Years Ended December 31, 1992)

	Final value of $10,000 investment	Annual rate of return
Management companies	$1,590,600	+65.9%
Equity funds managed	35,500	+13.6
S&P 500 Index	44,800	+16.2

At least over this time period, during which the mutual fund industry grew so substantially, the profitability of these advisers has been completely disproportionate to the returns of the funds they manage. Ironically, these two managers have enjoyed this enormous growth despite the fact that the aggregate performance of their managed equity funds fell far short of the performance of the unmanaged S&P 500 Index. (Incidentally, I am not recommending investments in management company stocks, in part because I see a new era of intense price competition ahead.)

---

solely in the interests of its shareholders. Independent directors must be asked questions like these:

- Are you honoring, in every respect, your fiduciary obligations to the fund shareholders you are responsible for representing?

- Are you negotiating fees with the same spirit and determination as if you were negotiating fees to be paid to your own trustees, responsible for your own and your family's investments?

- Would you terminate the services of your own trustee if your investment results were persistently inferior? Would you be willing to do the same with the fund's management company under the same circumstances?

- Have you considered the extent to which the substantial economies of scale resulting from the fund's growth are enjoyed by the fund's managers, as distinct from the fund's shareholders, for whom you are a fiduciary?

- Have you carefully evaluated what portion of the fees paid to the managers is expended on investment advice? On marketing and promotion? What portion remains as the manager's profit? Does the profit earned *before* the deduction of promotional expenses bear a reasonable relationship to the advisory fees received?

- Have you raised the issue of expenditures on distribution activities? Have you received a satisfactory answer to the question of why larger assets benefit the fund's shareholders? If they do, how and at what cost? Do you know if the 12b-1 plan is accomplishing its goals; if it is not, have you considered its termination?

- Do the advertising and marketing materials prepared by the sponsor to promote the sale of the fund's shares meet the standards of full disclosure you would insist on were you purchasing shares of the fund? Do you own shares in the fund? If it is a load fund, did you pay a commission to purchase your shares?

- How carefully do you read the fund's annual report? Is it candid, complete, and forthright, conveying bad news with the same emphasis as good news? Are the highlights of the fund performance comparisons that you review each year as a director presented to the *shareholders* you represent? Should they be? Are you aware of the potential conflict when the chief executive of the fund's management company writes the annual reports in his capacity as chairman of the fund's board?

- How often do you remind yourself that the express policy of the law of the land—the Investment Company Act of 1940—is violated "when investment companies are organized, operated, and managed in the interest of investment advisers, rather than in the interest of shareholders"?

CAVEAT EMPTOR: *Physician, Heal Thyself*

The following excerpts are from a recent speech by a mutual fund chairman speaking about the responsibilities of the directors of the corporations in which his funds own shares.

We want directors who will mind the store for us, making sure management's doing a good job. . . . Their final responsibility is to the shareholders. Too often they represent their own interests or the Chief Executive Officer's . . . (managers must be) the best available. If not, (the Board) has to fire, rehire, and pay new managers . . . diligently spotting issues where the interests of managers and shareholders may conflict and then taking the initiative to deal with them . . . (when the chairman sets the directors' pay) he can influence their loyalty . . . when it comes to an issue where shareholders' interests diverge from management's, which way will this person vote? . . . We should have intelligent national laws that spell out directors' accountability to shareholders . . . (We must) ensure better boardrooms—boardrooms that are responsible to shareholder interests and not passive rubber stamps for the chairman's agenda.

It is ironic that these comments were not directed to the independent directors of mutual funds. Rather, they were warnings to the directors of Fortune 500 corporations. As a legal matter their responsibilities are identical. Neither group should shirk these solemn responsibilities.

Such questions are not hypothetical. And, as a matter of law, they apply not only to the independent directors but also to the directors who are owners or employees of the investment adviser ("affiliated directors"). You should send to the directors you have elected a quiz asking them to answer these specific questions. I believe that, if asked to speak candidly, most directors would answer at least some of them in the negative. That response cannot stand.

BUILDING A NEW MUTUAL FUND INDUSTRY

It must be clear from this litany of cautions that many mutual fund sponsors have become aggressive marketing machines, clever to a fault, focusing on increasing their assets under management so as to increase the revenues they receive from management fees and sales commissions, the better to increase their profits.

CAVEAT EMPTOR: *More Sweeping Steps?*

In 1966, industry assets were $35 billion—a mere one-fiftieth of their $1.6 trillion total at the end of 1992. To solve the problems we have considered in this chapter, the Securities and Exchange Commission considered requiring compulsory internalization of the management function of mutual funds—having mutual funds operated by their own staffs rather than contracting out these responsibilities to a separate management company. The SEC noted that "such a step would deal most directly with the adverse consequences flowing from the external management structure of the industry," but expressed a desire to give the existing structure "a fair trial" to see if the problems relating to management compensation could be resolved. If not, the SEC concluded, "more sweeping steps might deserve to be considered." Nearly three decades later, the period of fair trial must finally have come to an end. The same problems remain, but in far larger magnitudes. It is difficult to imagine that the time for considering "more sweeping steps" has not arrived.

That objective, of course, is "the American way." And there is nothing fundamentally wrong with this phenomenon. The problem is that managing other people's money—managing *your* money—is a precious responsibility requiring, not only full disclosure of all known risks, rewards, and costs, but also high standards of commercial conduct and even higher standards of trusteeship and fiduciary duty. Trusteeship, indeed, has been part of the American ethic at least since Justice Samuel Putnam wrote his prudent man rule nearly 200 years ago, and part of British common law since time immemorial.

To the extent that asset gathering has superseded fiduciary duty as the industry's hallmark, fund shareholders are not well served. I emphasize that the spirit of fiduciary duty has not vanished. Rather, it has moved from the driver's seat to the back seat, subservient to the worship of market share. In the final analysis, as a mutual fund shareholder, you would be better served if these priorities were reversed. They will be, if only one or more of these three developments reaches fruition.

- First, mutual funds will respond if shareholders become more canny, more thrifty, more active, and more skeptical. If enough shareholders exhibit these traits, especially if enough are willing

---

CAVEAT EMPTOR: *The Center of the System*

History tells us that the 16th-century astronomer Nicolaus Copernicus was the first person to disprove the ancient belief that the earth was the center of our universe. The sun, he concluded, must be the center of the solar system. He doubtless would have been amazed at the perverse structure of the mutual fund industry. He would have hypothesized that the small satellite (the management company) would revolve around the giant sun (the funds themselves), not the reverse. In this light, the illustration below contrasts the total net assets of the mutual funds in the average major fund complex ($25 billion) with the net assets of their management companies ($50 million). It is drawn to scale. Which should be the center of the system? Logic compels the obvious answer: the fund and its shareholders must be the central focus of the mutual fund financial system.

Fund net assets

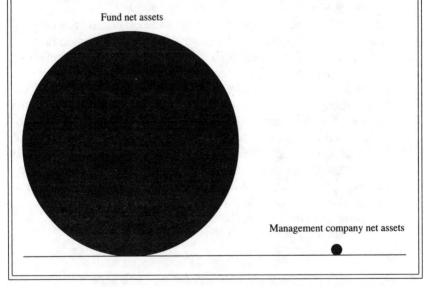

Management company net assets

---

to vote with their feet, the fund industry will quickly get the message. If you demand better disclosure, greater candor, lower cost, and a fair share of the economies of scale, the sponsors will provide all of them.

• Second, as shareholders make their opinions known, the independent directors of mutual funds should become more aware of the essential nature of their trusteeship and their fiduciary responsibilities. Many smaller shareholders—and more than a few larger shareholders—do not have enough financial experience, information, or financial sophistication to fully understand the risks, returns, and costs of the funds that they own. The independent directors must accept responsibility for the oversight of the proper management of shareholders' assets at a proper cost. That objective, indeed, is arguably the major purpose of the Investment Company Act of 1940. The independent directors must set fees at "arm's length." They must also assure themselves that the communications—advertising, marketing materials, and sales presentations—used to attract new shareholders are candid and complete, and that annual reports to the fund's shareholders are no less so. If an enlightened sense of self-interest on the part of fund directors does not soon force this change, a federal law establishing a statutory standard of fiduciary duty for fund directors should be enacted.

- Third, failing the success of the first two conditions, the very structure of the mutual fund industry must change, essentially placing the *fund* in the driver's seat and relegating the management company to the back seat. From a mutual fund standpoint, that indeed would be the world turned upside down. But it would be the functional counterpart of the time-honored structure of the ordinary business corporation, in which the owners of the corporation (in this case, the fund shareholders) control, through their board of directors, its affairs. Ordinary corporations do not need to go out and hire other corporations, with separate owners, to manage their affairs. Mutual funds do precisely that today; some combination of shareholder demand, enlightened self-interest, competition in the marketplace, and "more sweeping steps" under the law may someday compel a reversal.

SUMMARY

The quotation at the start of this chapter was incomplete. The full quotation is: "The fault, dear Brutus, is not in our stars, but in ourselves, *that we are underlings.*" In one way or another, the time for mutual fund shareholders to be underlings will surely end. You are the owners of the mutual fund corporation, and you are entitled to have it operated solely in accordance with your interests.

One would have to be an idealist to believe that shareholder activism will soon change the nature of the mutual fund industry. Failing that development, one would have to be even more of an idealist to expect that independent director activism will do so either, even by the end of this century. And failing that development, only a consummate idealist would expect that a structural change as fundamental as the reorganization of the very management structure of the industry—from external to internal—will occur in our lifetimes. But I believe that idealism has its place. Simply considering these issues will be a major asset for intelligent investors as you select the mutual funds in which to place your trust.

Epilogue

Twelve Pillars of Wisdom
Wisdom excelleth folly

"Wisdom excelleth folly as far as light excelleth darkness." My epilogue begins with this apt quotation from Ecclesiastes, and I must warn you that I shall end it with what I think is an equally apt quotation. Throughout this book I have tried to impart some wisdom to the intelligent investor in mutual funds and delineate some folly that should be avoided. And I hope that I have succeeded in shedding light on mutual fund issues previously shrouded in darkness. By way of summary, I close with the following "twelve pillars of wisdom" as lamps to guide you in your search for a sensible, productive investment program.

1. *Investing is not nearly as difficult as it looks.* The intelligent investor in mutual funds, using common sense and without extraordinary financial acumen, can perform with the pros. In a world where financial markets are highly efficient, there is absolutely no reason that careful and disciplined novices—those who know the rudiments but lack the experience—cannot hold their own or even surpass the long-term returns earned by professional investors as a group. Successful investing involves doing just a few things right and avoiding serious mistakes.

2. *When all else fails, fall back on simplicity.* If you have a major investment decision to make, there are an infinite number of solutions that would be worse than this one: commit, over a period of a few years, half of your assets to a stock index fund and half to a bond index fund. Ignore interim fluctuations in their net asset values. Hold your positions for as long as you live, subject only to infrequent and marginal adjustments as your circumstances change. Occam's razor—a thesis set forth 600 years ago and often affirmed by experience since then—

should encourage you: when there are multiple solutions to a
problem, choose the simplest one.

3. *Time marches on.* Time dramatically enhances capital accumulation as the magic of compounding accelerates. At an annual
return of +10%, the additional capital accumulation on a
$10,000 investment is $1,000 in the first year, $2,400 by the
tenth year, and $10,000 by the twenty-fifth year. At the end of
25 years, the total value of the initial $10,000 investment is
$108,000, nearly a tenfold increase in value. Give yourself the
benefit of all the time you can possibly afford.

4. *Nothing ventured, nothing gained.* It pays to take reasonable
interim risks in the search for higher long-term rates of return.
The magic of compounding accelerates sharply with even modest increases in annual rate of return. While an investment of
$10,000 earning an annual return of +10% grows to a value of
$108,000 over 25 years, at +12% the final value is $170,000.
The difference of $62,000 is more than six times the initial in-
vestment itself.

5. *Diversify, diversify, diversify.* It is hard to imagine that a principle as basic as investment diversification can be so valuable.
By investing in mutual funds you can eliminate the risk of
owning the stock or bond of a single enterprise that may deteriorate and never fully recover, or even fail altogether. The pas-
sage of time has no impact on this specific security risk. By
owning a broadly diversified portfolio of stocks and bonds,
only market risk remains. This risk is reflected in the volatility
of the total value of your portfolio and should take care of itself over time as reinvested dividends and interest are com-
pounded.

6. *The eternal triangle.* Never forget that risk, return, and cost
are the three sides of the eternal triangle of investing. Remember also that the cost penalty may sharply erode the risk premium to which an investor is entitled. This is not to say that
you should necessarily seek out the lowest-cost mutual fund option. Rather, you should understand unequivocally that investing in a fund with a relatively high expense ratio—more
than 0.50% per year for a money market fund, 0.75% for a
bond fund, 1.00% for a regular equity fund, or 0.30% for an
index fund—bears careful examination. Unless you are confident that the higher costs you incur are justified by higher ex-

The Eternal Triangle of Investing

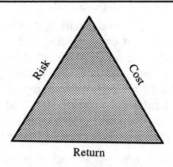

pected returns or enhanced value of service, select your investments from among the lower-cost no-load funds.

7. *The powerful magnetism of the mean.* In the world of investing, the mean is a powerful magnet that pulls financial market returns toward it, causing returns to deteriorate after they exceed historical norms by substantial margins and to improve after they fall short. The mean is also the powerful magnet that pulls the returns achieved by portfolio managers toward it, causing a fund's return to move, over time, ever closer to the average returns achieved by other funds. Regression to the mean is a manifestation of the immutable law of averages that prevails, sooner or later, in the financial jungle.

8. *Do not overestimate your ability to pick superior equity mutual funds, nor underestimate your ability to pick superior bond and money market funds.* In selecting equity funds, no analysis of the past, no matter how painstaking, assures future superiority. In general, you should settle for a solid mainstream equity fund in which the action of the stock market itself explains about 85% or more of the fund's return. Combining several low-cost equity funds to achieve this diversification is equally sensible; so is the holding of a single low-cost index fund. But do not approach the selection of bond and money market funds with the same skepticism. Selecting the better funds in these categories on the basis of their comparative costs holds remarkably favorable prospects for success.

9. *You may have a stable principal value or a stable income stream, but you may not have both.* Nothing could make this proposition more obvious than the contrast between a 90-day U.S. Treasury bill—with its volatile income stream and fixed value—and a 30-year U.S. Treasury bond—with its fixed income stream and extraordinarily volatile market value. Intelligent investing involves choices, compromises, and trade-offs, and your own financial position should determine which type of stability—or, more likely, which combination of the two—is most suitable for your portfolio.

10. *Beware of "fighting the last war."* Too many investors—individuals and institutions alike—are constantly making investment decisions based on the lessons of the recent, or even the extended, past. They seek stocks after stocks have emerged victorious from the last war, bonds after bonds have won, Treasury bills after bills have won. And they worry about the impact of inflation *after* inflation, having turned high real returns into so-so nominal returns, has become the accepted bogeyman. You should not ignore the past, but neither should you assume that a particular cyclical trend will last forever. None does.

11. *You rarely, if ever, know something the market does not.* It is really not possible to do so. If you are worried about the coming bear market, excited about the coming bull market, fearful about the prospect of war, or concerned about the economy, the election, or indeed the state of mankind, in all probability your opinions are already reflected in the market. The financial markets reflect the knowledge, the hopes, the fears, even the greed, of all investors everywhere. It is nearly always unwise to act on insights that you think are your own but are in fact shared by millions of others.

12. *Think long term.* Do not let transitory changes in stock prices alter your investment program. There is a lot of noise in the daily volatility of the stock market, which too often is "a tale told by an idiot, full of sound and fury, signifying nothing." (Macbeth would doubtless agree.) Stocks may remain overvalued, or undervalued, for years. Patience and consistency are valuable assets for the intelligent investor. The best rule is: stay the course.

As you go about investing for the future—a future surely filled with a full measure of reward and peril, optimism and pessimism, hope and fear—a

---

CAVEAT EMPTOR: *The Best Laid Schemes*

There are intelligent ways to go about investing and less intelligent ways. Although the odds are heavily against them, some foolish investors are ever seeking to grow rich, using Dr. Johnson's words, "beyond the dreams of avarice." In the real world of investing, such dreams rarely become reality. But even pursuing the sensible, time-honored policies of conservative investing is no guarantee of financial enrichment. The most intelligent of plans often go awry. As Robert Burns warned, "the best laid schemes of mice and men gang aft a-gley." So know yourself, educate yourself, determine for yourself the financial plan best suited to your own objectives, and have the wisdom, patience, and emotional discipline to stay the course that you have chosen. Finally, make your own careful judgments about all of the investment advice that you receive—including, dare I say, even the well-intentioned and experienced advice provided in this book.

---

final touch of philosophy may help you and other intelligent investors through the rough patches that inevitably lie ahead. As Ecclesiastes tells us:

> I returned, and saw under the sun, that the race is not to the swift, nor the battle to the strong, neither yet bread to the wise, nor yet riches to men of understanding, nor yet favor to men of skill; but time and chance happeneth to them all.

NOTES

Preface

P. x   Sources of most mutual fund data are Lipper Analytical Services, Inc. and Morningstar Mutual Funds. In a few cases, data are provided by the Investment Company Institute and CDA/Wiesenberger Investment Companies Services.

Chapter 1

P. 4   Total returns on cash reserves and common stocks 1872–1925 are from Cowles Commission; total returns on long-term bonds 1872–1925 are from Jeremy Siegel, Professor of Finance, The Wharton School of the University of Pennsylvania. All stock, bond, and bill returns 1926–92 are from Ibbotson Associates.

P. 9   All data on price, reported earnings, and dividends for the Standard & Poor's 500 Stock Index are from Standard & Poor's Corporation.

P. 10   Operating earnings for the companies that comprise the Standard & Poor's 500 Stock Index are from Goldman Sachs.

P. 12   For simplicity, the components of total return are combined using simple addition. The actual formula for combining the components of total return is:

(Initial yield) + [((1 + dividend growth rate) × (1 + multiple change)) − 1]

The results under each method differ marginally.

P. 16   All bond and bill yields are from Ibbotson Associates.

Chapter 2

P. 25   Inflation rate 1872–1925 is from the Cowles Commission; inflation rate 1926–92 is from Ibbotson Associates.

Chapter 3

P. 49   All data in Table 3–1 are from Lipper Analytical Services, Inc. Fund categories determined by The Vanguard Group.

P. 64   Data in Table 3–2 are from Morningstar Mutual Funds. Calculations of income return and capital return are from The Vanguard Group.

Chapter 4

P. 72   Small capitalization stock returns are from the Frank Russell Company.

P. 75   Foreign stock market returns and country asset weightings are from Morgan Stanley Capital International.

P. 84   Peer groups in Table 4–6 determined by The Vanguard Group.

P. 86   Mutual fund rankings compiled by The Vanguard Group using data from Lipper Analytical Services, Inc.

P. 90   Quarterly rankings compiled by The Vanguard Group using data from Morningstar Mutual Funds.

P. 91 Cumulative Honor Roll performance compiled by The Vanguard Group using data from *Forbes* yearly mutual fund issues dating back to 1974.

P. 93 Total returns for total stock market are from Wilshire Associates.

Chapter 5

P. 103 For simplicity, when adjusting yields for sales loads throughout the book, we assume the load is amortized on a linear basis (i.e., a 5% sales charge over 10 years results in a reduction of 0.50% annually). This methodology does not precisely reflect the impact of a sales load.

P. 105 Bond ratings are from Standard & Poor's Corporation.

P. 106 Fund examples in Table 5-3 are from Morningstar Mutual Funds.

P. 107 Bond yields and maturities in Table 5-4 are from Vanguard Fixed Income Group and Wellington Management Company.

P. 113 Capital returns calculated by The Vanguard Group using data from Morningstar Mutual Funds.

P. 114 Table compiled by The Vanguard Group using data from Morningstar Mutual Funds.

P. 116 Twelve-month yields are used as proxy for income returns.

Chapter 6

P. 122 CD yields are from Bloomberg Financial Markets Commodities News.

P. 124 Money market fund yields are from *Donoghue's Money Fund Report*; Money Market Deposit Account yields are from Bank Rate Monitor.

P. 129 Money market fund yields are from *Donoghue's Money Fund Report*.

Chapter 7

P. 142 Balanced fund categories determined by The Vanguard Group using data from Morningstar Mutual Funds.

Chapter 8

P. 163 Survivorship bias returns calculated by The Vanguard Group using year-by-year total return data from Lipper Analytical Services, Inc. Dollar-weighted return on short-term bond funds calculated by The Vanguard Group using data from Lipper Analytical Services, Inc.

Chapter 9

P. 171 Pension equity fund returns are from SEI Corporation.

P. 172 Performance of equity funds versus the stock market is from an article by Michael C. Jensen, "The Performance of Mutual Funds in the Period 1945-64."

P. 176 Quote taken from an editorial by Gilbert Beebower, Senior Vice President of SEI Corporation.

P. 180   Market capitalizations are from the Frank Russell Company.

P. 185   Total returns on Lehman Bond Index are from Lehman Brothers. Average bond fund returns compiled by The Vanguard Group using data from Lipper Analytical Services, Inc.

P. 186   Total institutional assets are from *Institutional Investor* magazine.

Chapter 10

P. 198   All data are from fund annual reports and Lipper Analytical Services, Inc.

P. 202   Expense ratios 1961–77 are from CDA/Wiesenberger Investment Companies Services; expense ratios 1978–82 are from Lipper Analytical Services, Inc.; expense ratios 1982–92 are from Morningstar Mutual Funds.

P. 206   Morningstar Mutual Funds were source of data for *Money* magazine article on expenses of mutual fund complexes.

Chapter 11

P. 209   Tax impact taken from a study done by Jeremy Siegel, Professor of Finance, The Wharton School of the University of Pennsylvania.

P. 210   Throughout this chapter, I have assumed that income is taxed at a 33% rate and capital gains are taxed at a 28% rate. The 33% tax rate assumption is somewhat arbitrary on my part, reflecting what I believe is a reasonable expectation over the coming years.

P. 214   Fund data are from CDA/Wiesenberger Investment Companies Services.

P. 215   Fund data are from CDA/Wiesenberger Investment Companies Services.

Chapter 12

P. 235   94% figure taken from an article by Gary Brinson, Randolph Hood, and Gilbert Beebower, "Determinants of Portfolio Performance."

Chapter 13

P. 276   Pension funds' percent of assets invested in equities from Goldman Sachs.

Chapter 14

P. 285   Data in Table 14–1 obtained by The Vanguard Group from fund proxies.

Index

A

Accumulation stage of life cycle
 goals, 22, 262
 investment strategies, 220–21, 238,
  259, 262–65
 risk-taking during, 33, 238
 stock fund choice, 73
Adjustable rate mortgage funds, 100
Advertising, 289–91
Advisory fees, 4
Aggressive growth stock funds, 68
 purpose, 71
 returns, 1978–1992, 73
Alpha concept, 83
Annual reports
 evaluation, 58–60
 information presented, 150–52, 285–88
ARM funds, 293
Asset allocation
 fixed versus variable-ratio programs,
  241–44
 investments graded, 47
 model portfolios, 240–41, 254–56,
  258–78
 and opportunity cost, 247, 272
 rebalancing, 235–36, 241–45, 261
 strategic versus tactical, 244–52
 strategies, 107, 236–57, 302
Asset allocation mutual funds, 137–38

B

Balanced index funds, 188, 240
Balanced mutual funds
 advantages, 135, 240, 260–61, 263
 asset allocation, 137–38, 140–41
 bond characteristics, 139

Balanced mutual funds—(Cont.)
 disadvantages, 136
 equity-oriented, 136, 140–41
 expense ratios, 290
 failure rates, 142
 historical background, 135–36
 income-oriented, 136–37, 140–41
 ownership costs, 139, 144–48, 190–
  208, 290
 performance evaluation, 140–43
 performance predictability, 142–43
 portfolio balance, 138–39
 portfolio statistics, 139–40
 selection strategies, 136–38, 144–46
 structural characteristics, 137–40
 tax considerations, 136
Bank services, 56, 192
Barron's, 159
Beta risk measurement, 82, 140–41
Bond index mutual funds
 advantages, 261
 purpose, 186–88
 target index, 185
Bond mutual fund "products," 100
Bond mutual funds
 age considerations, 100
 classifications, 97–98
 comparisons, 50
 derivative instruments, 108, 110
 diversification, 51–52
 effect of interest rates, 107–8
 importance of income returns, 112–13
 management fees, 51
 maturity level choice, 99, 106–8, 237
 municipal, 106, 196, 212, 227, 261
 ownership costs, 51, 102–4, 113–15,
  190–208, 282, 290
 performance evaluation, 111–15

311

Notes

Notes

Notes